Other books by Vic Carucci

They Call Me Dirty
(with Conrad Dobler)

By a Nose
(with Fred Smerlas)

THE BUFFALO BILLS

AND THE ALMOST-DREAM SEASON

Vic Carucci

SIMON & SCHUSTER
New York London Toronto Sydney Tokyo Singapore

Simon & Schuster
Simon & Schuster Building
Rockefeller Center
1230 Avenue of the Americas
New York, New York 10020

Designed by Caroline Cunningham
Manufactured in the United States of America

10 9 8 7 6 5 4 3 2 1

Library of Congress Cataloging in
Publication Data

Carucci, Vic.
The Buffalo Bills and the almost-dream
season / Vic Carucci.
p. cm.
1. Buffalo Bills (Football team) I. Title.
GV956.B83C37 1991
796.332'64'0974797—dc20 91-23919
CIP

ISBN: 0-671-74850-5

TO RHONDA, KRISTEN, AND LINDSAY—*the winning-est home team I know.*

ACKNOWLEDGMENTS

Although this marks my first solo book effort, no project of this kind is ever possible without help.

A great many people provided assistance in one form or another, beginning with Jeff Neuman of Simon & Schuster for believing there was a book in the Bills' 1990 season and in my ability to produce one under extremely tight time constraints; Stuart Gottesman, also of Simon & Schuster, for his brilliant editing and helpful advice from start to finish; Basil Kane, my literary agent, for talking me into the project in the first place;

I also want to thank Howard Smith, executive sports editor of *The Buffalo News;* Murray Light, editor of the *News,* and Foster Spencer, managing editor of the *News,* for their continued support through this project and the last ten years of my writing career; the talented and knowledgeable sportswriters with whom I have covered the Bills—Jay Bonfatti, Gary Fallesen, Larry Felser, Scott Kindberg, Sal Maiorana, Milt Northrop, Scott Pitoniak, Chuck Pollock, Leo Roth, Jerry Sullivan, Dick Usiak, Bill Wolcott, and Rick Woodson—for sharing valuable insight and information; *News* Super Bowl–coverage teammates Mike Beebe, Ray Bentley, Bob DiCesare, Donn Esmonde, Mark Gaughan, Susan Martin, and Gene Warner, and Bill Wippert for his photographic expertise.

I wish to give special thanks to other top-flight writers and reporters with whom it has been my pleasure to work—Charles Anzalone, Erik Brady, Dan Herbeck, and Mike Vogel.

In addition, I want to thank Todd Backes, Scott Berchtold, Rhonda Carucci, Linda Jozwiak, Linda Lisicki, Denny Lynch, Sally Schlaerth, Joe Shaw, and Fred Smerlas.

CONTENTS

MIAMI BLUES

The stitches were threatening to bust wide open, just as everyone figured they would. Let's face it, how much can a team's personality really change in one year—especially when its roster stays almost exactly the same? Even an expert mending job couldn't withstand the stress created by the Buffalo Bills' oversized egos and undersized maturity. That lethal combination couldn't be cleaned out of their dressing cubicles in a single off-season.

They were the Bickering Bills then. And just as almost every football journalist and fan in America had suspected, the 1990 incarnation was no less turbulent.

It was all starting to rip apart on the afternoon of September 16 at Miami's Joe Robbie Stadium. The encouraging memory of Buffalo players holding hands on the sidelines eight months earlier, watching Jim Kelly's valiant attempt to yank a play-off victory from Cleveland, was fading. All the encouraging statements from July and August about how the team had grown up, how they had learned from the previous year's mistakes, and how they vowed to erase all the embarrassment they had caused themselves, the franchise, and the city seemed hollow.

It was bad enough that the scoreboard showed the Dolphins ahead, 30–7, but now, with just under eight minutes to play,

Bruce Smith was about to make things worse. Marv Levy had just pulled Kelly and a couple of other offensive starters out of the game. It wasn't Levy's style to concede defeat so early, but the situation was hopeless. With the game out of reach, all he could do was avoid a serious injury to his star quarterback or someone else who would be difficult, if not impossible, to replace. At least, that was how the head coach saw it. Smith saw it as raising the white flag prematurely. Frustrated by the score and frazzled by the smothering South Florida heat, the 6′4″, 275-pound defensive end confronted the 5′10″, 170-pound Levy in front of the Bills' bench. With thousands of spectators in the stands and an NBC camera looking on, Smith yelled and flailed his massive arms as he tried to express his shock, anger, and bewilderment.

Levy never flinched. He told Smith to leave the coaching to him and sit down. Smith stormed away in disgust.

But that wasn't the end of it. A short while later, with Miami in possession, Levy began pulling several defensive starters out of the game. And strong safety Leonard Smith and cornerbacks Nate Odomes and Kirby Jackson refused to exit the field, making it clear that, like their agitated teammate, they too were not ready to surrender.

More than a half-hour after the game ended, with the 23-point loss still fresh in his memory, Bruce's disposition hadn't improved one bit. In the stunned Bills' dressing room he showered, donned his street clothes, and was retrieving his jewelry and other personal belongings when a reporter from *The Buffalo News* asked about his sideline display.

"We just fuckin' gave up," Smith said, adding that he had "no idea" why the substitutions came as early as they did.

When Levy saw the remarks (minus the profanity) in the next day's paper, he fined Smith five hundred dollars. He also fined the three defensive backs one hundred dollars apiece for hesitating to follow his directive.

This wasn't exactly another Bickering Bills player versus player showdown. It wasn't Jim Kelly publicly blaming Howard Ballard for a missed block against Indianapolis that resulted in the QB's separated shoulder. It wasn't Thurman Thomas publicly blasting Kelly to give him a taste of his own finger-pointing medicine. It wasn't Keith McKeller and Joe Devlin having to be pulled apart after a heated discussion about which players contributed more to the team's success—black or white. It wasn't Ronnie Harmon only allowing black teammates to autograph a football he brought to work one day and not permitting Andre Reed, whose parents are racially mixed, to sign it. It wasn't even the ongoing disagreement over the type of music that should blare from the speakers of the dressing-room stereo—rap or country—that Devlin once settled by yanking out the wires.

But Bills fans could hardly be comforted by the sight of Bruce Smith, one of the team's more vital cogs, taking on the head coach—especially after watching the club perform so dreadfully. There was a distinct sense of panic in the air. A blowout loss to the Dolphins, whom the Bills had beaten in six previous outings, simply wasn't expected. Not after the 26–10 season-opening victory over the Colts a week earlier. Not after all the preseason promises that the Bills had rid themselves of their self-destructive tendencies. The first two months of their schedule was supposed to be a walk in the park. They had four games at home, three on the road against beatable opponents (Miami, the New York Jets, and the New England Patriots) and a "bye" week to rest and heal.

The Bills were, on talent, the unanimous choice to three-peat as AFC Eastern Division champion. The team was, on talent, supposed to be a legitimate contender for the Super Bowl.

Ah, the Super Bowl. To Buffalo fans, it had become an almost mythical destination. Every season would begin with hopes and dreams of their beloved Billies playing in the game of games—with friends, neighbors, co-workers, and strangers telling each other, "Yep. This is the year. I can just feel it. We're going allllll the way." And every season would end, some later than others, with the same harsh reality: that the Super Bowl was someone else's party and that they could only watch from a distance.

It never seemed fair. No fans appreciated their NFL team more or supported it better. No professional sports franchise, with the possible exception of the Green Bay Packers, owned as large a slice of its city's identity. No town could be as deserving of the Super Bowl experience.

How important are the Bills to Buffalonians? When they are playing, home or away, the world outside of Western New York ceases to exist, while life on the inside enters a sort of suspended animation. Sure, taverns are open, but don't bother showing up if you're interested in anything other than watching The Game. And whatever you do, don't try and phone someone after the opening kickoff—unless the call somehow relates to the action on the field.

How important are the Bills to Buffalonians? As ridiculous as this might sound in other places, when the Bills do well, the city does well; when they do poorly, the city does poorly. There is ample proof. In 1976 the Bills had a 2–12 record and Buffalo's unemployment skyrocketed to 11 percent. It was the year heavy industry began to topple, with automobile workers comprising the bulk of massive layoffs. Unemployment also was high, between 8 and 9 percent, during 1984 and 1985. The Bills? Sure enough, they were staggering through consecutive 2–14 disasters. Then along came 1988. And as the Bills rose to the NFL's upper echelon with a 12–4 record, guess what happened to jobs in Buffalo? They soared right along with the team to record levels.

A study actually revealed significant differences in Monday factory production depending on the outcome of a Sunday Bills game. Wins made assembly lines hum. Losses brought them to a crawl.

"The Bills are like a blank screen on which people project all kinds of expectations about themselves," says Donald F. Sabo, associate professor at Buffalo's D'Youville College and sports sociologist.

The first of many unfulfilled Super Bowl expectations came in 1966, when the Bills lost the AFL championship to Kansas City for the right to face Green Bay in the NFL–AFL title game (also known as Super Bowl I). A long stretch of futility followed before their next play-off appearance in 1974—and their prompt elimination by Pittsburgh. The third chance came after the 1980 season, when the Bills were 11–5, but a sprained ankle limited Joe Ferguson's effectiveness as the

Bills lost a 6-point game to San Diego in the divisional round. The following year the Bills took a 10–6 record into the post-season, beat the New York Jets in the wild-card round, and advanced to Cincinnati. But there they proceeded to short-circuit a late drive with a delay-of-game penalty and lost by 7 points. File that one under "Thirty-Second Clock Disaster."

Another long stretch of futility followed before the success of 1988, when the Bills defeated Houston and reached the AFC Championship Game at Cincinnati. After dominating the first quarter against Anthony Munoz, Bruce Smith sustained a leg injury that slowed him down for the rest of the day. Then, late in the third quarter, Derrick Burroughs punched Tim McGee in the end zone, turning what should have been a third-and-goal at the 8 into a first-and-goal at the 4. Two plays later the Bengals scored the last touchdown of their 21–10 victory.

Finally came the frustration that would forever be known as "The Drop." Despite all the turmoil of the 1989 season, which ended with a 9–7 record and losses in three of the last four games, Buffalo's Super Bowl hopes and dreams remained alive in the final seconds of the divisional-round play-off game at Cleveland. Then a perfectly thrown Kelly pass bounced off Ronnie Harmon's fingertips in the end zone. On the next play Kelly's throw landed in Clay Matthews's hands, securing the Browns' 34–30 triumph, and Bills fans were left to ponder what might have been. One more time.

There was reason to suspect that, as the fans pondered, their faith did a little wavering. Season-ticket sales, which had increased every year since 1986, suddenly showed a decline. Nothing drastic, mind you, 47,865 to 46,037, but a decline nonetheless. It was an indication, perhaps, that there had been one heartbreak too many to endure. Or at least that forgiveness wouldn't come as easily to a team with a reputation for waging some of its more spirited battles in the dressing room rather than on the field.

All of which made the ugliness during and after the Miami game so unsettling. Were the Bills really going to come undone in only the second week of the regular season? Was all that talent going to be wasted foolishly again?

Ralph Wilson was concerned enough to issue, through

Levy, a stern warning to the players that the price for any further public criticism of a coach or teammate would be far greater than five hundred dollars.

"The next one of them that goes shooting his mouth off and disrupts the team will be suspended," the Bills' president and owner since their inception in 1960 later said to Will McDonough of the *Boston Globe.* "And then if they don't like it, we'll get rid of them. I'm sick of all this nonsense. I'm just not going to stand for it, and I told Marv to tell the players that."

Meanwhile, the national media couldn't pounce on the Smith-Levy incident fast enough. Crews from NBC and CBS were dispatched to Buffalo to get as many juicy details as they could from inside and outside the team. But the Bills were prepared and dropped a figurative cone of silence over Rich Stadium. Even O. J. Simpson, the most popular Bill of all time, was unable to get interviews with players or Levy for NBC. General Manager Bill Polian headed the damage-control effort by designating himself team spokesman. As could be expected, he played down the controversy, saying, "We need to put an end to all of this questioning. That has become a distraction in and of itself. We've just got to put that behind us and close the curtain."

Of course, that didn't stop either network from airing "Here Go the Bickering Bills Again" stories on their pregame studio shows the following Sunday, or similar newspaper reports from appearing around the country. And the national spotlight would only get brighter, as the Bills' next game was against the Jets—in the shadow of the world's media capital—on "Monday Night Football."

As game time approached you could almost hear the time bomb ticking from the Bills' dressing room at Giants Stadium.

WELCOME TO CAMP HARMONY

"There's a very fine line between winning and losing. Every team in the NFL has talent, but attitude is the biggest thing that counts—that and playing together as a team. If you can capture that feeling, then you'll have success."

—Bills linebacker Ray Bentley

For the 1990 Bills it was a case of trying to recapture that feeling.

And one of the larger questions of the off-season was how Marv Levy would respond to the challenge. His image, thanks largely to a Pat Paulsen–like face and gentlemanly demeanor, was that of a softy. Critics felt he created an atmosphere ripe for internal problems by often turning his back on situations that demanded discipline, such as a player's slacking off in practice or meetings—or publicly criticizing a teammate or coach. Even around the dressing room Levy was referred to as "The Master of Overlook," an expert in thc field of "scientific neglect," a graduate of the "Ronald Reagan School of Coaching." Somehow, no one seemed to remember that just two years ago his peers had named him *The Sporting News* 1988 NFL Coach of the Year. Everybody seemed to forget that

Ralph Wilson had once described him as "the best coach the Bills ever had" and gave him a lifetime appointment to the job five months after Buffalo's loss in the 1988 AFC Championship Game.

Media and fans kept calling for Levy to become a drill sergeant, but in forty years of coaching that had never been his style—and he wasn't about to change. Yelling and screaming simply weren't part of the way he did business, except on game day. And the targets then were usually officials, the berating of whom he did less out of genuine fury and more with a strategic eye toward influencing their judgment.

His was an intellectual approach, the kind you'd expect from someone who graduated from Harvard with a master's degree in English history. Someone who, in team meetings, often used words that prompted even his brightest players to later consult a dictionary. Someone who, at home, would curl up with all sorts of non-football-related reading material (Dickens's novels are his favorites).

So when minicamp arrived in May, Levy didn't give his troops an ear-blistering speech about avoiding the off-field problems of 1989. He just mentioned to them that they could expect plenty of references to the "Bickering Bills" in the media, with the first wave soon to come in preseason football magazines.

"And the only way to defuse it is to show people this is a team that's together," Levy said. "Don't let it eat at you. Don't be too responsive to it. There's probably going to be a sharper microscope on you this year than on most teams. And that's okay."

He also appointed nine players to a committee that would serve as a liaison between him and the team. Jim Kelly, Thurman Thomas, Kent Hull, James Lofton, Pete Metzelaars, Bruce Smith, Cornelius Bennett, Darryl Talley, and Mark Kelso were chosen to help the coach maintain order in the dressing room. In forming the group Levy sought a representative from each position, as well as an even blend of black and white players with various levels of experience. Lofton, thirty-four, was the oldest; Bennett, twenty-four, was the youngest.

The committee's responsibilities were outlined in the Bills' playbook: "Committee consideration should include, but not be limited to, topics such as training regulations, travel regulations, game-day policy, food, clubhouse policy and entertainment. . . . Suggestions, complaints or problems of individual players (other than personal), or groups of players shall be referred to the Players Committee. If the committee, in its discretion, believes they should be taken up with the coaching staff or management, a conference shall be arranged between the committee and head coach in order to discuss the matter."

It was Levy's way of addressing the perceived leadership void created by the off-season departures of two highly respected veterans: offensive lineman Joe Devlin, who was forced into retirement after thirteen years with the Bills, and nose tackle Fred Smerlas, who joined San Francisco as a Plan B free agent after eleven seasons in Buffalo. Most of the younger players had automatically taken their suggestions, complaints, and problems to them. And when either had seen a need for the air to be cleared by a players-only meeting, one was called.

Levy felt it was time for new leaders.

"Ones who relate to players who are at least closer to their own playing generation," he said. "They'll be better listened to, and they have a greater stake in the future of the team. Leadership isn't just a case of someone saying, 'Hey, you guys, come here! I'm calling a meeting.' It's the approach he takes to the game—work habits, setting a good example, how team-oriented he is.

"There's always a changing of the guard. In the past some players hesitated to exert positive leadership because they didn't want to step on anyone's toes. The time has come for them to step to the fore."

In July the Bills reconvened for training camp at Fredonia State College.

Everyone, right down to the kids collecting the dirty towels, seemed determined to undo the damage of the year before. You half expected the sign over the entrance to read "WELCOME TO CAMP HARMONY."

After one practice in the early going Darryl Talley couldn't help but notice two of his teammates, third-string quarterback Galc Gilbert and nose tackle Jeff Wright, climbing aboard a golf cart parked outside the dressing room. More specifically, he couldn't help noticing where they sat—Gilbert behind the wheel, Wright on the passenger side.

"How many times," Talley said with a wide grin, "are you going to see a quarterback driving around a nose tackle?"

It went on like that the rest of the summer, player after player citing examples of how drastically things had changed since 1989, how the Bickering Bills had become the Blissful Bills. They were proud of themselves. And they were eager to share their renewed unity with the rest of the world.

Defensive end Leon Seals: "You go to a restaurant, and you might take two or three guys with you instead of going by yourself. That just wasn't the case last year. Everybody's working for the same reason now, and that's the major difference. Last year certain people had their own individual goals and that made it divided."

Center Kent Hull: "You see a lot of different people hanging together who, in the past, maybe didn't. For instance, I've gotten to know players on this team who have been here for a couple of years who I really didn't know before. This football team is starting to grow up. We had a lot of people who, earlier, maybe weren't quite as mature as they needed to be. And they've accepted their roles like everybody else."

Linebacker Ray Bentley: "You just don't see the team as fragmented as it was. There are no real cliques any longer. It's more of a group feeling."

Some parts of the cleanup operation were more subtle than others. For instance, during prepractice stretching, the brain trust positioned players closer together—two and one half yards apart, rather than the standard five—and inside the white numbers on the field rather than scattering them from sideline to sideline. The idea was to promote social interaction.

And the players went right along with it.

"Before you were just talking to the two guys who were next to you, and that was about it," Bentley explained. "Now, you can talk to fifteen to twenty guys around you and get a better feel for each other."

Call it gridiron group therapy.

On the not-so-subtle side was Jim Kelly's new interview policy. Before a reporter could even utter one question, Kelly laid down the law: "I'm only going to talk about positive things." Known for shooting from the lip, he was measuring his words carefully now, being certain to say all the right things about all the right people. If someone did try to bring up any controversy, especially from the year before, he'd quickly change the subject. Or stop talking.

"Everybody realizes what we have to do and the things we have to say," Kelly said. "I don't think anybody's going to bad-mouth anybody this year."

Observed Bentley, "Jim has grown up as much as anyone has. I think he has bent over backwards to try to be accommodating to people and bite his tongue. And that's going to really help. It's important for how the fans are going to view us, but I think it carries over internally as well."

Convinced the media helped create much of the previous season's turmoil, Levy, in a move unprecedented in Bills history, barred reporters from the dressing room except after games. It was his feeling that the added distance between players and the press would reduce the chances of their sounding off about teammates and/or coaches and management, while keeping reporters from seeing or hearing something they shouldn't.

"It was a mistake to open the locker room up in the first place," Levy said. "Every place I've been [Kansas City in the NFL, Montreal of the Canadian Football League, Chicago in the United States Football League], I had a lot more serene, eye-on-the-target attitude amongst the players when we didn't have the media in the locker room during the week. Having the media in there is not a healthy environment. It allows very small issues to become big ones."

For instance, had the dressing room been off-limits to the media in 1989, one of the Bills' more embarrassing incidents that year—the fistfight between assistant coaches Tom Bresnahan and Nick Nicolau as they watched a videotape the morning after a blowout victory over the Jets—might never have been uncovered. It might have kept a reporter from seeing the turban-like bandage wrapped around Bresnahan's forehead that, along with his chin, sustained a cut requiring stitches. And it might have kept the same reporter from hearing about the wild brawl from several amused players who were all too eager to make it public.

Unlike most players, James Lofton felt there was more good than harm in the media's coverage of the Bickering Bills.

"It was almost nice that it all became public, because then everybody had to deal with it," he said. "Marv addressed it. People addressed it in team meetings and among their friends and family."

You might say that the players had been cleansed by the time they arrived at Camp Harmony.

Of course, getting along is easy for any NFL team in July and August. The games don't count, the team's record remains unblemished, and the emphasis is on assembling a forty-seven-man active roster instead of enduring the emotional ups, downs, twists, and turns of a sixteen-game schedule.

Sure, there might be a punch or two exchanged in practice. But such flare-ups tend to douse themselves in a hurry. They result more from the blazing sun and frustration of two-a-day workouts than bona fide hostility.

But what would happen when a different type of heat was felt?

"Like when we lose one of those games that we shouldn't have lost," Leonard Smith pointed out. "And you know that's going to happen; it always does in the NFL, because this is a game of bounces. I think everyone's wondering just how this team will react when the bad times set in."

Not that there weren't opportunities for dissension to rear its ugly head in the preseason.

Despite clearing a pair of major contractual hurdles in the off-season—a seven-year, $20-million agreement with Kelly and a six-year, $7-million deal with wide receiver Andre Reed—the Bills found themselves with three very significant holdouts: All-Pro halfback Thurman Thomas, linebacker

Shane Conlan, and offensive tackle Will Wolford. Each had plenty of friends on the team, several of whom showed their support by wearing the holdouts' jersey numbers in practice. And negotiations between Bill Polian, the Bills' pugnacious general manager, and the players' agents had their nasty moments. At one point Polian publicly referred to Thomas's representative, Dr. Charles Tucker, as a "charlatan and a fraud," and Tucker responded by calling Polian a "punk and a liar." In a rare move, at the start of training camp the GM also revealed details of his then top offer to Conlan, $850,000 per year. Polian's gambit demonstrated an obvious attempt to enlist public support in applying pressure to the Western New York native whose off-season home, overlooking Chautauqua Lake, was a twenty-minute drive from camp. He was close enough for an occasional boater cruising past his house to yell through a megaphone, "Hey, Conlan, I know you're in there. Get in camp!"

Of course, no sane person ever believed the Bills would enter the regular season without any of the three. True, Jim Kelly was the triggerman for the offense, which the year before had produced 409 points (the second-highest total in team history). True, except for a three-game slump late in the season, he had performed well in 1989, throwing for 25 of a club record 32 touchdown passes while being intercepted only 18 times. True, he had four touchdown passes and his first 400-yard game in the play-off game against Cleveland. But without Thomas the offense was going nowhere. Thomas had led the NFL in total yards from scrimmage with 1,913. He had rushed for 1,244 yards and 6 touchdowns, and caught 60 passes—a team record for running backs—for 669 yards and 6 more TDs.

The defense without Conlan? Get real. Although he missed much of the previous season with a knee injury, he was the best run-stuffer the Bills had. And as far as Levy was concerned, a team that couldn't stuff the run was a team that couldn't win.

But it was Wolford's absence that caused the largest immediate headache. If one area could least afford to be missing a proven starter it was the offensive line. Even before camp began there were major concerns over the unit's quality and depth. Most of the early hand-wringing centered around right guard, where Joe Devlin had started in 1989. Leonard Burton, who had spent most of his previous four seasons as a reserve, arrived at Fredonia as the number-one man at the position. But less than two weeks later he suffered a knee injury in practice that would sideline him for the rest of the year. At the same time veteran left guard Jim Ritcher was unavailable because of recent arthroscopic surgery to clean loose particles from his left shoulder.

All of a sudden the Bills found themselves with replacements at three of their five offensive line spots: rookie Glenn Parker for Will Wolford at left tackle; Mitch Frerotte, who had already made two unsuccessful bids to make the team, at left guard; and John Davis, who had yet to distinguish himself since joining the Bills as a Plan B free agent from Houston in 1989, at right guard. Kent Hull, at center, and Howard Ballard, at right tackle, were the only experienced members of the group. And the 325-pound Ballard, a.k.a. The House, was entering only his second season as a starter, with plenty of room to improve.

The most critical of the replacements was Parker, because, at left tackle, he was protecting Kelly's blind side. He also drew his share of attention as a curiosity, beginning with his face. It was big and round and much older looking than one would expect to belong to an NFL rookie, even at twenty-four years old. (His balding scalp and goatee merely added to the effect). Next was his body. It, too, was big (6′5″, 300 pounds) and round, and far less athletic looking than one would expect to belong to an NFL rookie—even an offensive lineman. Then there was his background. Parker didn't play organized sports in high school in Huntington Beach, California ("The time that I would have spent practicing football, I was pretty much practicing my suntanning, lying on the beach, and body surfing"). He went out for football on a friend's dare in junior college and played two seasons before transfering to the University of Arizona, from where the Bills made him a third-round draft pick. Those who saw Parker for the first time in Buffalo thought he had just stepped out of a motorcycle gang, and that was *before* he rolled up the right sleeve of his black T-shirt to reveal a tattoo of a red-and-blue capital "A" (for Arizona), with a tiny skull and crossbones inside the top of the letter, on his biceps.

In fact, the tattoo parlor in Tucson responsible for the work was across the street from a biker bar.

Even if the Bills managed to resolve all their contract disputes and pieced together an effective offensive line, they'd still have their share of challenges.

The only known quantity on the defensive line was Bruce Smith. His training camp workouts were limited by the aftereffects of off-season surgery on his right knee. But the arthroscopic procedure, for the removal of bone chips and other loose particles, left the knee feeling much stronger than it had in more than a year. Smith was in the best shape of his life. He was ready to dominate like never before. And that was a scary prospect for Bills opponents, considering he ranked second in the AFC in 1989 with 13 sacks, and that his career total was a club record 57½.

Gone from the front three were Smerlas and left end Art Still who, like Devlin, was shoved into retirement. Their replacements—Jeff Wright and Leon Seals—had a great deal to prove. Wright was taking over from one of the more popular players in Bills history, and his 6′3″, 270-pound frame was considered too small for the position, which the 6′3″ Smerlas had long filled at nearly 300 pounds. After coming up short in previous opportunities to establish himself as a full-time starter and pass-rushing ace, Seals was at the put-up-or-shut-up stage of his career. What was the prognosis going to be for the man nicknamed Dr. Sack?

A number of other questions lingered through the summer: Would James Lofton, at thirty-four, provide enough of a receiving threat to take at least some pressure off Andre Reed, who broke his own club record with 88 catches in 1989? Would Keith McKeller, a better pass-catching threat, displace Pete Metzelaars, a better blocker, as the starting tight end? Would thirty-year-old fullback Larry Kinnebrew, an old-timer for his position, hang on to his starting job? Would outside linebacker Cornelius Bennett rebound from a poor season in

1989, when he struggled with shoulder and knee injuries? Would number-one draft pick J. D. Williams unseat Kirby Jackson as the starter at left cornerback? Would Mark Kelso hold off the challenge of John Hagy at free safety? Would rookie John Nies, a sixth-round draft pick from Arizona, step into the punting vacancy created by the Plan B loss of steady John Kidd to San Diego?

By 1990 Marv Levy's list of preseason goals was painfully familiar to anyone in Buffalo who ever purchased an exhibition-game ticket at the full regular-season price: first, evaluate newcomers; second, give returning players enough of a tune-up for the regular season without overexposing them to injury or fatigue; third, win, but never at the expense of points one or two.

That was why, before the 1990 exhibition opener against the New York Giants on "Monday Night Football," Levy's August record as Buffalo's head coach stood at 3–10. That was also why no one seemed terribly surprised when the Bills suffered a 20–6 loss to the Giants.

Buffalo allowed 305 rushing yards and its defense was generally pushed all over Rich Stadium. But an asterisk belonged next to the performance, indicating that Smith was still resting his knee, Conlan was holding out, and Talley and Bennett did not play after the first quarter.

Not to mention the patchwork offensive line.

As always, the order of Levy's preseason goals rankled a number of fans who believed winning should always come first, regardless of a game's importance. As always, Levy was unfazed by their criticism.

"I'd rather have some fans upset now, in the preseason, than do something which I think minimizes our chance to win the opening game of the regular season," he said.

Four nights later, at the Pontiac Silverdome, Levy's point was dramatically brought home. Late in the first half of the Bills' exhibition encounter with the Detroit Lions, Darryl Talley was sidelined with torn cartilage in his right knee. He had suffered the injury while running full stride after Barry Sanders in the first quarter. At first he felt a little pain, but it quickly subsided and he stayed in the game for the rest of his scheduled appearance, which lasted until late in the second quarter.

Talley would require arthroscopic surgery to repair the damage. And although he vowed to be ready to play by the September 9 regular-season opener against Indianapolis, he couldn't help but feel discouraged, after having battled back from off-season operations on the same knee and both elbows.

If there was any bright spot in the Bills' 24–13 loss to the Lions it was the performance of third-string quarterback Gale Gilbert. He was supposed to relieve Kelly after the first quarter and give way to number-two man Frank Reich sometime in the second half. But with Reich sidelined with an inner ear infection that upset his equilibrium and left him feeling nauseated, Gilbert played three full quarters and completed 23 of 29 passes for 234 yards and 2 touchdowns.

Despite Reich's poor showing against the Giants earlier that week (4 of 12 for 14 yards and 2 interceptions), Gilbert wasn't any closer to being promoted to second string. Reich had locked up that job three months earlier when he signed a five-year contract worth $4.3 million. The deal, which included a guaranteed $1.2-million signing bonus, was his reward for guiding the Bills to three consecutive victories in 1989 while Kelly was sidelined with a separated shoulder.

On August 24, the day before the Bills' third preseason game, at New Orleans, the first of their three missing veterans returned to the fold. Shane Conlan agreed to a contract extension that would pay him an average of $867,500 per season through 1992.

"I didn't want to do it from day one," he said of the holdout. "I hated it. It was killing me. Enough's enough, and I want to start playing football."

But Conlan arrived too late to be part of the Bills' most entertaining effort of the preseason, as they fell just short on a fourth-quarter rally and suffered a 28–23 loss to the Saints.

Special-teams standout Steve Tasker recovered two onside kicks in the final five minutes to make things interesting. The first recovery, which followed a 34-four-yard Gilbert touchdown pass to rookie wide receiver Al Edwards, was at the

50-yard line and led to a 31-yard Scott Norwood field goal to cut the Saints' lead to 28–23. One play before the field goal James Lofton made what appeared to be a touchdown catch, but an official ruled the receiver was out of bounds after first indicating a score. After Tasker's second recovery, at the Buffalo 49, Gilbert moved the Bills to the Saints' 37. But he couldn't budge them any further and, with 49 seconds and no time-outs left, they turned the ball over on downs to give New Orleans the win.

The Bills' defense received a huge lift from the preseason debut of Bruce Smith. He played only one quarter, but in that time he made a sack and easily established himself as the most effective player on the field.

Two nights after the New Orleans game Thurman Thomas came to terms on a contract extension that would pay him an average of $1 million annually over four seasons. Earlier that evening, as he and his agent, Dr. Charles Tucker, gathered in Polian's office for what would be the final round of talks, Thomas told the GM he wasn't leaving without an agreement.

"Even if it took until three o'clock in the morning I was determined to get it done," Thomas said after emerging less than an hour later.

The next day brought an end to the final holdout, with Will Wolford signing a three-year contract that would pay him seven hundred thousand dollars per season. A collective sigh could be heard from the coaches—and especially from Jim Kelly—as the offensive line took a major step toward becoming whole again. But Bresnahan, in his second year as the Bills' offensive line coach, expressed concern over Wolford's ability to get ready for the regular-season opener, which was less than two weeks away.

"For an offensive lineman it's a killer to come in and be expected to perform up to potential in a week to ten days time," Bresnahan said. "It's going to be a struggle for him."

Conlan, Thomas, and Wolford accompanied the Bills to Columbia, South Carolina, for their preseason finale against the Chicago Bears. But they didn't play.

Of course, the same could be said for their teammates,

who did take the field at the University of South Carolina's Williams-Brice Stadium.

The nightmare began on the Bills' opening possession, which started on their 1-yard line. Kelly's first pass was deflected at the line and intercepted by rookie Mark Carrier at the 5. Two plays later Brad Muster scored to give the Bears a 7–0 lead.

On the second play after the kickoff Kenneth Davis fumbled and Chicago's Trace Armstrong recovered at the Bills' 26. The Bears proceeded to drive to another touchdown, a 1-yard sweep by Neal Anderson on fourth-and-goal, and added 7 more to make it 21–0 before the Bills scored their only points of the night.

With Kelly at the controls through one series in the second quarter, the Bills' first-team offense produced a mere 74 yards and 4 first downs. He completed only 4 of 10 passes for 27 yards, giving him a cumulative exhibition total of 9 of 25 (36 percent) for 104 yards, no touchdowns, and 2 interceptions.

Chicago put the finishing touches on the 35–7 humiliation with 14 points in the final 2:04. That gave the Bills an 0–4 exhibition record. And, for a while at least, Levy forgot all about his preseason goals and gentlemanly demeanor and told reporters exactly how he felt about his team's output.

"I'm sick and humiliated by the way our team played and the players should be also," he snapped. "I've coached a lot of years, and I don't recall being as angered over the type of performance that a team I was coaching turned in like I am tonight. I apologize to the people of South Carolina for it, I apologize to the Buffalo Bills fans, and I can say it damn well isn't going to happen again."

"I think I'm speaking for everybody when I say this," Jim Kelly said. "But I'm glad the preseason is over with."

Amen.

For all the wrong reasons one could feel more than the usual air of anticipation before the Bills' 1990 regular-season opener. Maybe it was anxiety.

First there was their 9–7 finish and early play-off exit in

1989. After a 7–8 record in 1987 and 12–4 mark and AFC Championship Game appearance in 1988, was that the first step off a cliff? Then there was their 0–4 preseason, capped by the disaster in South Carolina. Were they really as bad as they looked for most of the summer? And there were the preseason-long holdouts of Thomas, Conlan, and Wolford, plus Talley's knee surgery and Ritcher's absence for five weeks due to a shoulder operation. Would those key players be able to shake off the rust in time for the games that counted?

His angry reaction to the exhibition finale notwithstanding, Levy was irritated that such questions were being raised.

"We haven't gone as far back as people think," he said. "It's rare that a team improves its record three seasons in a row. Sometimes it's two steps forward and one step back. We hope to make that two or three steps forward this year.

"Right now, we're oh-and-oh, not oh-and-four. The thing that surprises me the most is the expectancy of impending disaster that seems to reign. There doesn't seem to me to be enough optimism and toughness that we'll bounce back if we lose a game."

Levy and his players insisted everything was under control, that they were ready for the real thing (even with Will Wolford missing from the lineup after aggravating a hamstring injury in practice and Parker's last-minute shift from number-one right guard to number-one left tackle).

Unlike the 1989 squad, this team was focused—so they insisted.

"The Super Bowl has not even been mentioned around here," Kelly said. "We know what we have to do before we even get to that point. We have to beat our conference rivals first. We have to concentrate on each game and not look ahead. We have to win the games we're supposed to."

Such as the opener against Indianapolis. Except for a game played during the 1987 players' strike, the Colts hadn't won in Rich Stadium since 1980. And they were going to try to beat the Bills with a rookie quarterback, Jeff George, who despite being the top overall pick in the draft was raw and working behind a shaky offensive line. Smith, Bennett, and the rest of the Buffalo pass-rushers figured to have a sack-feast.

What no one anticipated, however, was the Bills' opening the game in a no-huddle offense—a wild, pass-happy attack that seemed to fly in the face of the conservative, grind-it-out reputation shared by Levy and offensive coordinator Ted Marchibroda. Kelly threw on the first three plays, and the Bills sped from their 11 to the Indianapolis 13 before the Colts finally called a basketball-type time-out to regroup. After catching their breath they held the Bills to a 29-yard Scott Norwood field goal.

Now it was George's turn to show what he could do. And he responded on his first regular-season series by completing four of six passes for 53 yards as he guided the Colts on a 14-play, 67-yard drive that ended with a 24-yard Dean Biasucci field goal.

Norwood missed a 44-yard try, giving George a chance to show his stuff again. But the anticipated pass-rush began to have its way with him, as Bruce Smith stripped the ball from his grasp and Leon Seals recovered at the Indianapolis 22. A 12-yard Kelly pass to Thurman Thomas on third-and-four gave the Bills a first-and-goal at the 4. Two plays later Kelly rolled left and found third-string tight end Butch Rolle for a 3-yard touchdown toss that put the Bills in front, 10–3, with 5:14 left in the first half. Nicknamed "Mr. Touchdown," Rolle had made his sixth TD grab in as many receptions since 1987, his second year in the league.

The Bills made it 13–3 in the second quarter on a 31-yard Norwood boot set up by J. D. Williams's block of a Rohn Stark punt. They increased the lead to 16–3 before halftime when Norwood hit from 37 yards. But the Colts closed the gap to 16–10 early in the third quarter when George lofted a 25-yard scoring pass to Stanley Morgan, who was being covered as closely as possible by Williams—used as a nickel back after failing to unseat Kirby Jackson as a starter—in the end zone. Only a perfect throw could beat the coverage, and George delivered one.

The Colts threatened to move ahead early in the fourth quarter, but Jackson knocked down a third-down pass and Biasucci missed a chip shot from 29 yards. On the first play of the next Indianapolis series Cornelius Bennett blasted through the middle cleanly, placed his helmet squarely into George's chest just as he released a throw, and drove him to the ground hard enough to knock him unconscious. George was unable to return to the action, and whatever life he had given the Colts disappeared as soon as Jack Trudeau took over at quarterback. The Bills proceeded to get a third field goal from Norwood, from 47 yards, and sealed their 26–10 victory with a 6-yard Thomas touchdown run that followed a Mark Kelso interception with 5:10 remaining.

Although they didn't return to the no-huddle after the opening series, the Bills' early offensive fireworks left plenty of smiles throughout the stadium, as well as in the dressing room.

"That's my kind of football," said an excited Kelly, who called his own plays during the no-huddle. "It's something you haven't seen very much before, but Ted has confidence in me and the receivers and the offensive line so it probably won't be the last time you'll see it."

Kelly, who completed 14 consecutive passes before a drop by Reed in the second quarter, finished the day having connected on 28 of 37 (75.7 percent) for 283 yards and a touchdown without throwing an interception. Thomas caught 9 passes for 61 yards, while Keith McKeller—who started at tight end—grabbed 7 for 78 yards.

Besides keeping Kelly from being sacked, the offensive line had opened enough holes for Thomas to rush for 84 yards. So much for the fears about Parker, who handled himself well, or Ritcher's shoulder, or the alternating of John Davis and Mitch Frerotte at right guard.

"If we just stay together as a team, go out there each week and have some fun, and the defense plays great, who knows where we can go?" Kelly said. "This was one game. Hopefully, there'll be eighteen or nineteen more."

Next stop: Miami. Once considered a journey to hell, the trip had become a favorite of the Bills. It was a chance for a little sun, a little sand, and a sweet victory to savor on the long plane ride home.

The Dolphins used to own the Bills, beating them twenty consecutive times in the 1970s and in six of their first seven visits to Miami in the 1980s. But the tables turned in 1987, with the Bills winning six in a row through 1989. Since arriving in Buffalo in 1986, Levy had compiled a 6–1 record against the Dolphins' Don Shula, the winningest active coach in the NFL.

Levy was even a little smug before the game. He mentioned to reporters how he had come across a story in a Miami newspaper that quoted Shula as saying his team's goals in 1990 were to run, stop the run, and diminish turnovers.

"Sound familiar?" Levy said, flashing a wry grin to those in the media who had often heard him espouse that philosophy. "That's the way you win."

That was the way the Dolphins had defeated New England in their season opener. And that was precisely how they put an end to the Bills' three-year domination of the series. They rushed for 128 yards while allowing 44 on the ground. They lost the ball only once on a fumble, while the Bills coughed it up three times.

The game's turning point came in the Bills' first drive, when the Dolphins stuffed 260-pound Larry Kinnebrew short of a first down on fourth-and-one from the Miami 29. From that point on, the Bills never really posed a challenge. They simply melted in the 88-degree heat on the way to a 30–7 loss that gave Miami a 2–0 record and sole possession of first place in the AFC East. The 1–1 Bills were out of the division's penthouse for the first time since the end of the 1987 season.

"It was easy," boasted Tim McKyer, the Dolphins' outspoken cornerback. "The Bills are a very talented team. But in the NFL, if you don't show up to play, you get beat. You gotta show up every week."

From the start it was obvious the minds of Buffalo players were somewhere other than Joe Robbie Stadium. After Kinnebrew's fourth-down failure Dan Marino drove the Dolphins 71 yards to a touchdown, which Sammie Smith scored on a 2-yard run on fourth-and-goal. On the ensuing possession Pete Metzelaars caught a short Kelly pass, but was hit hard by John Offerdahl, fumbled, and the Dolphins recovered at the Buffalo 36. Marino led his club to the 5, but two of his passes fell incomplete before Pete Stoyanovich kicked a 23-yard field goal to make it 10–0. Two plays after the next kickoff a Kelly pass for McKeller was deflected by McKyer, and safety Louis Oliver made a diving interception at the Bills' 24. That set up a 29-yard Stoyanovich field goal with 5:47 left in the half. Then, with two seconds left in the second quarter, Stoyanovich hit a 48 yarder to give the Dolphins a 16–0 advantage.

Any hopes for a Bills rally died when, on their first series of the third quarter, Thomas fumbled at the Miami 49. Using a no-huddle of their own the Dolphins then marched 51 yards on 9 plays, with Sammie Smith scoring on a 1-yard run. On the first play of the fourth quarter, Marino threw a 17-yard TD pass to Tony Paige to give Miami a 30–0 lead.

The Bills' lone score came when Kelly, operating the no-huddle for the first time all day, moved the Bills 70 yards in 10 plays, the last of which was a one-yard TD run by Kinnebrew.

After that the game belonged to Frank Reich and other reserves, as Levy substituted liberally through the final eight minutes. In doing so, of course, he angered several of his players, who thought he was giving up too soon. Especially Bruce Smith, whose sideline confrontation with Levy and postgame remarks questioning the coach's decision to pull Kelly and other starters rekindled talk of the Bills' being a team in turmoil.

"It was coming, sooner or later," Kent Hull said, referring to the lopsided defeat.

There were a number of close and distant observers of the Bills who felt the same about the internal explosion touched off by the loss. They were never completely convinced by the things they had heard and seen at Camp Harmony. For them the only solid proof would be the way the Bills conducted themselves after their first encounter with adversity.

They gave an approving nod to Levy's swiftly issuing fines totaling $800 to Smith and the three defensive backs who hesitated to leave the field. They did the same to Ralph Wilson's stern warning that any future acts that proved disruptive to the team would result in a suspension or trade.

Now they wanted to see what would happen on the field when the Bills traveled to the Meadowlands to face the Jets for "Monday Night Football."

"The players have a chance to vindicate themselves in front of the entire nation and in front of their peers," Levy said. "Because when you play on Monday night, all the other twenty-six teams in the league are watching, and that should be very important to them. . . . I would hope so."

If the signs of insurrection and discord among the Bills weren't bothersome enough, there were plenty of reasons to worry about the 1–1 Jets. Although young and inexperienced they appeared to be rising from the ashes of their 4–12 finish in 1989. They had a new and progressive-thinking head coach in Bruce Coslet, and talented offensive weapons in receivers Al Toon and Rob Moore and running back Blair Thomas. They also would have the backing of a notoriously rowdy sell-out crowd.

A few days before the game Levy made repairs on the football side by releasing Larry Kinnebrew and filling his spot on the roster with punter Rick Tuten. Kinnebrew's fate was sealed after the fourth-and-one play in Miami—his inability to pick up the yard was a confirmation of eroding speed and strength Levy had seen in the preseason. Tuten had signed with the Bills in the off-season as a Plan B free agent from Philadelphia, then was released in August as the punting job was handed to Nies. But Nies had been unimpressive thereafter, and in his first five punts of the regular season, all against the Dolphins, he averaged only 34.8 yards. He was, though, kept as a kickoff specialist because of Norwood's inability to consistently boom the ball into the end zone.

Of course, the burning question on the night of September 24 centered around the work that had been done since minicamp to make the Bills more unified than the year before. Was it all for naught? Was the kingpin of the AFC East about to collapse?

The Jets were smelling blood. They figured—and reasonably so—if they could take an early lead and incite the crowd, the Bills would quickly fold. Sure enough, on New York's first possession, J. D. Williams drew a 29-yard pass-interference penalty that put the Jets on the Buffalo 1-yard line. Brad Baxter plunged for a touchdown, and the Bills were in a 7-point hole.

Unfazed by the Jets' quick score, the Bills went to their no-huddle offense and raced downfield for a tying touchdown, which came on a 1-yard run by Kenneth Davis. The Jets provided plenty of help on the drive by being penalized twice for too many men on the field—working to perfection, the no-huddle didn't allow them enough time to change defensive personnel—and once for defensive holding. They also had a blown coverage that left Keith McKeller wide open for a 43-yard pass from Kelly that put the ball on the Jets' 1.

On the Bills' next possession Thurman Thomas blasted for carries of 60 and 15 yards to help Buffalo reach the Jets' 5. However, New York's defense stiffened and forced a 24-yard field-goal attempt by Scott Norwood that was blocked by Ron Stallworth.

But the Jets couldn't capitalize and had to punt. The Bills' offense was back in business. First, Kelly threw 24 yards to Andre Reed to the New York 37. Two plays later Jamie Mueller ran 20 yards on a quick trap to the Jets' 8. And two plays after that McKeller went in motion to his right and Kelly rolled in the opposite direction, finding Butch Rolle wide open for a 2-yard TD, his seventh scoring catch in as many receptions since 1987.

The Bills cashed in on a Johnny Hector fumble for a 48-yard Norwood field goal that equaled the second longest of his NFL career, giving him 100 successful kicks as a Bill. Then, with 1:49 left in the half, Buffalo got the ball back and proceeded to move into position for another score, with Thomas rambling for 15 yards and Kelly gaining 2 on a fourth-and-one. On the same play Jets safety Erik McMillan was called for a personal foul, pushing the ball to the 27 and setting up a 42-yard field goal by Norwood, as time expired, to make it 20–7 at halftime.

On their first series of the third quarter the Bills found themselves backed up to their own 3. No problem. Thomas simply tore loose on a delay for a 39-yard gain to midfield. By then he had already joined Cookie Gilchrist, O. J. Simpson, Terry Miller, and Greg Bell in Buffalo's 200-yard-game club. Norwood eventually kicked his third consecutive field goal, from 27 yards, to increase the Bills' lead to 23–7. Midway through the fourth quarter Cornelius Bennett stripped Ken O'Brien of the ball and Chris Hale recovered at the Jets' 12. That set up a 6-yard touchdown pass from Kelly to McKeller for the final points of Buffalo's 30–7 victory—the identical score of the disaster at Joe Robbie Stadium eight days earlier.

In the best showing by a Buffalo running back since 1984, Thomas ran 18 times for 214 yards (a whopping 11.9 yards-per-carry average).

There was nothing complex about the Bills' running game. Most of Thomas's success came on a play called "Ride 16," where the offensive line blocks man-to-man. And it was still a line in transition, with Will Wolford, who had started against Miami, reinjuring his hamstring in the second quarter. Glenn Parker, who opened the game at right guard, took over at left tackle, while John Davis moved in at right guard. As they had in their previous games against Cincinnati and Cleveland, the Jets attempted to take away the run by bunching eight men up front. They often had McMillan on the line, along with three linemen and four linebackers. But the Bills used three wide receivers to force the safety back into coverage, and Parker, Ritcher, Hull, Davis, and Ballard proceeded to pound the Jets' defense into submission.

"I can remember some games where our line blocked well, but I just can't remember getting those long gainers like we did tonight," Hull said. "In fact, we ran the wishbone in college [Mississippi State], and I don't ever remember doing that."

"I didn't think anybody could really manhandle us like the Bills did," Bruce Coslet said. "Nobody should run through us like that. Nobody."

Besides athletic brilliance, Thomas also displayed a keen sense of the outcome's importance. And unlike almost everyone else connected with the Bills, he wasn't afraid to acknowledge it in public.

"If we would have lost this game, there's no telling what would have happened," Thomas said. "The team probably would have exploded and we probably would be bickering again. But we came out with fire in our eyes. We had it in the back of our minds that there was no way in the world we were going to lose this game."

Thomas, whose previous best outing was 148 yards against Miami in 1989, took most of the last quarter off, even though he knew, at 214 yards, he was within range of three single-game rushing honors—seven from Bo Jackson's "Monday Night Football" record set in 1987, 60 from O. J. Simpson's Bills mark set in 1976, and 62 from Walter Payton's NFL standard set in 1977.

Levy offered him a chance to return to the game, but Thomas declined. He saw no point in causing further humiliation to the Jets, whom the Bills would face again in four weeks, or risking an injury.

You read it right. This was a Bills player refusing to allow his ego to get the better of him. This was a Bills player whose personal glory didn't come before everything else.

"You can't go out and say you'll be the individual who makes all the big plays," Thomas said. "You've got to be a team. And that's what we were tonight."

"WHEN THE CLOCK STRIKES FOUR..."

In 1989 much was made about the Bills losing games they were supposed to win.

They were supposed to win at Atlanta, but lost, 30–28. They were supposed to win at New England, but lost, 33–24. They were supposed to win at Seattle, but lost, 17–16. And they were supposed to win at home against New Orleans, but lost, 22–19.

Those were the games critics pointed to when explaining why the Bills didn't secure the home-field advantage in the play-offs and had to travel to Cleveland, where they were bounced in the divisional round.

But the game with the greatest impact of all on events in the AFC in 1989 was the Denver Broncos' 28–14 victory over the Bills in week two at Rich Stadium. If Buffalo had won, the Bills, not the Broncos, would have hosted wild-card winner Pittsburgh in the divisional round. And instead of being home against the Bills, the Browns would have been forced to travel to Denver on the same weekend. And assuming the Bills would have knocked off the Steelers, *they* would have hosted either the Broncos or Browns in the conference championship game.

Not only did Denver snap Buffalo's nine-game home-win streak but, after an 8–8 finish in 1988, the Broncos suddenly reestablished themselves as a contender and rode the crest to an 11–5 record and a third Super Bowl appearance in four years. The Bills went on to spend another Super Sunday in front of their television sets.

Talk about your pivotal contests!

So it made sense that as their 1990 rematch with the Broncos approached Buffalo players spoke with flames in their eyes.

"It's payback time," Bruce Smith said. "They beat us last year in our stadium . . . and that doesn't sit too well with me."

Promised Shane Conlan: "You're not going to see another Miami game out of us. We seem focused. I think we'll look back at Miami as a wake-up call."

Nevertheless, the Bills appeared sound asleep after the opening kickoff on September 30 at Rich Stadium. The Broncos began with an easy-looking, 80-yard drive that ended with a 1-yard touchdown run by Bobby Humphrey (who would finish the day with 177 rushing yards, the most the Bills allowed by an individual since the Jets' Freeman McNeil had 192 in 1985). On that first drive Humphrey carried 6 times for 40 yards.

After a Rick Tuten punt the teams exchanged turnovers. Leonard Smith forced Humphrey to fumble, and Nate Odomes recovered at the Buffalo 29. Then, eight plays later, Greg Kragen forced Jamie Mueller to fumble, and Elliott Smith recovered at the Denver 35. The Broncos proceeded to march into Bills territory but were kept off the scoreboard when Darryl Talley blocked a 49-yard field-goal try by David Treadwell in the second quarter.

On the next series, the Bills squandered a scoring opportunity of their own when Scott Norwood hit the right upright (the first of three that would hit the uprights on the day) on a 37-yard field-goal attempt. The Broncos then punted the ball back with 4:23 left in the second quarter, but the Bills couldn't keep it long—three plays later Kelly was intercepted by Steve Atwater. That gave Denver the ball at the Buffalo 30, and on the first play Elway found Vance Johnson for a 25-yard completion to the 5. Two plays later Steve Sewell ran for a 2-yard touchdown to make it 14–0.

With 1:51 left in the half, Kelly drove the Bills 53 yards to the Broncos' 19, setting up a 27-yard Norwood field goal to cut the margin to 14–3 at halftime.

After failing to capitalize on a Kirby Jackson interception the Bills picked up another turnover in the third quarter when Bruce Smith forced Elway to fumble and Darryl Talley recovered at the Denver 10. On third-and-twelve, Kelly audibled from a pass to a direct snap to Don Smith, who broke through the middle to score, leaping over Dennis Smith for the final four yards. Frank Reich mishandled the extra-point snap, so the Bills could only reduce the gap to 14–9.

They next got the ball back with 5:24 remaining in the third quarter, but Thomas fumbled a first-down handoff from Kelly. The Broncos recovered at the 19, and a late-hit penalty on Shane Conlan moved them to the Bills' 3, from where Sammy Winder ran into the end zone to make it 21–9.

That was still the score as the Broncos lined up for a 24-yard field-goal attempt by Treadwell with less than eleven minutes remaining. It was a "gimme" kick, a chip shot that, for all practical purposes, would put the game out of reach.

The last thing anyone expected was a block, but that was exactly what happened after Nate Odomes came flying around Rick Dennison from the right corner to put himself between the ball and the uprights. The ball took a towering bounce, Cornelius Bennett grabbed it in midair and took off down the left sideline. Gary Kubiak, the holder, gave chase for a while, then made a hopeless dive at Bennett's feet. Eighty yards later Bennett was in the end zone.

Denver 21, Buffalo 16.

"I was just standing there watching and saying, 'Oh, oh! This kick is going to put us away,'" Ralph Wilson said. "And then they blocked it."

Odomes credited Talley's earlier block, on which he had also beaten Dennison from the right side of the Bills' defensive line, for his success.

"So, when they lined up for that second field goal, he [Dennison] gave Darryl, who was still lined up on my side, a lot more attention, which made my path to the ball a lot cleaner," Odomes explained.

Of course, no path was as clean as Bennett's after he grabbed the ball out of the sky.

"It seemed like it took forever for the ball to come down," Bennett said. "I almost jumped for it too soon. I even had a chance to look up and look back down to see where [the] Denver guys were. And I saw right away that, if I got the ball, I could score.

"Once I caught the ball, there was no looking back . . . and there was no catching me."

On Denver's next play from scrimmage the Bills' defense smothered running back Bobby Humphrey after a 1-yard gain. Then, on second-and-nine, John Elway released a pass to his right. Leon Seals jumped and tipped the ball with his left hand, Leonard Smith intercepted and ran 39 yards for a touchdown with 9:27 remaining, exactly one minute after Bennett's TD. The crowd let loose with a roar that rattled eardrums even after Scott Norwood's extra-point try hit the left upright.

Buffalo 22, Denver 21.

On the next kickoff Don Smith buried Vance Johnson at the Denver 10 after his 4-yard return of a squibber by John Nies. An illegal-block penalty pushed the ball back to the 5. Now the crowd was really into it. Elway pleaded with referee Bob McElwee for relief, and the official flipped on his wireless microphone to announce he had asked the Bills to help quiet the fans—the next step would be the loss of a Buffalo time-out. The noise subsided, but only slightly. And Elway was so shook, he dropped Keith Kartz's snap at the Broncos' 2. Bennett pounced on the ball. One play later Kenneth Davis plowed through the left side for another score with 9:10 to play.

Buffalo 29, Denver 21.

Seventy-seven seconds. Five plays. Twenty points.

A crowd of 74,393—many of whom had already started packing their thermoses and rain gear—had witnessed one of the most dramatic turnarounds in the seventeen-year history of the stadium. Perhaps even in the history of the NFL.

But there were more sparks to come.

The Bills had a chance to increase their lead, but Norwood hit the right upright on a 48-yard field-goal attempt with 3:37

left. Denver took over, and Elway, after having another pass batted away by Seals and throwing two others incomplete, converted a fourth-and-ten with a 20-yard throw to Ricky Nattiel. After three more completions and a pair of runs Elway found Nattiel for a 10-yard touchdown to cut the margin to 29–28 with 1:25 on the clock.

Treadwell tried an onside kick. The ball took a big hop over the head of Andre Reed, and 6′7″ Pete Metzelaars, a former basketball standout at Wabash College, dove through several Denver players running past him to recover for the Bills.

All Jim Kelly had to do after that was kneel twice.

"In all my life I've never seen a game change that rapidly, from almost-certain defeat to a victory," Wilson, the Bills' seventy-one-year-old owner, said after his team's 29–28 win. In the blink of an eye the Bills went from being victims of their second thrashing in three weeks to owning a 3–1 record and maintaining a first-place tie with Miami in the AFC East.

Besides the miracles, Denver coach Dan Reeves saw his team outgain the Bills, 410 yards to 197, and 28 first downs to 15. The Broncos also had four sacks (thanks largely to Glenn Parker's trouble replacing Will Wolford at left tackle) to the opponent's two. And they still lost.

"It was one of those crazy games," Reeves said, still looking and sounding shocked several minutes after the final gun. "If you're around long enough, you'll see everything."

Even a spectacular touchdown run by Cornelius Bennett.

Before the game there were some fans and media who sarcastically considered reporting the Bills' linebacker to the authorities as a missing person. They referred to him as "Bisquit," a cruel takeoff on his nickname, "Biscuit." They looked at his disappointing 1989 season and his 14 tackles and zero sacks through the first three games of 1990 and declared him a bust.

In what he called "probably the greatest win I've ever experienced in the game of football," Bennett quieted the critics with a performance that more closely resembled those he gave in the season and a half after the Bills acquired him in a 1987 blockbuster trade with Indianapolis. His 80-yard TD was only the fourth such recovery in team history and the longest ever.

He also was in on 7 tackles, broke up a pass, and twice forced Elway to unload early.

"This is to everybody who doubted me, everybody who wanted to ship my ass out of here," said Bennett, who had cost the Bills two first-round draft picks, a second-rounder, and running back Greg Bell. "You can knock me down, you can kick me, but don't ever count me out."

Then, in a bit of sarcasm of his own, he offered thanks to reporters (who, after a sudden change of heart by Levy, would be allowed to enter the dressing room on Wednesdays) for helping to motivate him.

"I appreciate you guys for criticizing me," Bennett said. "If that's what it takes, keep doing it. Because sooner or later, the good things will start happening again.

"Since 1987 I've had a shoulder that didn't allow me to lift weights in almost two years. I don't care what kind of talent you have. When you're going up against a two-hundred-eighty-five-pound, three-hundred-pound guy, there's nothing you can do when you don't have any strength. I've tried to run around them, I've tried to run through them.

"I apologize to the fans for me being injured and not being able to give it my all. But as long as I stay healthy, you never have to doubt Cornelius Bennett again."

Maybe not. But there were some doubts about the Bills' overall quality. The miraculous victory over Denver couldn't hide the fact that for much of the game the Bills played poorly enough to lose. Through four games they had had 8 turnovers and were allowing opponents to run with relative ease. The next day Levy reminded his players about how lucky they had been against the Broncos.

"But, to your credit, you won because you kept plugging," he told them. "You deserved to win, you earned it. But we have to get better than that. As hard as you try, you're not going to be able to count on that many big plays being made."

Nevertheless, with the Los Angeles Raiders coming to town on Sunday night, October 7, the Bills figured to need all the help they could get.

The Raiders entered the game with a 4–0 record. They were

big. They were physical. And they were as intimidating as ever, especially on defense. Despite injuries to defensive end Howie Long, defensive tackle Mike Wise, cornerback Garry Lewis, and strong safety Mike Harden, the Raiders had allowed only 35 points in their first four games, the fewest in the NFL, and had registered 17 sacks, the most in the league.

This wasn't the poor imitation of the team that once routinely collected victories and championships. This wasn't the club that, after 1985, suddenly stumbled into mediocrity with four consecutive nonwinning, non-play-off seasons—8–8 in 1986, 5–10 in 1987, 7–9 in 1988, and 8–8 in 1989.

After the disastrous 1987 season, Tom Flores retired as head coach and, instead of hiring a replacement within the Raider family, managing general partner Al Davis chose Denver assistant Mike Shanahan. It proved to be the worst decision ever in Davis's otherwise brilliant career of player and coaching moves. Then midway through the 1989 season, he made a family member, Art Shell, a Hall of Fame offensive tackle who had worn the silver and black for fifteen years, the NFL's first black head coach.

The Raiders went on to win seven of their remaining twelve games. Unlike Shanahan, who imposed rules such as no sitting on helmets during practice, Shell allowed his players to have fun. He restored much of the freewheeling atmosphere that had helped put and keep the Raiders on top.

"They're a typical Raiders team now," Kelly said. "They're like they were back in that era when they were rough and tumble. The Raiders controlled the whole league then."

And for the first three and a half quarters against the Bills, they controlled the game. They took the opening kickoff by Norwood—who returned to that duty after Nies was cut a few days earlier—and moved with relative ease from their own 26 to the Buffalo 33. The Bills' defense finally tightened, forcing a 50-yard field-goal attempt by Jeff Jaeger, which was wide left. However, the Bills' offense went three and out, and the Raiders were on the move quickly again. Marcus Allen ran for 14 yards on the first play, Jay Schroeder threw 29 yards to Mervyn Fernandez on the second, and Allen ran three more times for 15 yards to give Los Angeles a first down at the Buffalo 11. On the next play Schroeder threw a touchdown pass to Willie Gault.

The Bills' next series was stopped when Jim Kelly was intercepted by Eddie Anderson, but the Raiders failed to capitalize. The Bills, though, made good on a Raider turnover when Steve Tasker forced Tim Brown to fumble and Chris Hale recovered at the Los Angeles 15. After a 2-yard Thurman Thomas run and an incomplete pass, Kelly fired for Andre Reed in the end zone. The ball was underthrown, but Reed, showing the grace of an acrobat, reached over the back of cornerback Terry McDaniel to grab the ball and tie the score at 7–7 with 4:09 left in the second quarter.

A punt gave the Bills possession at their 12-yard line with 1:43 remaining in the first half. But on the first play Kelly, throwing despite the poor field position, was again picked off by Anderson, whose 31-yard return put the Raiders at the Buffalo 2. The Bills' defense tightened again, forcing Jaeger to kick a 19-yard field goal that made it 10–7 as time expired in the first half.

On the second-half kickoff, a holding penalty by Pete Metzelaars helped bury the Bills at their 6. And after another three-and-out series the Raiders took over at the Bills' 47. Once again they mixed Allen's running with Schroeder's throwing and advanced to the 1, from where Allen ran off tackle to increase the lead to 17–7.

But Kelly brought the Bills right back, hitting Thomas on a 13-yard pass and James Lofton on a 23 yarder. After 8- and 9-yard carries by Thomas, Kelly connected with Reed for a 10-yard gain that put the Bills at the Raiders' 15. On the next play Kelly found McKeller for a touchdown to cut the margin to 17–14 with 1:57 left in the third quarter.

The Raiders kept fighting back and pulled away one more time on an 11-play, 69-yard scoring drive. For a moment the Bills appeared to be dodging a bullet when, on third down at the Buffalo 9, Schroeder threw incomplete. But Kirby Jackson was called for holding, giving the Raiders a first down at the Bills' 4. Two plays later Schroeder threw a touchdown pass to

Steve Smith to make it 24–14 with 10:35 remaining in the fourth quarter.

Then came the fireworks.

Kelly ignited them with a drive that began on his 20. He threw passes to Reed and Thomas for a combined 24 yards, then ran for 6 of his own to the 50. Thomas blasted up the middle for 7 more yards. Then, on first down at the Los Angeles 42, Kelly fired a perfect touchdown bomb to Lofton, a Raider castoff, whose score closed the gap to 24–21.

On the Raiders' next possession Steve Tasker came swooping in from the left side of the Bills' defense and got his left forearm in front of a Jeff Gossett punt. J. D. Williams picked up the ball on a bounce and ran for an easy 38-yard score to put the Bills in front for the first time, 28–24, with 6:52 left in the game.

"They were in a man-for-man blocking scheme and we overloaded the one side," Tasker later explained, proudly displaying a large red welt where the ball struck his arm. "No one blocked me, and that gave me a clear path to the punter. I blew in as fast as I could, but I didn't know if I was going to get him because he's one of the fastest punters in the league, and he usually steps and kicks toward the side away from the unblocked end. This time he happened to step more toward the center of the field, and I happened to be there."

After the blocked punt the roar of the second-largest crowd in Rich Stadium history (80,076) seemed to confuse and disorient the Raiders. You just knew that, at any moment, the Bills' defense was going to come in for the kill. Sure enough, two plays later Bennett sacked Schroeder and won a scramble for the ball at the Raiders' 21. The Bills cashed in with a 23-yard Norwood field goal that made it 31–24.

After that came the clincher. On the third play of the next series Schroeder completed an 18-yard pass to Gault. Then, in a move that shocked the fans almost as much as the Raiders, Nate Odomes yanked the ball right out of Gault's hands and took off for 49 yards and his first NFL touchdown, with 2:34 remaining.

"I just happened to see the ball open, got my hand on it, and was able to get it away from him," said Odomes, who throughout the game exchanged words and shoves with Gault. "I think it kind of surprised him, as well as surprised me."

The Raiders, presumably too stunned to move, barely gave chase. The crowd was so shocked, the cheering was nowhere near as loud as one would have expected for such an amazing feat. Fans just sat with their jaws dropped, as they had a week earlier.

This time, it was 24 points in a span of 6:03 that gave the Bills their third consecutive win, 38–24.

"I don't know why," Talley said, "but when the clock strikes four [as in fourth quarter], everybody's eyes light up and their tails go up, and we just come out from under the woodwork."

For the Bills, though, victory carried a price. In the final two minutes, Mark Kelso had suffered a fractured and dislocated ankle when he landed awkwardly while making the twenty-first interception of his career. In the midst of the postgame celebrating in the Buffalo dressing room was the sobering sight of Kelso wincing and holding his head as he was wheeled on a stretcher to the trainer's room. A number of teammates stopped what they were doing, stared, and shook their heads, realizing he would be out of action for several weeks. Kelso had just been making progress in his bout with migraine syndrome, a condition that had been causing him to have recurring headaches and blurred vision.

He was a favorite among his teammates and highly popular in the community because of his tireless charity work, especially on behalf of children with cancer. In fact, as he awaited the stretcher on the field, he asked one of the trainers to look after a sixteen-year-old boy suffering from cancer, whom Kelso had invited to the game and planned to take into the dressing room afterward. The injury forced him to break the engagement, but to make it up, he arranged for the boy to receive a game ball.

Meanwhile, the Raiders were still trying to figure out what had hit them in that six-minute, three-second flurry. Shock and bewilderment filled their dressing room, where Al Davis, who refused to speak with reporters, could be heard cursing the team's fate from the trainer's room.

"They didn't beat us heads-up," Los Angeles defensive end Greg Townsend argued. "They didn't sit there and play football on the line of scrimmage with us. They just beat us with fluke plays."

The frustration was understandable. For the second week in a row the final numbers on the Rich Stadium scoreboard contradicted every other game statistic. The Raiders gained 347 yards to Buffalo's 280. The Raiders' time of possession was 39:14 to Buffalo's 20:46.

Levy used a boxing anecdote to make the point that numbers don't always add up the way they should: "Billy Conn beat the hell out of Joe Louis for twelve rounds, but Louis knocked him out in the thirteenth."

Someone asked Levy if he felt fortunate that his team was 4–1 instead of 2–3. The coach bristled.

"Not at all. I consider it an 'earned' four and one. Every inch."

That seemed to be the prevailing attitude in the dressing room. The players didn't want to hear even the slightest suggestion that their success was more a case of being lucky than good.

"A lot of people are counting us out," Reed said. "When we're losing they're counting us out left and right. But we're no quitters. We're not going to be counted out. We have a don't-die attitude."

The Monday night pounding of the Jets had been an impressive response to the Miami debacle. But back-to-back displays of so much grit and determination provided even stronger evidence that the Bills had, indeed, turned over a new leaf. If anything requires a team to be unified, it is the challenge of overcoming a huge deficit.

Without a doubt the driving force behind the Bills' gritty comebacks against Denver and Los Angeles was their special teams. Counting J. D. Williams's punt block in the season opener, the Bills' special teams had erased 4 kicks the first 5 games. They directly or indirectly had produced 24 points, while eliminating 6.

Considering Marv Levy's background it wasn't surprising that the Bills' special teams have consistently ranked among the NFL's best. He began his pro coaching career by overseeing Philadelphia's kicking teams in 1969. He then joined George Allen's staff as special teams coach for the Los Angeles Rams in 1970 and followed him to Washington in the same capacity a year later, where his unit played a key role in the Redskins' drive to Super Bowl VII. Levy may be the only man on earth ever to describe the double thud of a blocked kick as "the most beautiful sound since Glenn Miller."

To say the Bills are committed to having great special-teams play would be a gross understatement. They're obsessed.

Case in point: Shortly before the Raiders' game Levy had any number of places he could have been making last-minute checks on the field. He could have been standing with Jim Kelly, talking about how to attack Los Angeles' smothering defense. He could have been standing with his defensive linemen and linebackers, talking about how to stop the Raiders' running backs. Instead, Levy was on the other side of the field, holding a stopwatch as he viewed the opposition practice field goals and punts. He was double-checking the speed with which they made their kicks—their "get-off" times.

For the record, neither Shell nor any of the Raiders assistant coaches did the same on the Buffalo side. For the record, few if any opposing coaches have ever been seen on the Buffalo side before a game.

"We convey, as a coaching staff, three equally important departments of play—offense, defense, and special teams," Levy said. "We keep players on our team because of their special teams contribution, even more so than maybe if they would have been rated one hundred percent only on how they could play their offensive or defensive position and might have been a hair ahead of someone else. Because a big play in the kicking game, somehow or other, has a more uplifting effect than in almost any other area where it occurs."

Steve Tasker, the Bills' 5′9″, 185-pound special-teams captain, whose boyish features belie the nature of his work, has made a science of special-teams play.

"It's as technical as any other part of the game; it's just not as complex," Tasker said. "We have specific assignments and things that we look for opponents to do and things we try to get done. And if we see a weakness or someplace where we can exploit their special teams or personnel, we're just like any other facet of the game.

"Of course, you have to take the time to know what you're doing. You have to watch a great deal of film. A lot of guys sit through a special-teams meeting with their head against the wall, sleeping. But if you sit up and take notice, you'll see there are keys and facets of that part of the game that can make a difference in what you do.

"For instance, when we rush a punt, I'll study the guy I'm going to rush against. I'll watch him against two or three different opponents, and I can tell what move he's going to be the most susceptible to. Such as an up-and-under move. That's where I start to rush outside, the guy steps outside to get me, and I step underneath him inside. And you don't always have to get a block to be successful. Sometimes you can draw a holding penalty, which is also very damaging to the other team.

"A lot of people can't understand why the Bills wouldn't keep a better player at a position as opposed to another guy, just for the fact that he can cover kicks. But watching the Denver and Raider games, I think, finally, it dawned on the average fan that players like myself and Butch Rolle and Mark Pike are important to have on the squad. Special teams aren't to the point that offense and defense are, and they probably shouldn't be. But when you see that, sometimes, one out of every four plays in a game is a kicking play, it makes you stop and think. I mean, there could be as many as twenty-eight kicking plays in a game. That's like three or four drives."

When the Bills punt, Tasker lines up wide to the outside in the "gunner" position, which is every bit as aggressive as it sounds. His job is to race downfield and put the hardest hit he can on the return man—provided a fair catch hasn't been called, of course. Knowing this, the opposition usually has two men trying to stop Tasker at the line of scrimmage. More often than not, they fail.

Speed has something to do with it. Tasker was a high school sprint champion in Kansas, and by NFL skill-position standards, he has a decent 40-yard dash clocking of 4.5 seconds.

But he gives most of the credit to the time he spends in practice at his "regular" wide receiver position.

"I get a lot of work releasing off the line as a wide receiver, with a guy in my face," Tasker explained. "And I don't think the defensive backs covering me on special teams spend that much time working on double-teaming somebody at the line, because they're usually working on regular defense in practice. There's just no defense that calls for them to cover a guy two-on-one at the line, except the punt team. And no team spends much time on that with their defensive backs.

"I just rely on quickness at the line of scrimmage. Most of the time I'm able to get enough of an edge, where I can turn the corner. And once I get by them they can't legally hit me in the back and they can't grab me. All I really have to get is a half step, and I should be safe. After that, if I can, I take a peek up at the punt to see where it's going. But I usually just watch the return man, because if I just go to him, I'm going to go to the ball. If he calls for a fair catch near the end zone, I go past him looking for the ball to go over him and try to down it as close to the goal line as possible. If we're out toward the middle of the field and he calls for a fair catch, I stay as close to him as I can because if he fumbles it, I'll be in a position to grab it."

Levy may make last-minute "get-off" checks, but the man he entrusts to guide his special teams is Bruce DeHaven. Since Levy hired DeHaven in 1987, the Bills had built a three-year streak leading the NFL in kickoff coverage, and they appeared well on their way to making it four seasons in a row in 1990.

It's not unusual for someone to want to grow up and coach football. But who ever heard of anyone wanting to be a special-teams coach? That chore usually is given to the junior member of the staff until he proves himself worthy of "real" coaching duties, such as designing blocking schemes, pass patterns, and blitzes. And then it will be passed on to the next sucker who comes along.

DeHaven had always thought that way until he received some career advice from John Madden. When DeHaven was coaching high school football in Oxford, Kansas, he attended a clinic in Oklahoma City where Madden, then head coach of the then Oakland Raiders, was the featured speaker.

"I got to talking to him after his speech, and I asked him what would be the best way for a guy to break into coaching professional football," DeHaven recalled. "He said, 'To me, the best door right now is special teams. Boy, those guys are really starting to do lots of things, and more and more teams are going to be looking for them.' That always was kind of in the back of my mind after that."

In 1985, while his Chicago Blitz squad was inactive, Marv Levy was a color commentator on USFL cable telecasts. One weekend he was assigned to a game involving the Orlando Renegades.

"They did not have a very good team overall," Levy said. "But I was very impressed with their special teams." He took note of the fact that the unit was coached by DeHaven, who had previously guided the special teams of the USFL's New Jersey Generals and Pittsburgh Maulers.

Two years later, with the USFL's folding, DeHaven was out of professional football and back to teaching high school. When restructuring his staff for his first full season with the Bills, Levy remembered the Renegades' game and brought DeHaven to Buffalo.

The head coach's emphasis on special teams would figure to make DeHaven's life miserable. But he insisted it is more of a help than a hindrance.

"I think there's a pretty good correlation between the time you spend and the results you get," DeHaven pointed out. "If you're working for a head coach who affords you the meeting time and time in practice to work on them, you've got a pretty good chance to have good special teams."

"Our special-teams game plan is ninety-five percent Bruce's," Levy said. "He's successful because he's a good teacher. He organizes very well. He has a good touch with the players. He does a good job of prescouting."

Although DeHaven puts a great deal of stock in Xs and Os, he puts even more in the sheer guts (insanity?) required to run full speed and hurl one's body into another's. All while receiving far less pay and recognition than the regulars on offense and defense.

"There's a group of about seven or eight guys—guys like Steve Tasker, Butch Rolle, Mark Pike—who have been around for three or four years and who take a great deal of pride in what the special teams do," DeHaven explained. "And the more success they have, it's that much easier to motivate the whole group the next time out. This is their only chance to play in a ball game if they're not a starter, so they want to make the best show they can out there.

"Speed and toughness are two of the prime prerequisites. There are just some guys who have a certain enthusiasm for playing special teams that makes them better than what they should be."

Not that that's any guarantee kicks will be blocked, touchdowns will be scored, and games will be turned around.

As Tasker pointed out, "You can go a whole season without making as many big special teams plays as we've made in the last two weeks."

And you can go a lifetime without seeing two more electrifying fourth quarters.

GONE FISHIN'

The week after the Raiders game posed a different kind of challenge for the Bills: maintaining momentum while standing still.

In a new twist, the NFL had created a regular-season bye week for each team so that its sixteen-game schedule could be stretched over seventeen weeks. The idea was to provide more action for the television networks, which, in the spring, had agreed to pay the league a record $3.65 billion for broadcast rights. For that kind of money the NFL was only too quick to oblige. It even threw in a pair of extra wild-card play-off games.

Each club's blank spot was determined by division and the final 1989 standings. As a top-four finisher in the AFC East, the Bills were off the weekend of October 14, along with Miami, Indianapolis, and New England. Because they finished fifth in the division, the Jets' bye wouldn't come until week fourteen, along with the league's other fifth-place finishers: San Diego, Tampa Bay, and Dallas.

The thought of their season coming to a screeching halt after five highly emotional games left everyone a little uneasy. No one could help wondering if the Bills would stay focused. Could they keep the edge from their three-game winning streak alive until October 21, when they would face the Jets again at home?

After scaled-down practices Wednesday through Friday, Levy gave his players the bye weekend off. Before doing so, he also gave them something to ponder: "This is a chance to rest and regenerate a little bit. You don't have quite the same there's-a-game-this-Sunday pressure on you. By the same token, don't take it as an excuse to vegetate and degenerate. Refresh, but don't let it take you down."

Some players visited family and friends out of town. Others took the kids to the zoo. Still others played golf.

Bruce Smith did a little fishing in his hometown of Norfolk, Virginia. Jim Kelly handled the coin toss for the homecoming game at his high school alma mater in East Brady, Pennsylvania. Keith McKeller and his wife tried out their new video camera at Niagara Falls. Leon Seals put together the crib for his soon-to-arrive baby.

Even Marv Levy managed to pull himself away from the stack of Jets videotapes on his desk. He paid a visit to Letchworth State Park for a breathtaking view of fall foliage.

"It's funny, but I didn't even know what autumn was like, because you're in the stadium all the time," he said. "You come to work in the morning and it's dark. You go home at night and it's dark."

One player who couldn't take his mind off football during that time, however, was John Hagy. Because of Mark Kelso's ankle injuries he was about to get his big chance to start at free safety.

"I really feel bad for Mark, but I'm here to play, too," Hagy said. "I feel confident. Mentally, I know what I'm doing. I just need to get out there and play."

Believe it or not, the Bills' coaches were worried about the 2–4 Jets. Even after watching their team humiliate them, 30–7, a month earlier. Even after watching the Jets lose to San Diego 39–3 while the Bills enjoyed some R&R. The coaches' concern seemed to go beyond the usual phobia those in their profession have about every opponent, regardless of its record.

First, there was the bye week. True, it allowed injuries to

heal and tired legs to become fresh again. But it also posed a real threat to the Bills' progress. After all, they hadn't exactly cruised to most of their victories. Their success took everything they could give, physically and emotionally, and the timing of a first-ever week off during the season (excluding strike years) seemed to invite a letdown.

Second, there was the rematch factor. Usually it is a struggle for an NFL team to beat an opponent twice in the same season. The losing club can correct coaching and player mistakes made the first time, and tends to be driven by revenge (in the Jets' case, there was the added incentive of trying to snap a six-game losing streak to Buffalo). And the winner might be lulled into not taking the second game as seriously as the first.

Third, there was the rebound factor. NFL teams, especially in the early part of the 1990 season, seemed to be bouncing back from poor showings with inspired ones. The Jets had already done so once, after their loss to the Bills. The Bills had also rebounded against the Jets, after losing to Miami. So had Cleveland, after being shut out by Kansas City, and the Chargers, after a disastrous showing against Pittsburgh.

Finally, there was the Bills' tendency to win the big ones and lose the small ones. In 1988 they squandered a chance to capture home-field advantage in the play-offs by losing to lowly Tampa Bay. In 1989 they dropped four games to teams at or below .500.

Levy continued to be bothered by those inexcusable flops.

"It's a hurdle we're going to have to get over in order to be a championship-level team," he admitted. "We haven't arrived anywhere yet. We're still struggling to get better. To say this team is strong, dominant, and has a killer instinct is premature."

But in their upcoming four-game stretch against the Jets, New England, Cleveland, and Phoenix—teams with a combined record of 8–19—the Bills would have an excellent chance to prove themselves. They'd also have an excellent chance to damage their credibility.

Which path would they follow?

After the teams exchanged punts on their opening drives it seemed as if the Bills might have chosen the latter. Ken

O'Brien got the Jets in gear from their own 37, throwing a 25-yard pass to Al Toon. Five straight running plays moved the ball to the Buffalo 13. On second down Cornelius Bennett was called for unnecessary roughness while forcing O'Brien to throw incomplete, and the Jets had a first down at the 7. Freeman McNeil carried for 2 yards on the next play and followed it with a 5-yard touchdown run with 5:21 left in the first quarter.

Two plays later Jim Kelly was intercepted by Erik McMillan, whose 19-yard return put the ball at the Bills' 30. A 2-yard run by O'Brien kept the drive alive on third-and-one, and an 8-yard carry by holder/punter Joe Prokop on a fake field goal gave New York a first down at the 3. After a 1-yard run by McNeil, O'Brien found tight end Mark Boyer for a touchdown, to make it 14–0 three seconds into the second quarter.

The situation looked even bleaker for the Bills because, during McMillan's interception, Thurman Thomas suffered an injury to his right knee. He would return for a 2-yard carry, then spend the rest of the game on the sidelines. But during the series after the Jets' second score, the Bills, with a strong effort from number-two running back Kenneth Davis, moved easily into Jets territory from their own 36. A pass-interference penalty by Brian Washington, while covering Keith McKeller, turned a third-and-seven at the New York 19 into a first-and-ten at the 16. Two plays later Kelly found Andre Reed for a 19-yard touchdown pass.

The Jets wasted no time regaining control. Starting from their own 29, they put together an impressive scoring march, helped by a face-mask penalty committed by Leonard Smith and a 17-yard O'Brien pass to Al Toon on fourth-and-five from the Buffalo 34. After a 3-yard McNeil run and a false start penalty on left offensive tackle Jeff Criswell—who was having his typical long day against Bruce Smith—O'Brien connected with Toon for a 19-yard touchdown pass to give the Jets a 21–7 lead with 5:24 remaining in the second quarter.

Again the Bills bounced back, although the drive had its shaky moments. First, on second-and-eight from the Buffalo 41, Jim Ritcher was called for a 10-yard holding penalty on an incomplete pass. Then, on the next play, the Bills were flagged

5 yards for delay of game. Faced with a second-and-twenty-three from his 26, Kelly scrambled for a 9-yard gain. One play later Reed exploded for 26 yards on a reverse, giving Buffalo a first down at the Jets' 39. Kelly then threw a 25-yard pass to James Lofton, followed by a 14-yard TD toss to Reed to cut the margin to 21–14.

Despite regaining possession at the New York 47 with 1:31 to go in the second quarter, the Bills were unable to get into the end zone. But they did pick up a 29-yard field goal by Scott Norwood just before halftime.

The Jets' first series of the second half didn't look promising after a 53-yard Tuten punt and an illegal block penalty pinned them at their 8. But O'Brien fought his way out by completing several big passes—14 yards to Terance Mathis on third-and-seven from the New York 11; 20 yards to Rob Moore on second-and-twenty-five from the New York 41; and another 25 yards to Toon on the next play. But the march stalled at the Buffalo 11, and the Jets settled for a 28-yard Pat Leahy field goal to make it 24–17 with 7:27 remaining in the third quarter.

Thanks to Carlton Bailey's holding penalty on the ensuing kickoff, the Bills would have to start from their own 9. Kelly wasn't bothered in the least. He quickly fired 12- and 19-yard passes to Reed. Then, on first-and-ten from his 40, he threw a magnificent 60-yard touchdown bomb to James Lofton, who was wide open after beating John Booty's bump-and-run coverage. In three plays and 1:09 the score was tied at 24–24.

After trading punts the Bills appeared in position to move ahead early in the fourth quarter when Kirby Jackson intercepted an O'Brien pass at the Jets' 49. A 12-yard reverse by Andre Reed and Kenneth Davis runs of 3 and 12 yards put Buffalo at the New York 22. Changing a call at the line, Kelly then faked a toss and ran 11 yards on a bootleg, and Jamie Mueller carried for 5 more to the 6. When the Bills could advance no further, out trotted Norwood for a 24-yard field-goal attempt. But the chip shot sailed wide to the left, leaving most of the 79,002 fans in Rich Stadium wondering whether this was a game the Bills just weren't meant to win.

The Jets took over at their own 20, and after a 1-yard gain by Brad Baxter, O'Brien connected on passes of 10 and 22 yards to McNeil and Moore to put the ball at the Buffalo 47. Three runs advanced the Jets to the 38, and after a 9-yard O'Brien throw to Boyer and a 9-yard carry by Johnny Hector, they were at the 15. The Jets called a time-out, then ran three straight times to set up a 25-yard Leahy field goal that put them ahead, 27–24, with 2:46 left in the game.

But Bills players weren't about to concede the end of their three-game winning streak and six-game dominance of the Jets, not as long as Jim Kelly was still breathing.

"Three minutes is like an eternity for a guy like Jim," Kent Hull would remind reporters afterward.

Actually, only 2:38 remained when the Bills' offense took the field at their own 29. After a first-down incomplete Kelly found Reed for a 9-yard pass, and on third-and-one, Don Smith plunged for 5 yards. Kelly then hit Pete Metzelaars on two consecutive passes and called a time-out with 1:29 showing on the clock, before throwing 11 yards to Reed to give Buffalo a first down at the Jets' 29. A pair of incompletes followed, then Kelly hooked up with Reed—for the eighth time that day—on a 16-yard curl pattern before calling the team's second time-out with 48 seconds showing.

When a pass in the flat to Jamie Mueller lost a yard the Bills had a second-and-ten from the New York 14. They came out in a four-wide-receiver formation, with Jamie Mueller as the lone back. Kelly took the snap and immediately looked for one of his two primary targets—slot men Andre Reed and Don Smith—but both were covered. So he scrambled to his left. Mueller's first responsibility on the play was to block any linebacker pass-rushing from the weak side. None did, so he drifted out of the backfield trying to find an opening in the secondary in case Kelly was desperate for someone to throw to. And Kelly would have to be very desperate, considering how infrequently the 225-pound blocking fullback caught the ball. Spotting Mueller, Kelly waved him one way, then another, and after what seemed like several long minutes, zipped a perfect pass to him in the end zone to give the Bills a 30–27 lead with 19 seconds left.

"It's definitely not supposed to go to Jamie Mueller," the quarterback confirmed.

"This was the last thing I ever expected," Mueller confessed.

How improbable was Mueller's being a hero with his hands? In a postgame news conference a disbelieving reporter couldn't resist asking if, in fact, he had actually tried to get open. Without missing a beat, Mueller replied sarcastically, "Nah, I wasn't trying to get open. Actually, I was going for some water on the sidelines."

The touchdown reception was the first of his four-year NFL career. The only other time as a pro he had even reached the end zone with the ball was in 1987, his rookie year. And the last time he had caught a pass there was in 1986, while playing for Benedictine College in Atchison, Kansas.

The only imperfection in the score against the Jets was Norwood's extra-point try, which, like his 24-yard field-goal attempt, was wide left. That gave the Jets a small prayer with 12 seconds on the clock but, for some strange reason, they managed to get off only one play, with O'Brien being sacked by Bruce Smith for a 4-yard loss to ice the Bills' 30–27 win.

The touchdown pass to Mueller was Kelly's fourth of the day, his most in an NFL game since the play-off defeat at Cleveland. Picking up the slack for Thurman Thomas, Kelly threw for a season-high 297 yards while completing 19 of 32 attempts.

Was a third consecutive nerve-fraying, cardiac-arresting win too many for Levy to handle? "You wouldn't know, looking at me, that I'm thirty-one years old," cracked the sixty-two-year-old coach.

The victory also kept the Bills apace with the Dolphins, who had improved their record to 5–1 with a 17–10 win over New England the previous Thursday night.

Unfortunately, the game did have an ugly moment. As the teams headed for their dressing rooms, a scuffle broke out in the tunnel when Bruce Smith confronted Mark Boyer, whom Smith accused of trying to injure his knees during the game. They exchanged words, but were separated before trading any punches. Smith had told the Jets' tight end repeatedly that if he didn't stop blocking at his knees, he was "going to kick his ass in the tunnel." Boyer ignored the warnings, as well as those he received from officials responding to Smith's complaints.

"It's flagrantly going after a person's knees, and if he'd have caught me flush on my knee, he'd have ruined my career," Smith said. "The league ought to do something about it, because it's ridiculous. Apparently, he was taught to do that."

The other downer from the game was Norwood's performance. The field-goal miss was his sixth in sixteen tries since the beginning of the season, while his extra-point failure was his second in eighteen. Three weeks earlier he had experienced a kicker's nightmare when he hit an upright on two field-goal tries, as well as on a point-after attempt.

But after what had happened against the Jets, Norwood was convinced he knew the cause of his problems: the angle of his soccer-style approach wasn't wide enough. By extending it a mere five inches he was certain he could escape his first serious slump since joining the Bills in 1985.

"You set yourself up for failure if your angle is too shallow, if you're not out far enough," Norwood said. "If you start out straight, your hips have only one way to go, and it sets you up for a hook, whereas if I'm over more, the hips can't go through that far. It takes a few misses like that to come up with such an evaluation."

The first person to notice the flaw in Norwood's approach was his father, Del, a retired high school football coach who serves as his son's holder during off-season practices in his native Virginia. His father had pointed it out a few weeks before the second Jets' game, but Norwood didn't pay much attention. He felt the one big plus from reducing his angle—increased power—outweighed any minus.

"My father's a hawk for that type of thing," Norwood said. "He drives eight hours, one way, from Virginia to our home games, and he'll just sit there and watch everything I do through his binoculars. I really respect his opinion."

So did special-teams coach Bruce DeHaven. He spotted the shallow angle on his own and couldn't help but smile when Norwood told him of his father's observation. He also wouldn't express anything but absolute confidence in Norwood's ability to make the correction and return to his dependable form.

"If I had to have someone in the NFL kick a field goal to get us into the play-offs tomorrow, Scott Norwood is the guy I'd want kicking it, regardless of what's happened in recent weeks," DeHaven said. "There isn't a kicker in the league who hasn't had a time when he's struggled a bit. It's a confidence thing. Miss a couple, and maybe you think a bit. But I think we're on the right track with Scott."

Scott Norwood might have been struggling, but his kicking problems looked like a tiny molehill compared to the recent fortunes of the Bills' next opponents, the New England Patriots. Led by thirty-seven-year-old veteran Steve Grogan, it seemed appropriate that the teams' first encounter, on October 28, would be played at decaying Sullivan Stadium. And like their stadium, where in 1989 the artificial turf was coming unglued in chunks, the Patriots were, to put it mildly, a mess. For openers, they were 1–5, their poorest start since their 2–14 season in 1981. Their fans were staying away by the thousands. They were being mocked and scorned by local and national media also.

Worst of all, losing was only one of their problems.

NFL commissioner Paul Tagliabue was awaiting an investigator's report on allegations of sexual harassment by five New England players of *Boston Herald* sportswriter Lisa Olson, as well as on the team's handling of this incident. As if that hadn't been enough, two weeks before their game against the Bills, Patriots wide receivers Irving Fryar and Hart Lee Dykes were involved in a brawl outside a Providence, Rhode Island, nightclub. Fryar was charged with illegal possession of a loaded, semiautomatic pistol and suffered a cut on the back of his head. Dykes sustained an eye injury that would sideline him against Buffalo. Both were also fined by coach Rod Rust for missing a meeting the day after the altercation.

Looking to shake things up in the throes of a four-game losing streak, Rust decided to bench starting quarterback Marc Wilson and replace him with Grogan. In his sixteenth NFL season, Grogan began the year as New England's number-one quarterback, but suffered a neck injury in week two in a 16–14 victory over Indianapolis. After Wilson took over the offense floundered. With Grogan at the controls through the years, the Patriots had won 74 games and, in the first two weeks of the season, had scored 40 points. With Wilson starting they had only one win and had scored a mere 37 points in their previous four outings.

"I don't care if he's sixty-seven, the guy still scares the hell out of me," Darryl Talley said of Grogan. "He still has a strong arm; he's still very mobile; and he's damn smart. Some quarterbacks you can make mistakes with. Make a mistake against Grogan and he'll beat you. Beat you bad."

Despite his 13–6 lifetime record against the Bills, Grogan shook his head when told of the concern being voiced by Buffalo defenders. "I think they're feeding you guys a line," he told reporters. "I don't know why anybody would be afraid of me right now."

He had a point. In fact, before the Patriots would even allow him to take the field against the Bills, they made Grogan sign a letter acknowledging he had received written advice from a neurosurgeon that he shouldn't play football because of recurring spinal trouble. As a reminder of how cold things could get in the world of professional sports, the team wanted to protect itself from a potential lawsuit in the event Grogan suffered a serious neck injury or something of that nature against Buffalo or any future opponent.

Still, the thought of facing the Patriots made the Bills uneasy. For one thing, they had lost twelve of their previous fifteen meetings with them, including ten of twelve on the road. For another, in their 1989 game at Foxboro, Massachusetts, when Buffalo was 7–3 and New England was 3–7, the Patriots scored 20 points in the final 8:46 for a 33–24 win.

"When I think of New England, I always think of a tough game," Kent Hull said. "It's not the same rivalry as us and Miami, but there's some strong feelings in there. And, historically, we just don't play well in Foxboro."

Sure enough, cloud-covered and rain-drenched Sullivan Stadium looked as gloomy as usual for the Bills' annual visit. It seemed a perfect setting for the hopeless, hapless Patriots to score another upset.

But the Bills made it clear from their opening series, which started on the Buffalo 32 after a punt, that they had come to play.

Beginning with a 19-yard completion to Andre Reed on third-and-nine, Kelly connected on five consecutive passes to drive the Bills to a first down at the New England 3. Jamie Mueller carried to the 1, and on the next play Don Smith crashed through the middle to give the Bills a 7–0 lead.

After the ensuing kickoff Grogan managed to guide the Patriots to the Buffalo 5, but a pass for Greg McMurtry was intercepted by Nate Odomes in the end zone for a touchback three seconds into the second quarter. The Bills failed to get any points out of the turnover, though.

Playing despite the bruised knee that caused him to miss most of the Jets' game the week before, Thurman Thomas opened Buffalo's third possession by taking a pitch for 9 yards. Mueller then ripped off 14 more, and after tripping and falling for a 9-yard loss, Kelly completed two passes into a stiff wind. The first was a 10-yarder to Keith McKeller. The second was a 52-yard bomb to James Lofton, who was so wide open that he slowed down and waited for the poorly thrown ball to float into his hands before being tackled at the Patriots' 14. An incomplete followed, then Thomas ran off right tackle for 11 yards. On the next play he took a pitch to the same side for a 3-yard touchdown to make it 14–0 with 7:04 left in the first half.

No one appreciated the fast two-touchdown cushion more than members of Buffalo's defense. "I've been saying the whole year that we need to jump up on people early so we can do what we do best, and that's get after people, and go out there and have fun," Bruce Smith said afterward.

There appeared to be plenty of time for the Bills to extend their lead before halftime. However, the Patriots took the next kickoff and devoured the rest of the quarter with a 14-play, 54-yard drive that ended with a 32-yard Jason Staurovsky field goal. One play earlier John Hagy had saved a potential touchdown by diving to deflect a Grogan pass to Eric Sievers at the goal line.

After punts were traded on the first two possessions of the third quarter, the Bills slowly but surely took command. On their next series Scott Norwood made the initial step out of his slump by hitting a 35-yard field goal. Two plays later Grogan fumbled and Ray Bentley recovered at the New England 30. Three minutes after that Norwood again booted a 35-yarder to give the Bills a 20–3 advantage.

The Patriots punted once more, and the Bills took over at their own 30 with 4:02 remaining in the third quarter. Four runs by Thomas gave Buffalo a first down at the New England 29. Kelly then threw a 14-yard pass to Lofton, and after a 5-yard penalty on the Bills, he found McKeller for a 20-yard touchdown to make it 27–3. The final points in Buffalo's 27–10 victory came on a 19-yard Grogan touchdown pass to Sammy Martin early in the fourth quarter.

"As a team, we felt this was a must win," said Thomas, who rushed for 136 yards. "We couldn't let a one-and-five team beat us. In order to be a championship team, you've got to put away teams like New England."

In putting away Grogan, however, most Bills defenders tried to be gentle. Leon Seals, for one, couldn't help but squirm at the thought of causing the injury for which the Patriots were going to such great lengths to avoid liability. And he couldn't help but feel relieved after the game when he saw Grogan exit the field in one piece. In fact, Seals confessed he had done everything humanly possible—short of staying on the sidelines or standing still on the field—to avoid delivering a crippling hit to Grogan.

"I'm just going to be honest about it, I wasn't going in there for the kill," Seals said. "A couple of us talked about it before the game even started, and everybody said, 'I just hope I'm not the one to go in and hit him and have him stay down. If I ever get a sack, I hope he gets back up.' With any kind of hit, the guy could go down for good. And for you to deliver that hit, it's going to be something you're going to have to live with the rest of your life."

Seals did have one of the Bills' three sacks—Bruce Smith and Carlton Bailey had the others—but he didn't put the usual steam into it.

"I went back there and got him, but I wasn't saying, 'I'm going to kill you,' and that kind of stuff," he said. "It's a touchy situation, because as a defensive lineman, you're taught to go in there and rip a person's head off. But in a situation like that, you have to kind of low-key it. You have to have respect for a guy like that."

With their fifth consecutive win the Bills were 6–1, and continued to share first place in the AFC East with the Dolphins, who the same day had pounded Indianapolis, 27–7.

The Bills' eighth opponent, Cleveland, didn't look a whole lot tougher than the seventh. Plagued by age, injuries, poor drafting, and some horrible luck, the Browns were 2–6 and threatening to go belly-up in the Cuyahoga River.

Their once powerful running game had vanished, averaging a mere 68.5 yards per game. Their once proud defense, the cornerstone of the Browns' franchise, was allowing 295 yards and 24 points per outing.

To put it another way, the Browns were headed for the dogs. Not the Dawgs, as in the nickname their defense had acquired in happier times, but D-O-G-S. And change was in the wind. The benching of quarterback Bernie Kosar, whose poor mobility rendered him ineffective behind a line that had already given up 23 sacks, seemed inevitable (in a Cleveland newspaper poll of 800 fans, 90 percent called for Mike Pagel to start). So did the firing of head coach Bud Carson, in only his second season at the Browns' helm.

In 1989 Cleveland owner Art Modell had hired Carson to finish the job Marty Schottenheimer started before leaving for Kansas City. Carson responded by guiding the team to a third appearance in the AFC Championship Game for a third showdown with Denver since 1986. As in the first two, the Browns lost. But it seemed like a good rookie season for Carson, something upon which he figured to build.

Instead, 1990 brought a collapse.

Nevertheless, they were the Browns. They were the team responsible for bringing Buffalo's 1989 season to a terribly disappointing end. They were a club the Bills hadn't beaten since 1981. And Cleveland Stadium was a place they hadn't won in since 1974.

The night before each game, Bills players usually are shown, as a group or by position, videotape from their last encounter with the next day's opponent. Depending on the footage they've seen during the week, it will either be first- or second-half action. On the Thursday before their November 4 rematch with the Browns they saw the first 30 minutes of the gut-wrenching, heartbreaking play-off loss ten months earlier. On Saturday night they saw the final two quarters. And that, of course, gave them one more look at The Drop, The Interception, and all the other frustrating moments that caused the 34–30 defeat to remain lodged in their throats every day since.

They watched in silence, especially when the final two plays appeared—Ronnie Harmon's touchdown drop and Kelly's pass into the hands of Clay Matthews. "Everywhere you turned," Reed said, slowly shaking his head, "those plays were there for at least a month and a half after the season was over."

When they stopped showing up on TV and in magazines, they continued to show up in dreams. Make that nightmares.

"I don't really think about those last two plays or the other [eight] dropped passes as much as I do about that kickoff return," Steve Tasker said, referring to Eric Metcalf's 90-yard touchdown that broke the game open for the Browns in the third quarter. "I replay that in my mind all the time. The things that stay with you are the things that go wrong when you're on the field. And that's when I was on the field."

"In life, you don't get many second opportunities," Leon Seals said. "Just getting a second opportunity to play Cleveland is motivation in itself. We knew we were a better team, and the score didn't represent that. Now there's a chance to redo it, and hopefully we'll come out on top."

Added Jamie Mueller, a Cleveland native, "I'm sure the thought of that last game is going to give everybody that little extra push that we're going to need. Especially if it's a close ball game."

On Buffalo's opening drive Kelly completed three passes, including a 20 yarder to Reed. Two runs by Mueller and an 8-yard carry by Thomas put the ball at the Cleveland 3. On the next play the Bills lined up with their "Elephant" personnel, using 300-pound Glenn Parker and 285-pound Mitch Frerotte as tight ends and 235-pounder Carwell Gardner at fullback. The big men blew open the left side, and Thomas ran through the arms of safety Thane Gash for a touchdown.

Early in the second quarter Thomas scored on an 11-yard counter play to the same side, with 310-pound John Davis and 325-pound Howard Ballard pulling from the right to clear the way. Davis plowed into 190-pound cornerback Raymond Clayborn, while Ballard flattened the 200-pound Gash. (Afterward, none other than Kelly would present Ballard a special game ball for his blocking.)

The Browns controlled the rest of the quarter but had nothing to show for it. Mike Pagel threw passes of 21 yards to Ozzie Newsome and 26 to Brian Brennan as he moved his team to a first down at the Bills' 7. Then, two plays later, Webster Slaughter beat Nate Odomes on a slant pattern for an apparent touchdown, but the score was rubbed out by an interference penalty on Newsome. Cleveland ended up attempting a 35-yard field goal, but Jerry Kauric's kick was blocked by Shane Conlan and John Hagy returned the loose ball to the Buffalo 40.

After the Bills went three and out, Pagel had the Browns moving again. He drove them from their 40 to the Buffalo 9. But a botched third-down play out of shotgun formation resulted in an incomplete. Cleveland then lined up for a 27-yard field-goal try by Kauric, but it was foiled when Mike Morris's snap sailed over Pagel's head.

Taking over at his 32 with 1:05 left in the half, Kelly ran the hurry-up to perfection, completing four straight passes before spiking the ball at the Cleveland 25 to stop the clock at eight seconds. But Norwood's field-goal attempt from 42 yards was wide to the right, and the first half ended, 14–0.

Once the second half began the Bills proceeded to put the Browns out of their misery. Kelly passes of 16 and 43 yards to Reed, and a penalty on Raymond Clayborn for interfering with Lofton put the ball at the Cleveland 1. On the next play Jamie Mueller followed Jim Ritcher into the end zone to make it 21–0.

Buffalo began the fourth quarter with a 53-yard drive that was capped by Thomas's third touchdown on an 11-yard throw by Kelly. Eight days earlier Thomas had ignored the aftereffects of a bruised right knee he sustained against the Jets. Against the Browns he did the same mind-over-matter routine.

This was the same man who, as a rookie in 1988, was criticized for being too easily bothered by injuries.

"The guy I'm starting to take after right now is Darryl Talley," said Thomas, who despite limping on the sidelines would rush 17 times for 58 yards and catch 5 passes for 65 yards. "He plays hurt all the time, so I basically just follow him. He has been in the league longer than I have. And if you want to stick around for a long time and be successful in this league, you have to learn to play with a little pain. If I can run, I'm going to play."

Frank Reich replaced Kelly, who finished with 14 completions in 19 attempts for 200 yards and a TD, for the Bills' second possession of the fourth quarter. And he moved them just as efficiently, from midfield to the Cleveland 3. Kenneth Davis then scored on a second-down sweep to give the Bills a 35–0 lead.

As if that weren't humiliating enough for the Browns, on fourth down from the Buffalo 48, Pagel had his second pass of the day wind up in Talley's hands. This time the Cleveland-born linebacker ran 60 yards for the first touchdown of his eight NFL seasons to put the finishing touches on the Bills' 42–0 victory. The last man with a chance to stop him was his brother, John, a Browns tight end and the intended receiver. But he was taken out on a block by Dwight Drane.

By winning their sixth in a row—and setting a team record for largest margin of victory while handing the Browns their third-worst defeat ever—the Bills remained deadlocked with Miami atop the AFC East at 7–1. (On the same day the Dolphins beat up on Buffalo's next opponent, Phoenix, 26–3.)

"It was a very emotional game," Talley said, still holding the football after changing into his street clothes. "And it was important, because it showed that everybody dug down deeply. Overall, defensively, this may have been our best game. It just seemed like everybody was making the tackles. We didn't have many missed tackles, and everybody was in the right gaps."

Revenge will do that to a team. For the Bills and Buffalo, the blowout began to make up for decades of football mistreatment from their neighbors across Lake Erie. Besides The

Drop and The Interception, it helped ease the pain of other bad memories, such as Otto Graham's screen pass to Mac Speedie that resulted in a record 99-yard touchdown against the old All-America Conference Bills. And it applied salve to the many slow-healing emotional wounds inflicted by the likes of Marion Motley, Lou Groza, and Dante Lavelli.

Midway through the fourth quarter most Browns fans gave up and went home. That left virtually all of the cavernous, 80,098-seat stadium to an estimated twenty thousand Buffalo supporters. Only ten months earlier a deafening roar had rolled over dejected Bills players and coaches as they filed into the visitor's dugout and up the tunnel. This time around it was their fans breaking into song at the Browns' expense:

Nah Nah! Nah! Nah!
Nah Nah! Nah! Nah!
Hey! Hey-ey!
Goodbye!

Then, after Talley's touchdown, the singing stopped and the Buffalo contingent turned its attention toward the future. Through the game's final 2:31, and as the Bills players and coaches filed into the visitor's dugout after the final gun, a chant echoed through Cleveland Stadium.

Super Bowl!
Super Bowl!
Super Bowl!

AS GOOD AS THEY WANT TO BE

After hitting midseason with their sixth consecutive victory and most resounding win ever, the natural question was asked: Just how good are the 1990 Buffalo Bills?

Never one to avoid a chance to boast, Bruce Smith was quick with the natural answer: "The sky's the limit."

As far as Smith was concerned the Bills could take care of themselves. They didn't need help beating Miami or any other club that might rise to challenge them in the AFC East. He wasn't at all bothered by the neck-and-neck race with the Dolphins and saw no reason to divide his attention between what the Bills were doing on the field and what Miami was doing on the out-of-town scoreboard.

"We control our own destiny," Smith said. "Miami has to come up to Buffalo and play (December 23). So if we screw it up, it's our fault.

"But I don't see us screwing it up."

Such were the sentiments throughout the team and most of Western New York. Even the harshest critics had to be impressed with the Bills. And it wasn't only the sparkling record, or the winning streak, or the fact they had outscored their last six opponents 196–96 that made everyone stand up and take notice. It was the manner in which that success had been achieved. In some games the Bills relied on offense. In others they relied on defense. In still others they relied on special teams.

If ever a club had struck a perfect balance in all phases, the Bills were it. At least, through midseason.

"That's the mark of a champion," Darryl Talley said. "And it builds confidence for us. When a game gets tight and it's on the line, we know there are different facets we can go to that might provide us with a big play. We're learning that we can win a game in more ways than one."

But some parts of the lesson had come harder than others.

It took three consecutive heart-stopping victories—over Denver, the Raiders, and the Jets—for the Bills to realize the full extent of their many strengths.

It took back-to-back road blowouts—over New England and Cleveland—for them to discover their capability of playing well outside the friendly confines of Rich Stadium.

And it took a disaster on the road—week two at Miami—for them to understand that every bit of their success would have to be earned. (Even if luck did play a small part against Denver and Los Angeles.)

"I think the Miami game woke us up," Jim Kelly said. "We realized, in order for us to get as good as we want to be, as good as we think we are, we were going to have to work at it. And I think, when we stepped on the field in Miami, we automatically thought we were going to do well just because of the names we had out there."

The first corrective step was taken on the practice field. To Marv Levy and several returning veterans the workouts leading up to the Indianapolis and Miami games provided frightening flashbacks to the year before. Frightening, because during the 1989 season practice for many Bills players meant honing their skills as joke tellers and pranksters. Concentration was in short supply in most corners of the squad. And the boiling point was reached after a 33–24 upset loss to the Patriots, when Levy went public about his players' cavalier approach to preparing for the game.

Now he was praising them for being a mostly serious-minded bunch, beginning with the week before the Monday night game against the Jets. From that point on workouts were more businesslike—and far more productive. In fact, they were running about thirty minutes shorter than in 1989, while covering the same amount of material.

"It's quality time, not quantity," Jim Kelly pointed out. "Everyone's concentrating. We're in and out of the huddle, just like it was a game."

"It's the best practicing team I've had in coaching professional football," Levy said. "They really work, concentrate, and keep their eye on the target."

Ralph Wilson was excited about the Bills at midseason, too. Not just their record. Not just their winning streak. But the team itself—the quality of the players in whom he had invested $20.6 million.

"I'm not getting carried away when I say this," Wilson said. "But I've seen thousands of pro football games and we have some of the best players I have ever seen. They're not good players; they're great players."

That list of great players began with Wilson's biggest investment of all, Jim Kelly. More than a few observers had questioned the whopping new contract the quarterback had received in the spring, saying his accomplishments didn't warrant the NFL's second-highest salary at $3 million per year (behind only the $4 million of San Francisco's Joe Montana). But after eight games Kelly was the top-rated passer in the AFC at 95.1. Only the Giants' Phil Simms (104.4) and Montana were ranked higher in the league. And by doing more with his arm than his jaws, Kelly established himself as a strong leader and had the respect and following of most, if not all, of his teammates.

"There's no question in anybody's mind that Jim Kelly has arrived as a first-rate professional quarterback," Bill Polian said.

The rest of the offense was also distinguishing itself at the halfway mark. Thurman Thomas led the AFC in total yards from scrimmage with 972—623 rushing and 249 on 30 pass receptions—and had 5 touchdowns. Don Smith, a Plan B acquisition from Tampa Bay, was far more productive as a pass-catching running back and return man than Ronnie Harmon, a Plan B loss to San Diego. Andre Reed had caught 40 passes for 520 yards and 4 TDs. James Lofton emerged as the team's long-ball threat with a 21.4 yards-per-catch average, while Keith McKeller became one of its more dangerous receivers ever at tight end. The offensive line was performing superbly, allowing only 14 sacks and opening big holes for Thomas.

The defensive line was getting another All-World year out of Bruce Smith (42 tackles, 8 sacks, 5 QB pressures, 3 batted-down passes, and 4 forced fumbles) and workmanlike efforts from Jeff Wright and Leon Seals. Darryl Talley was having his best season ever (56 tackles, 2 interceptions, 1 fumble recovery). Cornelius Bennett was back from his shoulder problems—with a vengeance. Leonard Smith led the team with 63 tackles. John Hagy had filled in admirably for Mark Kelso. Nate Odomes had been tough to beat at right cornerback, while the left side was holding up despite Kirby Jackson's nagging hamstring problem and J. D. Williams's limited experience.

And even with Scott Norwood's slump and Rick Tuten's inconsistency, the special teams were, as always, very special.

"I'm not saying we're going to the Super Bowl, because we've played only half the season and a lot of things can happen," Wilson said. "But we have a good football team. You don't get to seven and one in this league by being a bunch of sandlotters."

Wilson couldn't recall another time when he felt as good about his club. And that included 1988, when the Bills were 12–4 and played in the AFC Championship Game. The basic problem then was that they weren't ready for the success they experienced. Several key performers—Kelly, Smith, Bennett, and Thomas among them—had still had plenty of room to mature, on and off the field. But an inordinate amount of good fortune in close games had caused the Bills to appear further along than they actually were. At the core, they probably had been a solid 8–8 or 9–7 team, as opposed to a bona fide Super Bowl contender. And as they would demonstrate in 1989, they simply weren't emotionally prepared to handle being everyone's choice to reign as AFC champions.

Since issuing a stern warning to his players about their

conduct after the Miami game, Wilson had seen a definite attitude adjustment.

"I think the players' sights are set on the goal they want to reach [Super Bowl XXV]," he said. "There's not a lot of jumping up and down after games. Not that that's out of order, because everybody wants to celebrate. But I don't see them celebrating before they reach their goal."

"The team has, to this point, kept very good perspective," Levy said. "They've gotten a lead and haven't gotten giddy about it. They've gotten behind and haven't lost their poise. And I think it has been a more opportunistic team than in the past. But I also know it's only half a season."

Which was another way of saying he had seen his club play well through the first eight games before, only to watch them flop through the last eight. Second-half collapses—and the resulting loss of home-field advantage in the play-offs—had become almost synonymous with the franchise. In 1988 the Bills had been 11–1 before losing three of their final four games. In 1989 they had been 6–2 before losing five of their final eight.

With the Bills there always seemed to be something to worry about. Even as they prepared for their November 11 home clash with the 2–6 Phoenix Cardinals, the Bills remained uneasy.

This time the concern centered around the Bills' consistently poor record against the dreaded NFC. The Cardinals were the first of four NFC teams the Bills would face in the second half of the season. Since finishing 3–1 against the NFC West in 1980, the Bills had not posted a winning record against the NFC, going 1–3, 1–2, 1–3, 1–3, 0–2, 1–1, 1–2, 2–2, and 1–3. They were also in the midst of a three-game NFC losing streak.

Weren't the lopsided triumphs over New England and Cleveland convincing enough evidence of how the Bills could handle a weak opponent? Didn't the fact they were playing at Rich—site of only two Buffalo losses in three seasons—against a warm weather team in November weigh heavily in the Bills' favor?

Still, sound arguments could be made on the Cardinals'

behalf. Despite the similarity of their records, they did not appear quite as hopeless as the Patriots or Browns. Those teams had uncertain quarterbacking and were distracted, if not demoralized, by controversies swirling around them. Under first-year coach Joe Bugel and with Timm Rosenbach over center, the Cardinals were seen as a young team with a promising future, as opposed to an aging club going nowhere but down. Also, they had already faced some tough competition. Their previous three games, all losses, were against the Giants, Chicago, and Miami—teams with a combined record of 22–2.

"They're the type of team that slips up on people," Kent Hull said.

Or, given the blustery weather on game day (a wintry smorgasbord of wind, rain, sleet, and fierce snow squalls), suddenly blows into their faces.

And that was exactly what happened on the first Bills series. On third-and-seven from the Phoenix 49, Cedric Mack blew in from left cornerback and blindsided Jim Kelly like a 6′0″, 185-pound missile. Kelly fumbled. Mack picked up the ball at the Buffalo 24 and, with Kelly miraculously back on his feet and giving chase, ran 17 yards to the Bills' 7. Three plays later rookie running back Johnny Johnson ran for a 1-yard touchdown to give the Cardinals a 7–0 lead.

Just like that.

Despite facing 29 mph wind gusts that threatened to uproot the goalposts, the Bills had a nice drive going on their second possession. Thomas exploded for 43 yards on first down, then carried to the Cardinals' 24. But on the next play Kelly threw a low pass to Keith McKeller, who in trying to scoop up the ball, let it slip from his hands and into those of linebacker Anthony Bell. And that wasn't the only disastrous occurrence on the drive: While blocking for Thomas's 43-yard run Andre Reed suffered a sprained ankle that would sideline him for the rest of the day.

With 4:40 left in the first quarter and the wind still in their face the Bills began their third offensive series at their 25. Five running plays advanced them to their 40, from where, on third-and-six, Kelly threw a safe look-in pass to McKeller for

22 yards to the Phoenix 38. Three plays later, in the second quarter, Kelly tossed a 15-yard screen to Don Smith to put the ball at the 22. Then, after an incomplete and a 4-yard throw to Pete Metzelaars, Kelly connected with McKeller for an 18-yard TD to tie the score at 7–7.

Disaster struck at the end of the Cardinals' next drive. As he made his drop, punter Rich Camarillo had the ball ripped out of his hands by the wind. He retrieved it, but by that time Steve Tasker was there to strip it free. Tasker fell, but bounced back up for the recovery and 5-yard return to the Phoenix 6. On third down Kelly threw a 1-yard touchdown pass to Butch Rolle, his third in as many catches in 1990, to make it 14–7, with 9:25 left in the second quarter.

"The wind was so strong, it almost knocked guys off their feet," Camarillo said. "How am I going to have any luck kicking a football into something like that?"

After he and Tuten each managed to get off a punt the Cardinals had the ball at the Buffalo 49 with 2:07 remaining in the first half. Rosenbach threw 11 yards to Walter Reeves, and after a pair of incompletes, the quarterback ran to the 32. On fourth-and-four, Cornelius Bennett, wearing a six-hundred-dollar downhill-skier's waterproof bodysuit under his uniform, made the defensive play of the day when he stopped Johnny Johnson a yard short of the first down.

The final twenty-four seconds of the first half were an indication of how aggressive the Bills' offense had become in 1990. Leading 14–7, they had a second-and-twelve at their own 27. In the past they probably would have played it safe and avoided a turnover by running out the clock. Even Kelly, who is always ready to go deep, thought the best idea was to kneel. However, on the sidelines, Levy told him, "I don't know. We have pretty good field position." So they decided to go for it, and on the next play, Kelly connected with Don Beebe for a 49-yard gain to the Phoenix 24.

Beebe developed a muscle cramp on the play, which forced him out of the game temporarily. With Reed already sidelined, that left Steve Tasker to play receiver, something he had rarely done in his six NFL seasons. On the next play Kelly threw between two defensive backs to—who else?—Tasker for a touchdown that gave the Bills a 21–7 halftime lead. As the wild end-zone celebration (involving almost every Buffalo player on the field and the sidelines) indicated, this was no ordinary score. It was Tasker's first touchdown as a pro and first regular-season reception since joining the Bills off waivers from Houston in November 1986. The last time he had caught a ball in the end zone he was playing for Dodge City (Kansas) Community College, from which he transferred to Northwestern.

"It was six years in the making, I guess," Tasker said. "It hasn't been my role to catch passes, but I'm glad that, when I got in there, I was able to make it work. Because if a guy like me gets in there and drops that ball, he might not see the field again."

The touchdown catch would earn Tasker a game ball, but he easily could have received one for the thing that earned him a Pro Bowl trip after the 1987 season—kick coverage. Besides causing and recovering Camarillo's fumble, Tasker recovered another loose ball in the third quarter when a punt bounced off the helmet of return man Vai Sikahema as Tasker zeroed in for a tackle. That put the Bills at the Cardinals' 31, but on a fourth-down pass, Beebe had the ball knocked loose by Mack and Tim McDonald recovered.

For a moment it looked like it might have been a struggle to the end when the Cardinals cashed in on the turnover and drove 74 yards for their second touchdown. The 29-yard Rosenbach pass to Ernie Jones cut the Bills' lead to 21–14 with 7:42 left in the third quarter.

But the Bills bounced right back with the most impressive scoring march of the game. Much of it was against the wind, including an 18-yard run by Thomas and clutch 12- and 11-yard catches by Lofton to get the Bills out of a second-and-seventeen from midfield. By the time Scott Norwood came on for a 25-yard field goal the fourth quarter had begun and the Bills were going the other way.

Buffalo added three more touchdowns in the fourth quarter. John Hagy's first NFL interception set up the first, an 11-yard Kelly pass to Beebe. A fumble recovery by Leon Seals set up the second, a 1-yard run by Jamie Mueller. And the second of two wind-stifled, 12-yard punts by Camarillo set up the third, a 13-yard run up the middle by Kenneth Davis for the final points of the Bills' 45–14 victory.

It was their seventh straight win and their first against an NFC opponent since their 1989 Monday Night Miracle over the Los Angeles Rams. Naturally, Miami didn't blink, beating the Jets 17–3. Now the Bills and Dolphins shared first place in the AFC East with 8–1 records.

Against the Cardinals the Bills did what a team is supposed to do without its top receiver and with a relentless wind howling through the stadium: They ran 51 times for 211 yards (112 by Thomas). They used rushing plays to pick up 11 of their 20 first downs. Although Kelly threw only 16 passes, he completed 11 for 165 yards and 4 touchdowns.

Levy sympathized with the Cardinals' problems with Mother Nature's fury. "Even though you live here and you play here and you practice here, it isn't easy to play in that kind of weather," he said.

But as the Cardinals packed up for the return trip to the warmth of Arizona, a frustrated Tim McDonald told reporters, "You can have Buffalo. You can have this whole city. Whenever we come here in November or December again, it'll be too soon."

How volatile were conditions at Rich Stadium that day? All 59 points were scored in the east end zone, when each team had the wind at its back. And during pregame warm-ups, several of Tuten's punts were blown into the middle of the marching band as it tuned up at midfield.

Not that any complaints were heard from the Buffalo dressing room.

"This was Buffalo Bills weather," Kelly said proudly. "This was Buffalo Bills football."

In 1990 that meant threatening to blow the circuits of scoreboards in every stadium they played. Never before in their thirty-one-year history had the the Bills scored 40 or more points in back-to-back games. And their two-game total of 87 broke a club record of 85 that had stood since 1966. And their three-game total of 114 was the most they had scored in that stretch since 1979.

You want more?

With 274 points through the first nine weeks, the Bills were leading the NFL and averaging 30.4 per game—a pace at which they would surpass the single-season club record of 420, which they set over 14 games in 1975. In 1989 they had their second-highest total ever at 409.

The Bills' schedule featured another cream puff the following Sunday, as the 1–8 Patriots visited Rich Stadium. Levy knew that convincing his players to take the game seriously would be even harder than the previous two weeks. At least he could call upon legitimate rallying points before facing the Browns (revenge for a play-off loss) and the Cardinals (a losing record to NFC teams). Now he faced an opponent whose ineptitude his players had already witnessed first-hand only a few weeks earlier. He also had a team that knew it was one of the NFL's best.

So Levy hit his troops with an all-out propaganda blitz. First, he plastered the dressing-room bulletin board with newspaper clippings from a previous Buffalo–New England encounter. Not the Bills' 27–10 victory on October 28, but their 33–24 loss in 1989—when the Patriots were allegedly struggling at 3–7 and the Bills were 7–3. Then he kept the straightest face possible while telling the media the Patriots were a team to be reckoned with.

"Anybody is dangerous, even a team that has a one and eight record," Levy declared. "Dallas was one and five [in 1989]. They won one game—they beat the Washington Redskins. And that took Washington out of the play-offs.

"The Patriots are not a bad team. They are a very capable team. They really outplayed Indianapolis [in a 13–10 loss on November 11]. They outrushed them badly [175–54], they outgained them considerably [247–156]."

A few Bills players recited the company line. But for the most part it sounded, at best, semiforced.

"Who knows?" Seals said. "They might be able to put it together this weekend."

Even the New England coach, Rod Rust, had quit trying to put up a brave front. When a reporter asked before the game if he thought the Patriots were the worst team in the NFL, he replied, "I wouldn't argue that. That's what the record says. They keep score for a reason."

Odds-makers favored Buffalo by 14½ points, which meant, like everyone else, they expected a rout.

And at the beginning it appeared certain the Bills were indeed headed for a third consecutive bloodletting. On their first possession Kelly threw a third-down pass to Reed, playing despite an aggravated sprained ankle he had suffered the week before, for 25 yards to the Patriots' 34. Thomas, who would finish the day with 165 yards on 22 carries, took over from there. He ran six consecutive times, the last a 5-yard trap to the left for a touchdown. The score seemed like child's play, with House Ballard pulling from right tackle and clearing away 6′2″, 245-pound linebacker Vincent Brown and 5′10″, 185-pound cornerback Maurice Hurst as if they were twigs.

But things would become increasingly difficult for the Bills.

Late in the first quarter Marc Wilson got the Patriots moving from their 45 with an 18-yard pass to Irving Fryar. Mosi Tatupu and Marvin Allen combined for three running plays that produced another first down, at the Buffalo 27. Wilson then threw a 28-yard pass to George Adams, putting the ball at the 1. A motion penalty shoved it back to the 6, but after three more Allen runs, New England had a fourth down at the two-foot line.

Before the play Ray Bentley, the Bills' defensive signal-caller, alerted his teammates to watch for a play-action pass. But all that changed once he saw the Patriots break from their huddle.

"You could see it in their eyes: They were going to try and run," he recalled.

Sure enough, Wilson, struggling to call signals over the roar of more than seventy-four thousand fans, handed off to Allen, who ran right. H-back Marv Cook had gone in motion to that side to block, and left guard Chris Gambol pulled to be Allen's chief escort into the end zone. But Allen never had a chance. Before he could even turn upfield, Bentley, coming from the opposite direction, clobbered him shoulder high, while Talley clawed at his ankles. Allen was dropped for a 1-yard loss, and the Bills took over at the 2.

Bentley's great anticipation allowed him to make the play look embarrassingly easy. The instant he saw Gambol pull, he knew what was coming and shot through the opening untouched.

"Actually, about four blockers hit me and I shed 'em all," he joked. Then turning serious, he explained, "Anytime you have a goal-line stand, it has a massive psychological effect on a team. It brings us up, knowing we can stop them. And it kind of makes them scratch their heads and wonder if they can score."

Wilson, for one, did a great deal of head-scratching. But it had less to do with the Bills' defense than with the refusal of referee Johnny Grier to do something about the crowd noise.

"I had asked him three times, and on all three plays he said, no, it wasn't loud enough for him to take action," Wilson said. "Clearly, we could not hear the snap count. And it took any advantage that we had away from us."

After the Bills took over they drove to the New England 12. But on third-and-four Kelly was pressured into an incomplete by Mickey Washington's cornerback blitz. Kelly would throw only 15 times on the day, completing 5 for 79 yards—both NFL-career lows. He also would be sacked twice and generally absorb more punishment than in previous outings. (Of course, he could have had Wilson's protection and been dumped four times.)

After Kelly's third-down misfire Norwood sent a 30-yard field-goal try wide to the left, and that seemed to kill any notion the Bills would cruise to their eighth consecutive victory. Noted Levy, "It would really have helped to break the Patriots' morale if we had scored then."

Hagy appeared to break a lot more 4:29 later when he delivered a vicious head blow to Fryar while causing a third-down incomplete. Hagy timed the hit perfectly, uncoiling just as the ball arrived in Fryar's hands deep in Buffalo territory. Fryar remained on his back for several minutes before walking off the field under his own power. At least Hagy was compassionate enough to check on the receiver's condition while he was down.

"I want to play physical and try to make people not want to

catch the ball," he said. "But I don't want to hurt anybody seriously."

In the third quarter the Bills had the ball twice and twice punted—from their 38 and 35. The Patriots crossed midfield on their first two series of the second half, but also punted. This dreary volley continued in the fourth quarter, with the Bills punting from the New England 37, the Patriots from their 17, and the Bills from the New England 45.

With 1:51 left in the game, J. D. Williams, starting in place of the injured Kirby Jackson, picked off a 38-yard Wilson pass for Fryar in the end zone to stop a Patriot drive that threatened to force overtime. Wilson and Fryar had worked on the rookie all day, hooking up for short and intermediate passes in hopes of suckering him into closer coverage and, at the right moment, beating him deep. Fryar wound up with 8 catches for 85 yards. But he couldn't get his hands on Wilson's 38-yarder, because Williams soared in front of him to make the second pickoff of his career.

"There wasn't very much time on the clock, so the best chance for them was to go deep," Williams explained. "And they tried for me, because I was a rookie. It's only natural. Why not?"

"The guy's cool under pressure," Bills defensive coordinator Walt Corey said of Williams. "He's taking his lumps, but it doesn't affect him. If a corner gets down on himself, he's not worth a darn the rest of his career."

On the next play Thomas wheeled around the right side, shrugged off a necktie tackle by free safety Fred Marion, got a partial block downfield from Lofton on Maurice Hurst, and tightroped the right sideline for an 80-yard touchdown to give the Bills a 14–0 lead with 1:38 remaining. It was the longest carry of Thomas's three NFL seasons and Buffalo's longest scoring run since Greg Bell went 85 yards against Dallas in 1984.

"They had been running an even defense all day, and the offensive line was on the sidelines talking about what they were doing," John Davis said. "We knew, if we could get their guys going in one direction, we would cut Thurman back against the grain for a long run. And it worked."

Still, the Patriots weren't quite dead yet. Starting from his 34, Wilson completed three passes in a row—12 yards to Allen, 19 to Fryar, and 22 to Greg McMurtry. All of a sudden, New England had a first down at the Buffalo 13 with fifty-two seconds left.

Wilson tried throwing twice more to McMurtry but couldn't connect. The Patriots lost five yards on a false-start penalty, but Wilson got them back with a pass to Cedric Jones. With thirty-two seconds showing, Wilson dropped back on fourth-and-ten and fired toward the end zone, but David Pool, a rookie reserve defensive back, intercepted the pass, and Kelly killed off the remaining twenty-five seconds.

The final score showed the Bills winning by two touchdowns, but it was hardly reflective of the game's competitiveness. Meanwhile, the Dolphins were left with something to ponder in the twenty-four-plus hours before their Monday night game against the Raiders. And this time the Fish would blink, losing 13–10. At last, the Bills were alone in first in the AFC East.

After the New England game Levy couldn't resist the opportunity to remind reporters of his futile attempt to awaken them to the truth about the Patriots.

"It was every bit as tough as I thought it would be," he said. "And we weren't flat. We weren't anything. They just played hard, they played sound, they knew us a little better than the first time. And they did a good job."

During his postgame press conference Rod Rust spoke about how his team had played "quite well" and worked "very hard" and that he was "very proud" of the effort. But at least one New England player, linebacker Richard Harvey, refused to accept any consolation in losing a tight, low-scoring game to the high-scoring Bills.

"If they outscore you, you didn't play well enough to win," said Harvey, whom the Patriots had signed away from Buffalo in the spring as a Plan B free agent. "And if you're not looking at it like that, you've got the wrong attitude. Our objective is to stop them from scoring. Period. It doesn't matter what else happens."

Nor, in the Bills' case, did it matter whether they won 14–0 or 44–0. They were still on a roll. And nowhere was this more apparent than on the offensive line, which was emerging as one of the best the Bills ever fielded. It had the size and strength to consistently plow open holes for the running game and enough quickness and agility to offer strong pass-protection. It also had done a good job of avoiding drive-killing penalties.

"We're not real fancy in what we do," center Kent Hull said. "We don't have a lot of blocking schemes. It's just a matter of getting on somebody and pushing."

Not that he had always felt so comfortable about the unit.

In August, with the regular season quickly approaching, it seemed everywhere Hull looked on the line there was something that made him queasy. To his left were two vacancies—tackle Will Wolford, embroiled in a contract dispute, hadn't reported to training camp and guard Jim Ritcher was recovering from arthroscopic surgery on his left shoulder. To his right was another void: Guard Leonard Burton, the top candidate to replace retired Joe Devlin, had suffered what would prove to be a season-ending knee injury in the second week of camp.

"I can't even say what I was saying then because it wasn't very pretty," Hull recalled. "I mean, we were down to two experienced linemen, me and Howard Ballard. I've always believed that an offense is only as good as its line. So I thought we might have some problems if we didn't make a turnaround—quick."

By the end of the preseason things began looking up in two of the trouble spots, with Wolford coming to contract terms and Ritcher receiving medical clearance to play. John Davis, a seldom-used Plan B free agent in 1989, had been penciled in as a starter at right guard, but offensive-line coach Tom Bresnahan had so little confidence in him, he alternated Davis with Mitch Frerotte and even briefly made rookie Glenn Parker the number-one man at the position. Eventually, however, Davis took control and became as much of a solid starter as any of the other offensive linemen.

"There were a lot of questions early on, and the unknown quantity in the whole thing was John Davis," Wolford said.

"No one had seen much of John; he didn't really play much the year before, and no one was really sure if he could come in and do the job. But John came in and has done one hell of a job. He's played as well as anybody on the line."

Ritcher, the senior member of the group with eleven years of experience, had been particularly impressed by the nimbleness of the 310-pound Davis and 325-pound Ballard. At the beginning of the season, on counters and traps, the Bills pulled to the right, with the 275-pound Ritcher and/or 295-pound Wolford leading the way.

"But starting with the Cleveland game, we began pulling John and Howard to the other side, and they were hitting the holes and staying on their feet and getting their blocks as well as Will and I were doing, if not better," Ritcher pointed out. "Howard just totally smashed some people."

Not coincidentally, the Bills were doing the same to most of their opponents.

MELTING THE DECEMBER JINX

Now came the hard part.

Almost every patsy was behind the Bills. For the next six weeks their schedule would grow teeth. Make that fangs. And the Bills would be able to prove themselves as a member of the NFL's upper echelon to any nonbelievers still out there—or expose themselves as a team capable of bullying only the meek and mild of the league.

The statistics were too revealing to ignore.

Bills' opponents since their October 14 bye owned a combined record of 9–32. Through the next six weeks, that would change to 39–21, beginning with a Monday night game against the Oilers at the Houston Astrodome. After that the Bills would host Philadelphia, face Indianapolis and the New York Giants away, return home to play against Miami, and close the regular season at Washington.

So far the Bills had beaten only one winning team—the Raiders. Since 1986, when Marv Levy had taken over as head coach, their aggregate record for the final third of the season was 9–15. Throw in their 7–11 record on "Monday Night Football" and 5–13 mark in domed stadiums, and one could see where there was at least a little room for skepticism.

Unless you were talking to Thurman Thomas. He didn't want to hear even the slightest suggestion that the Bills were about to be dismembered by the meat-grinder portion of their schedule.

"Everyone's looking at us like we're going to fall apart these last six games, and it's just not going to happen," Thomas said. "We're so focused right now, it's unbelievable. I know our track record isn't good late in the season, but this is a different year, a different team.

"We feel we can play with anybody in the league, regardless of who it is or what their record is. We know we're not going to score forty points against the Giants. We know we're not going to score forty points against Philadelphia. But if we can be consistent on offense, defense, and special teams, we'll be in those ball games."

"Actually, I think this part of our schedule works to our benefit," added Nate Odomes. "We're going to play a lot of play-off teams, and if we can come out on the better end, I think that will make a big statement going into the play-offs. I don't think it's a situation where we're in over our heads."

Of course, Odomes played cornerback. Most of the upcoming opponents were big and physical, especially on their defensive lines. The real challenge would be faced by Buffalo's offensive linemen, who on the night of November 26 in the Astrodome were to face the fourth best run-defense team in the AFC.

"This is where, I think, the test of our offensive line is going to come—how well we can do against those larger defenses," John Davis said. "It's going to be interesting to see the outcome."

There was no question the Oilers were far more dangerous than their 5–5 record implied. They had one of the NFL's best quarterbacks in Warren Moon. And they had an offense that, in a climate-controlled setting, was nearly impossible to stop. It was the run-and-shoot, which Kelly had made famous while playing for Oiler coach Jack Pardee with the United States Football League's Houston Gamblers. Kelly hadn't operated it since joining the Bills in 1986. The Bills hadn't faced it all year.

And because so few NFL teams employed it, Buffalo's defensive strategists and defenders had limited knowledge about how to deal with it.

They would also have only a week to learn.

"If there's one disadvantage going against the run-and-shoot, it's having just that one week of preparation," Walt Corey said. "The whole thing is a nightmare, because it's a possession type of offense that's being executed very well. It's such a fast offense. Everything is predicated on quarterback-receiver relationships—on where the receivers run and how and when the ball is thrown."

"It's a stretch system," explained Pardee. "You try to stretch the defense, instead of condensing it, to try to create some holes to work in. All the run-and-shoot does is create balance. We cover the whole field with our positioning of receivers. We don't want to let them get five defenders where we have three receivers or get three where we have two. It creates a balance where we have an area to work, where we have a one-on-one or a [favorable] matchup and our guys get to make a play."

A late entry to the NFL via the Canadian Football League, Moon had just turned thirty-four, yet was only in his seventh NFL season. He had been in the league a year less than twenty-nine-year-old Dan Marino, but was seriously threatening to break the Miami quarterback's 1986 records for attempts (623) and completions (375). Moon led the league with 406 attempts, 253 completions, and 3,152 yards, putting him in range to become only the second quarterback in NFL history to throw for 5,000 in a season. Marino totaled 5,084 in 1984.

Moon's favorite targets were Ernest Givins and Curtis Duncan, who shared the AFC lead with 51 receptions each. They were followed by Drew Hill, who was fourth in the conference with 45, and Haywood Jeffires, tied for sixth with Reed, the Bills' leading receiver, at 43.

"I really think we're a lot better team than five and five," Moon said. "And I think we can have a respectable season if we just continue to play the way we did last week [in scoring a 35–23 victory over Cleveland] and continue to execute once we get the scoring opportunities and avoid giving up big plays, which we haven't been doing enough of this year."

The game opened with a Moon pass to running back Lorenzo White for 22 yards. It was the beginning of a very busy night for White. On the next play, he ran to his left for 9 yards, up the middle for 2, and up the middle again for 9 to the Buffalo 37. Moon then threw to Jeffires, who slipped behind Nate Odomes and John Hagy for a touchdown with only 3:18 expired.

The Bills answered with a much slower and more methodical drive that began at their 25. Using an even mix of passes and runs, plus an 11-yard pass-interference penalty on Richard Johnson, Kelly moved them all the way to the Houston 1. Along the way Jamie Mueller converted a third-and-one and Kelly, who for the game would complete 23 of 34 passes for 224 yards and 2 touchdowns, had 11-yard throws to McKeller and Reed. On third-and-goal from the 1, the Oilers stuffed Don Smith's attempted dive into the end zone. On fourth down Kelly faked a handoff to Smith, rolled right, and threw to a wide open Pete Metzelaars to tie the score at 7–7 and cap the 15-play, 9:11 journey.

But the Oilers zoomed right back on their next possession. White ran 12 yards, Moon scrambled for 6, then White exploded for 22 to give Houston a first down at the Bills' 28. After an offsides penalty on Cornelius Bennett, Moon threw a 20-yard pass to Givins to put the ball at the 3. On the next play, White ran for a touchdown, but the play was erased because center Jay Pennison was penalized 10 yards for holding Bruce Smith, who would finish the game with 8 tackles and 2 sacks. Two plays later White ran 10 yards on a delay, but on third down, Moon was sacked by Smith for a 5-yard loss. Out came Teddy Garcia for a 26-yard field goal that made it 10–7.

After a Buffalo punt the Oilers quickly moved to the Bills' 37. But Moon made a bad pitch on an option play to White, and Leonard Smith recovered at the 47. Four plays later, however, on a first-and-ten from the Oilers' 35, Kelly overthrew McKeller on a deep pattern and free safety Terry Kinard intercepted. His 26-yard return put the ball at the Houston 33. Moon promptly threw 11 yards to Hill, White ran a delay for 16, and Moon connected with the running back on a 29-yard screen to the Buffalo 11. But on the next play, Bruce Smith tripped Allen Pinkett for no gain. Then after the Oilers were penalized 5 yards for illegal procedure, Bruce dumped Tony Jones on a reverse for a 2-yard loss to the 18.

"That was incredible," Bills defensive line coach Chuck Dickerson marveled. "The flow was going away from Bruce and, based on everything the scheme was showing, he should have run like hell on a flat course to get to the ball carrier from the back side. But all of a sudden he planted his foot, turned straight upfield, and made the tackle for a loss. He saw the reverse before the reverse even began. Not only that, but he took a guy who runs a four-four forty and stopped him in wide-open territory. Just incredible!"

On third-and-seventeen Moon threw incomplete for Hill in the end zone. Out came Garcia again, and his 36-yard field goal gave Houston a 13–7 lead with 3:07 left in the second quarter.

Starting at their 35, the Bills went into their hurry-up offense. Kelly completed a 14-yard pass to Thomas, and on the next play, Chris Dishman, Houston's notorious cheap-shotting cornerback, picked up a 7-yard pass-interference penalty that gave Buffalo a first down at the Oilers' 44. After a pair of short throws Kenneth Davis converted a third-and-one with a 4-yard run to the Oilers' 31. Kelly then connected with Reed for passes of 13 and 11 yards to put the ball at the 7. An incomplete and a 5-yard illegal procedure penalty on Howard Ballard gave the Bills a second-and-goal from the 12. Under pressure Kelly rolled right, began directing traffic, and threw a high pass that McKeller leaped to catch in the back of the end zone. That put Buffalo in front, 14–13, at halftime.

After the second-half kickoff the Bills put together a 49-yard scoring drive that saw three big third-down conversions. On third-and-ten from the Buffalo 25, Don Smith took a direct snap in shotgun formation and ran 10 yards. On third-and-eight from the Buffalo 37, Richard Johnson again was flagged for pass interference, putting the ball at the Houston 49. And on third-and-six from the 45, Kelly threw a 13-yard pass to Don Smith. Two plays later he found Lofton for a 9-yard gain that gave the Bills a first down at the 17. But after a pair of incompletes and a 9-yard loss on a sack, Norwood was called upon for a 43-yard field goal to increase the lead to 17–13.

But the Oilers couldn't be stopped. After Bruce Smith dumped him for a 6-yard loss to the Houston 15, Moon completed a 15-yard pass to Drew Hill and ran 2 yards to convert a third-and-one from the 30. Moon then passed 15 yards to Hill, White ran for 4, and Moon again found Hill to put the ball at the Bills' 1. On the next play White plunged for a touchdown to give Houston a 20–17 lead with 3:14 remaining in the third quarter.

The Bills couldn't move on their next possession, but Rick Tuten's 31-yard punt appeared to have the Oilers buried at their 12. No such luck. White was at his most effective here, picking up 53 yards—31 on two pass receptions and 23 on four carries. His 28-yard catch on third-and-three gave Houston a first down at the Buffalo 5. Three plays later, Moon, buying time with Bruce Smith in hot pursuit, threw 3 yards to Leonard Harris for a touchdown to make it 27–17 with 7:21 left to play.

Going to the hurry-up again, Kelly had the Bills streaking downfield. He threw to Don Smith for 39 yards, then hit Reed for gains of 8 and 6, to put the ball at the Oilers' 23. On third-and-eight Kelly found Don Smith again, for 15 yards, to the 6. After two more passes Thomas ran around the left side for a 2-yard score to cut the margin to 27–24 with 3:29 left.

The Bills' defense would, once and for all, have to stop the Oilers. Or, to be more precise, Lorenzo White. But he ran for 6 yards on first-and-ten from the 24, and the Bills called time-out at 3:10. Then he ran for 1, and the Bills stopped the clock at 3:04. Then he caught a pass for 7 to give Houston a first down at their 38. Shane Conlan dropped White for a 1-yard loss on the next play, and the Bills called their final time-out at 2:08. White then sprinted for another 5 yards, but lost the ball while being tackled by Jeff Wright; after a scramble, the Bills recovered. Although referee Jim Tunney ruled White down by contact, television replays seemed to clearly show that Ray Bentley jarred the ball loose before the running back ever hit the ground. There was no reversal by replay officials, because—as is too often the case—they said a whistle had blown and the play was dead, making their review moot.

At the two-minute warning the Oilers faced a third-and-six

at their 42. But Moon did it again, hooking up with Givins for a 28-yard gain. With no time-outs left the Bills were helpless as Houston killed off the final 1:40 to hand the Bills a 27–24 loss.

With millions of TV viewers and the second-largest crowd in Astrodome history (60,130) watching, the Oilers had piled up 411 yards in ending Buffalo's eight-game winning streak. They also sent the Bills, 9–2, back into a tie with Miami for first place on the AFC East (the Dolphins had beaten Cleveland the day before, 30–13). And the game capped a rare weekend when all six NFL division leaders suffered defeats.

Afterward the Bills argued they were the victims of a bad call on White's separation from the ball—one that might have allowed them to, at the very least, force overtime with a tying field goal.

"There's no question it was a fumble," Bill Polian said. "I don't know how you can rule down by contact when, in fact, the ball was out before he hit the ground."

"The ball was definitely loose," Wright said. "And when he [White] fell back on it, he didn't have control of it. It was still moving around. We all thought it was a fumble . . . but maybe we shouldn't have been in that position in the first place."

And maybe they wouldn't have been had they not faced the run-and-shoot. Or been able to handle it better.

"I hate the run-and-shoot," Bentley grumbled. "It's not football; it's a damn track meet."

Actually, it was the run more than the shoot that did the Bills in. White, who entered the night averaging only 31.2 yards per game, rushed for 125 yards and a touchdown, and picked up 89 more yards on 5 receptions.

"This offense is twice as hard to stop when we run well," White understated. "It felt good to be able to carry the ball like I did back in my days at Michigan State."

Moon had a typically brilliant performance, completing 16 of 22 passes for 300 yards (his fourth consecutive 300-yard passing game) and two touchdowns. He could also be held responsible for making Walt Corey yank out the few remaining strands of hair on his head. By the end of the game the perplexed defensive coordinator had been through every page of his playbook—twice. Most of the night he and the rest of the Bills' defensive coaches took a calculated gamble by going with five men up front. Their hope was that the defense would be strong enough to stand toe-to-toe with what had been a meager Houston running game, while reinforcing downfield coverages against the Oilers' four-wide-receiver formations.

It failed on both counts. Miserably. The Oilers' burly offensive line overpowered Bills defenders, leaving White with plenty of room to run and catch, and Moon with plenty of time to do pretty much as he pleased against the Buffalo secondary.

"We tried everything," Corey said. "We tried blitzing them with man-for-man coverage. We tried three-deep zone, two-deep zone. Then, at the end, we even tried some regular stuff. We gave them the whole shmear.

"But if the run-and-shoot's clicking on all cylinders, you'd almost have to have a rifle and shoot those guys. It's a high-efficiency offense. And that's why they're number one in efficiency in the National Football League. You just hope that they screw up. When they got in trouble in other games, they put themselves there. And they didn't do that tonight."

But consolation was plentiful in the Buffalo dressing room. First, there was the fact that the Bills wouldn't see another run-and-shoot team for the balance of the regular season. Next was the fact that in losing their second game, they didn't come anywhere near the embarrassment suffered in losing their first. In fact, offensively, they were as proud as ever of their accomplishments.

"If we continue to play like this the rest of the year," Kelly said, "we'll be hard to beat."

After their loss to Miami the Bills won eight games in a row. How they would respond this time was anybody's guess.

After the Dolphins the Bills couldn't have picked a better opponent than the struggling Jets. But after Warren Moon and the run-and-shoot, they had a date with Randall Cunningham and the run-and-shoot-we-can't-catch-him. Moreover, Cunningham's team, Philadelphia, had a 7–4 record and the NFL's longest winning streak at the time (five games). Some of the more fanatical residents of the City of Brotherly Love had gone from looking to string up controversial head coach Buddy Ryan by his toes (after the Eagles' 2–4 start) to nominating him for mayor.

That was a lot for the Bills to ponder. So was the fact the game would be played on December 2, because since 1985 Buffalo's December record was 3–15, worst in the AFC and second only to Tampa Bay (2–16) for worst in the NFL. The last time the Bills had posted a winning record for the month was 1981, when they went 2–1. Oh, and they still had the curse of the NFC to overcome. Beating Phoenix didn't count.

It was another matchup of scoring machines: the Bills at the top of the league with an average of 28.4 points per game, the Eagles close behind at 25.6. It also figured to be another defensive nightmare for the Bills. Amazingly, Cunningham was the seventh-leading rusher in the National conference with 607 yards, 115 more than the Eagles' most productive running back. He was well ahead of his 1988 pace, when he ran for a personal single-season best of 624 yards. So far, he had been the team's leading rusher in six games, including the last five in a row.

But Cunningham wasn't all feet. He had a 58.2 completion percentage for 2,480 yards and 21 touchdowns, while throwing only 8 interceptions. "He's multifaceted, maybe the most multifaceted quarterback in the league," Levy pointed out.

Cunningham also had an extensive receiving corps, with running back Keith Byars (60 catches), tight end Keith Jackson (32), and rookie wide receivers Calvin Williams (25) and Fred Barnett (21).

"It's a wild offense, man," Cunningham said. "People don't know what we're doing. They think they can guess. But I can throw it to Byars and throw it to Jackson and—boom!—they're seeing Freddie and Calvin catching bombs for touchdowns."

The Bills would also be up against the league's second-best run defense, which had been allowing an average of 77.6 yards per game on the ground. Only San Francisco (75.9) was permitting fewer.

But as the first quarter opened, the Eagles offered almost no resistance. After taking the opening kickoff the Bills, starting at their 34, needed only forty-five seconds and two plays to take a 7–0 lead—a 3-yard run by Thomas and a 63-yard touchdown pass from Kelly to Lofton. Operating the no-huddle offense to perfection, Kelly would go 8-for-8 for 229 yards in the opening quarter, and wind up with his first 300-yard game of the season, as he completed 19 of 32 passes for 334 yards.

The Eagles went three and out on their first series, and Buffalo was on the march again from its 36. After Kenneth Davis leaped just far enough to convert a third-and-one, Kelly found Lofton for 20 yards to give the Bills a first down at the Philadelphia 34. But Kelly couldn't move the Bills any closer, so Norwood was called on to bang through a 43-yard field goal to make it 10–0.

The Eagles then went three and out again, and the Bills took over at their 35. This time Buffalo needed only twenty-seven seconds to score on two plays—a 9-yard run by Thurman Thomas and a 56-yard touchdown pass from Kelly to Reed to give the Bills a 17–0 advantage.

On the next possession the Eagles actually held the ball for more than four plays—they had it for six before Jeff Feagles was forced to punt it away for the third time.

With 2:45 left in the first quarter the Bills started their fourth possession at their 17. On third-and-two from the Buffalo 25, Kelly connected with Lofton for a 71-yard gain to the Philadelphia 4. The Bills called a time-out to assess their goal-line options, then Kelly threw to Thomas in the end zone to make it 24–0 with 1:23 left in the first quarter. For fifteen minutes the Bills had been unstoppable. Everything was working. But even though they seemed to be in complete control, there were three long quarters still to be played.

"The biggest thing was, even though we scored twenty-four points, it didn't run any time off the clock," Kent Hull said. "And when you're playing a football team with Randall Cunningham in the backfield, you never feel safe."

The Bills found out just how unsafe they were after Rick Tuten, a former Eagle, came on for his first punt of the day early in the second quarter. On second-and-nine from the Philadelphia 28, Cunningham dropped back to pass, found no one, and turned on the jets for 51 yards to the Buffalo 21. Anthony

Toney pounded out 3 yards through the middle, then Cunningham fired a touchdown pass to Keith Jackson. Roger Ruzek's extra-point attempt was no good, and the Bills led, 24–6.

Buffalo quickly gave the ball right back on a punt, but not before missing a perfect opportunity to deliver a knockout punch. On third-and-eight from the Bills' 30, a wide-open Don Beebe dropped a would-be touchdown bomb from Kelly that would have given the Bills a 25-point lead.

Instead, the Eagles took over with 9:38 remaining in the first half. With an even blend of runs and passes, Cunningham moved them to the Buffalo 3. On first-and-goal, however, he was sacked by Bruce Smith for an 8-yard loss. Then he fumbled the snap and Heath Sherman recovered all the way back at the Bills' 22. Finally, Cunningham scrambled for 8 before Ruzek trotted out to kick a 32-yard field goal to make it 24–9.

A career-long, 53-yard punt by Tuten pinned the Eagles at their 9 with fifty-four seconds left in the first half. On third-and-fourteen from the 5, Bruce Smith smelled a safety as he bore down on Cunningham in the middle of the end zone. But the quarterback ducked under him, scrambled to his left, avoided more pressure from Leon Seals, and unloaded with all his might to Barnett, who was standing near midfield with J.D. Williams. The pass was a little short, and had Williams not jumped a hair too early, he probably would have intercepted. Instead, Barnett made a leaping catch facing Cunningham at the Buffalo 46, turned upfield, and ran untouched for the 95-yard score, after which he collapsed from exhaustion—and disbelief—in the end zone. That pulled Philadelphia to within 24–16 at halftime.

"Are you kidding me?" Smith said. "I almost had to change my pants after that play."

"Out of the corner of my ear hole," Cunningham joked of eluding the defensive end, "I saw a '7' and part of an '8.' "

The Eagles weren't finished. They began the third quarter at their 23, and, with the help of a couple of big third-down conversions, drove for a third unanswered score. The first came on third-and-eleven from the Philadelphia 11, when Cunningham threw 13 yards to Calvin Williams. Then, on third-and-ten from the Buffalo 18, a pass-interference penalty on Leonard Smith put the ball at the Bills' 1. Three plays later Cunningham fired a touchdown pass to Keith Byars. Now Buffalo clung desperately to a one-point lead.

All of a sudden things didn't look so good for the Bills. They stopped tackling. They couldn't cover receivers. And the Eagles were no longer baffled by Buffalo's no-huddle offense. Then, somewhere in the middle of the third quarter, the Bills came out of their slumber. For the final 24:28, what had been a shoot-out between the NFL's two top scoring clubs turned into a defensive tug-of-war.

Buffalo's first possession of the second half began at its 22, and Kelly finally got the no-huddle in gear again. On third-and-four he hit Reed with a 12-yard pass. Then, on second-and-eight, he connected with Thomas for 35 yards to the Eagles' 23, setting up a 21-yard Norwood field goal that widened the gap to 27–23.

After that the Bills' defense grabbed the game by the throat. Rookie nose tackle Mike Lodish made his first sack as a pro, dumping Cunningham for a 6-yard loss on third-and-three at the Philadelphia 33, to force the Eagles to punt.

One play after Tuten kicked the ball back Cunningham was intercepted by Ray Bentley, whose 13-yard return gave the Bills a first down at the Eagles' 27. Thomas was stuffed for no gain, and Kelly threw two incompletes before Norwood booted a 45-yard field goal to make it 30–23 with eleven seconds gone in the fourth quarter.

Cunningham then drove the Eagles from their 28 to the Buffalo 42, but Cornelius Bennett's 12-yard sack pushed them back to the other side of the field. On the next play it appeared the officials might take the victory away from the Bills when they called a roughing-the-passer penalty on Leon Seals for his halfhearted shove of Cunningham. The infraction wiped out John Hagy's breakup of a deep pass for Calvin Williams, turning a third-and-eighteen from the Philadelphia 46 into a first down at the Buffalo 40.

"Terrible call," Seals growled. "When I hit him, it was in front of the Philadelphia bench, and Buddy Ryan started jumping his fat ass up and down. And the referee just threw the flag."

After an illegal-shift penalty on Keith Jackson (read: makeup call), a 4-yard run by Sherman, and a 7-yard pass to Byars, the Eagles had a third-and-four at the Bills' 34. That was when Talley, on what might have been the game's biggest defensive play, crashed through on a blitz to throw Cunningham for a 14-yard loss and force a punt.

If Cunningham's safety-turned-touchdown to end the first half was the most bizarre play of the game, a close second had to be Seth Joyner's fourth-quarter interception-turned-fumble. Thanks to a blocked punt by Tasker the Bills were driving at midfield with 8:57 left. On a third-and-six from the Philadelphia 46, Kelly was flushed from the pocket. He waved to Thomas to get open over the middle, then threw—right into Joyner's hands. But as the linebacker was about to be tackled on his 9-yard return, he tried to lateral to teammate William Frizzle. Showing remarkable alertness, Thomas knocked the ball free, and after a mad scramble in which it slipped through the hands of Eagle defender Eric Allen, Lofton recovered at the Eagles' 49. Santa had made an early delivery to One Bills Drive.

"I don't know what he [Joyner] was thinking," Jim Ritcher said. "It was a silly play. But I'm glad he did it."

"Looking back," Joyner said, in a voice that was barely audible, "if I could do it all over again, I would have just fallen on the ball."

The Bills proceeded to run 6:12 off the clock, making a pair of critical third-down conversions with Kelly's 8-yard throw to Lofton and 7-yard completion to Reed. When Philadelphia got the ball back, after Norwood missed a 36-yard field goal, only thirteen seconds remained—enough time for Cunningham to throw an 8-yard pass and an incomplete before time expired, giving the Bills a 30–23 triumph.

The victory, which lifted their record to 10–2, helped the Bills regain sole ownership of first place in the AFC East after Miami was humiliated by Washington, 42–20.

"We showed strong willpower," Bennett said. "They had taken the momentum right away from us. But we came back and got it."

On a day that would produce all sorts of surprises, the Bills' defense created one of their own by swarming all over Cunningham and catching him for a Buffalo season high of 6 sacks.

"We didn't expect to do that," confessed Talley, who along with Bruce Smith twice dumped Cunningham for losses. "It's like trying to chase a halfback around the field."

As it was, Cunningham finished as the game's leading rusher with 71 yards on 7 carries, including a 51-yard gain. And he completed 15 of 25 passes for 231 yards and three touchdowns.

Thurman Thomas finished the day with 53 rushing yards, helping him reach the 1,000-yard mark for the second consecutive year and become only the third rusher in Bills history to record back-to-back 1,000-yard seasons. O. J. Simpson had five in a row, from 1972 to 1976, while Joe Cribbs had two straight, in 1980 and 1981.

On defense Bruce Smith overcame a sore knee to boost his season sack total to 15, which equaled his own club record. He was having such an easy time against left tackle Ron Heller that the Eagles yanked the reputed cheap-shot artist and replaced him with Daryle Smith for the rest of the day. Bruce and Heller had jawed and shoved after several plays in the first half, and Smith later explained, "Some of the things that he was doing were just ridiculous. The play's over, I'm down on my knees trying to get up, and the guy comes and hits me under my chin while the referee is looking right at him. And he did that several times."

Meanwhile, the Eagles didn't get a single sack, which was amazing considering that Reggie White, their All-Everything defensive end, entered the game with 10. Howard Ballard, who blocked White for most of the game, pitched a stunning shutout as the Bills went through a third game without Kelly being tackled behind the line.

"If you were to tell me before the game that I wasn't going to be sacked, I wouldn't have believed you," Kelly said. "I figured I was going to get hit a couple of times, but our line did one hell of a job."

By beating a worthy opponent in the first of five December games the Bills couldn't help but feel vindicated. Well, most of them couldn't. Cracked Tasker, "What will people say now? That this doesn't count because it's too early in December?"

The most critical game remaining for the Bills' Super Bowl aspirations was their December 23 showdown with Miami. But the second-most critical was their December 9 meeting with the Colts at the Indianapolis Hoosier Dome.

Victories over the Colts and Dolphins would give Buffalo its third consecutive AFC Eastern Division championship and home-field advantage in the play-offs. Period. It wouldn't matter what happened against the Giants, a far more prominent opponent, or in the regular-season finale at Washington.

The Colts had a 5–7 record. They had already lost to the Bills by 16 points in the season opener. Yet there was no sense of this being an automatic Buffalo victory.

For the Bills the Hoosier Dome was not a friendly place. In six previous trips there they had come away with only one victory. In 1989 they had not only lost the game, 37–14, but also Jim Kelly for three weeks with a separated shoulder—and the rest of the year to the Bickering Bills.

An ugly loss had become almost a given whenever the Bills traveled to Indianapolis. In the first three years after the Colts moved there from Baltimore, the Bills lost 31–17, 49–17, and 24–14. In 1987 the streak was snapped with a 27–3 Buffalo win, but that was followed by a 17–14 loss in 1988 and the 1989 debacle.

"Last year we came out flat, and they womped us," Tasker said. "If we go out ready to play this time, it should be a lot different."

But the Colts were expected to be ready, too. Before losing a close game to Phoenix in their previous outing they had beaten New England, the Jets, and Cincinnati. They figured to want nothing more than to be the foot that tripped the Bills on their way to the postseason.

Looking back at the first game, the Colts couldn't help but feel frustrated by the thought of what might have been had Cornelius Bennett not put rookie quarterback Jeff George out of the game with a concussion while victory was in their reach in the fourth quarter. Up to that point, George described it as his best game of the season, because he "was throwing to all the right people, and doing it under pressure."

But that was then. As he approached the December 9th game George seemed a bit apprehensive about facing the Bills' pass rushers a second time.

"The pressure is unbelievable," he said. "You're more concerned about the pass rush sometimes than you are with your own receivers running down the field."

From the very start of the rematch it was obvious George was preoccupied with the thought of going home with all of his body parts intact. And that Eric Dickerson wasn't interested in running his hardest. And that, overall, the Colts were flat and dispirited. They missed blocks. They missed tackles. If one didn't know better, one would have sworn the entire team had also missed a night's sleep.

The Colts stumbled through their opening series, advancing only three yards before a Rohn Stark punt. For the second week in a row the Bills, beginning at their own 34, came out sizzling in their no-huddle offense with the number-one-rated passer in the NFL at the controls. Kelly threw a 13-yard screen pass to Thurman Thomas on the first play, and Thomas ran twice for 11 yards to put the ball at the Indianapolis 42. On third-and-nine Kelly connected with James Lofton for 12 yards on a sideline pattern. And after losing 4 on a pass to Thomas the Bills lined up with three wide receivers to one side and Keith McKeller to the other, which forced the Colts to single cover one of the wide men with a safety. Keith Taylor, who, like most strong safeties is built to cover tight ends and other slower targets, never had a prayer as Andre Reed broke free to catch Kelly's 34-yard touchdown pass.

The Bills' pass rush wasted no time getting in Jeff George's face. On the first play of the Colts' next series Jeff Wright pressured the rookie into an incomplete. On second-and-nine from the Indianapolis 42, Leon Seals and Wright combined to force another incomplete. One play later George was intercepted by Kirby Jackson, whose 14-yard return gave the Bills a first down at the Colts' 37 (while causing Jackson to sustain yet another hamstring pull.)

Kelly kept the hurry-up motoring with a 12-yard pass to Reed and an 18-yard throw to McKeller that moved the ball to the 7. Kelly then connected with Reed in the middle of the end zone (making him the team's all-time leader in touchdown receptions), and the Bills were in front, 14–0, with 7:21 left in the first quarter.

On their next possession the Colts were single-handedly destroyed by Bruce Smith, who sacked George on two consecutive plays for 19 yards in losses. Smith would drop him twice more before the five-minute mark of the second quarter—a single-game career high of 4 sacks in twenty minutes.

"I think George was a little rattled," said Smith, whose 19 sacks for the season were three shy of the NFL record set by Mark Gastineau with the New York Jets in 1984. "If you get constant pressure on any quarterback, he's going to start wondering where it's going to come from next. And I think that's what happened to him."

Especially after the fourth sack, on which Smith blew in without a blocker within five feet and did a belly flop on the quarterback for a 7-yard loss. George had lost all poise by then, which he proved on a nonsack pursuit by Smith in the fourth quarter just before the defensive end would be given the rest of the day off.

"He saw me coming," Smith said. Then, widening his eyes to recapture the look on George's face, he added, "I heard him say, 'Ohhh shit!' "

"I'm just glad he's wearing a Bills jersey and helmet," Levy said of Smith.

After Smith's second sack, the Bills looked as if they were going to build a 21–0 lead before the end of the first quarter. But they gave the ball back when Don Smith, on a 6-yard shuttle pass from Kelly, fumbled while trying to vault over free safety Mike Prior at the Indianapolis 2.

It wasn't until late in the second quarter that Buffalo had its three-touchdown advantage. Beginning at their 36, the Bills smashed away with three Thomas runs for 15 yards and a 9-yard carry by Mueller to reach the Colts' 35. Kelly then completed passes of 6 yards to Reed and 14 to Beebe, on third-and-four, to give Buffalo a first down at the 15. After being dumped for a 7-yard loss, Kelly threw a 7 yarder to Reed, and two plays later Thomas crossed the goal line from 5 yards out to make it 21–0 at halftime.

Looking as if they finally meant business, the Colts came out for their first series of the second half—after a 20-yard punt return by Clarence Verdin—in a three-wide-receiver formation. Eric Dickerson remained on the sidelines, while Albert Bentley, the best pass catcher among their running backs, was used in a single-back set. Now the Colts were on the move, converting a third-and-five from the Buffalo 40 with a 6-yard George pass to Billy Brooks and a third-and-four from the 28 with Bentley's 18-yard carry on a draw. George then threw another 6 yarder to Brooks to put the ball at the 4. A 3-yard Bentley run set up a 1-yard quarterback keeper by George to reduce the margin to 21–7.

But Kelly and Thomas answered by hooking up for a 63-yard pass on the first play after the kickoff, giving the Bills a first down at the Indianapolis 17. Thomas was only supposed to have been a decoy on the pattern, with the throw going to either Lofton, Reed, or McKeller. Kelly and the running back saw the Colts' playing a deep zone, however, and knew there would be plenty of green in which to operate underneath. The Bills couldn't get any closer than the 5, but were satisfied to have Scott Norwood kick a 25-yard field goal with 3:35 left in the third quarter.

"To me, that was the biggest series in the game," Kelly said. "We didn't get the TD, but we got three points, and that took a little air out of them."

Make that a lot of air.

Late in the third quarter the Bills received an unlikely turnover when Leon Seals made the first interception of his four-year career after a pass was deflected to him by Clifford Hicks, a free-agent defensive back signed only four days earlier.

"It shocked the hell out of me," Seals said. "As a defensive lineman, you expect to get fumbles, maybe, but not an interception."

Starting at his 49, Kelly came out firing again with a 9-yard pass to McKeller, followed two plays later by a 12-yard throw to Reed. On third-and-nine, Thomas completed the 31–7 rout by streaking 23 yards for a touchdown at 2:08 of the fourth quarter.

The December collapse would have to remain on hold, as the Bills clinched at least a wild-card play-off berth with an 11–2 record. With the Dolphins beating Philadelphia that night, 23–20, Buffalo maintained a one-game lead in the AFC East. The Bills also were 2–0 in December, 4–2 on the road, 6–1 in the division, and 9–2 in the conference.

George's postgame perspective on the Bills didn't change a whole lot from his pregame version: "You hope they don't kill you."

Dickerson, who carried 12 times for a mere 33 yards, also pulled no punches in his assessment: "We were no match for Buffalo."

Throughout the league the notion began to spread that future opponents would be in the same sinking boat unless they could find a way to stop Buffalo's no-huddle offense. Smith was an intimidating force by himself, but the Bills were making him even more effective with their early leads. Opponents were forced into a throwing mode sooner than they preferred, allowing Smith and the other pass-rushers to simply tee off. The Bills opened each of their last two games with the pass-happy, fast-breaking attack, and the results were staggering. They had a 24–0 advantage before the Eagles knew what hit them. They were ahead, 14–0, before the Colts realized the game was under way.

So how and when did this no-huddle mania begin?

Kelly deserved the bulk of the credit. Early in his NFL career he demonstrated a knack for successfully operating without a huddle under the usual circumstances that called for a quick score—late in the game, or the half, with the Bills trailing. And as the years passed he became known as "The Master of the Two-Minute Drill." Eventually Kelly concluded that it would be equally, if not more, effective to use the no-huddle earlier in the game. Cincinnati had proven as much during the 1988 season, after they defeated the Bills in the AFC Championship Game. But the Bengals' primary motivation was to draw 5-yard penalties by catching defenses—as they desperately tried to substitute run-stuffers with pass-coverage specialists before the snap—with too many men on the field. Kelly saw that as a plus, too, but he was more interested in making big plays while an out of sync, gasping defense struggled to keep up.

It was in a 1989 overtime triumph against Houston that Kelly first ran the no-huddle as something approaching a standard offense. And after the 47–41 shootout he went public with his desire to employ it on a regular basis. Levy and offensive coordinator Ted Marchibroda took it under consideration. But they decided a radical change in the offense during the season would do more harm than good. Then, after watching Kelly's brilliant execution of the no-huddle late in the play-off loss to Cleveland, the coaches embraced the idea for 1990.

"It was an evolvement from the Houston game to the Cleveland game, and the Cleveland game definitely set the tone," explained Marchibroda. "There were just so many games in which Jimmy was so successful in two-minute situations to begin with, we thought, 'Why wouldn't he be successful at it during the regular course of the ball game?' You do what you do best, and that's something Jimmy does extremely well."

What makes the no-huddle so effective?

"Number one, it creates confusion," Marchibroda said. "They [opposing defenses] don't have time to get the call in from the sidelines, so there's a possibility we can hold them in a particular defensive scheme. Number two, fatigue sets in quicker on the other team and we feel that's an advantage we have because our guys are in excellent shape. And three, there's the unknown factor, with the opposition saying, 'How long are these guys going to keep this up?' "

Earlier in the season Levy picked his spots when to use the no-huddle and avoided doing so through most or all of any single game, including the season opener against the Colts when it wasn't seen after the first series. But as the year progressed he saw greater benefit in employing it for long stretches. And the greatest was that it brought the best out of Kelly. He would get hot, find a rhythm, and become virtually unstoppable, such as when he went 8-for-8 in the 24-point run against Philadelphia and 7-for-9 in the 14-point eruption against Indianapolis.

The thing Kelly liked best about the no-huddle was that it allowed him to call his own plays. And that, of course, made him one of a kind. Since Paul Brown started sending instructions to the huddle with messenger guards in the 1940s, play calling gradually was taken away from quarterbacks and put into the hands of coaches. Today the sight of an NFL quarterback looking to the sidelines for hand signals telling him what to call next is as common as the three-point stance. Joe Montana does it. Some, like Pittsburgh's Bubby Brister, can even be seen moving their lips as they decipher the information.

After a week of intensive film study and meetings with Marchibroda, Kelly's brain was loaded with thirty to forty plays, plus five to ten formations. The rest was up to his mouth. As the rest of the offense took its place before the snap (in shotgun or over center) he barked a series of numbers or code words. His play selection depended on down-and-distance and how he anticipated the defense to react. In addition, Kelly called the pass routes, the blocking schemes, and any necessary adjustments based on his presnap reads. To prevent defenders from picking up plays simply by listening to the signals, Kelly had numerous "dummy" calls to throw them off.

Play calling gave Kelly a chance to improvise and use his own experience and wisdom. Now he could run the plays that *he* liked. And they weren't all passes. Quite often he'd spot something in the defense that told him it was a good time to run, either with a handoff to Thomas or a direct shotgun snap to Don Smith. He also could utilize his sense for when to show confidence in a certain player, who might have flubbed an earlier play, by calling his number again. If Kelly ever experienced a problem he could always look to Marchibroda or Frank Reich for help from the sidelines. But that rarely happened.

"In the no-huddle I'm in total control of the offense," Kelly said. "Whether we score points or don't score points is in my hands. When we have to do it, I love to be the guy who has to get it done. It's something I've thrived on ever since I was in Little League football and up through high school and college. If I made the big plays we usually were very successful. If I didn't, we usually lost."

"Jim's like the NBA player who wants the ball at the end of the game," Marchibroda said. "He's our Michael Jordan, our Magic Johnson. And that, first and foremost, is why the no-huddle has been so successful for us."

Of course, it wasn't all Kelly. The no-huddle would be no dice without pass catchers the caliber of Reed, Lofton, Thomas, and McKeller. The whole premise was to force teams, through the hurried pace that limited their changes in personnel and strategy, to cover some or all of the receivers one-on-one. Given their great speed and athletic ability, Kelly would almost always find an open man. And his protection was as good as any in the NFL, giving him time to make the correct choice.

"A lot of teams use the no-huddle, but it's the way you execute it that makes the difference," Reed said. "We believe that if we don't beat ourselves, nobody can beat us. We're unstoppable."

Unstoppable was also a word more and more offensive linemen and their coaches were using to describe Bruce Smith. No longer was he satisfied with being recognized as the best defensive end in the league. He felt he had already surpassed Philadelphia's Reggie White for that honor.

Now he wanted to be known as the NFL's best defensive player. Period.

Three days before the Bills' December 5 game against the Giants at the Meadowlands Smith took his campaign to the place he knew it would have its greatest impact—New York City. For one thing, he could count on the media there to gobble up juicy quotes from an opposing team's star player. For another, he realized that the man long regarded as the top defensive player in the league was Giants linebacker Lawrence Taylor. It took a lot of nerve for Smith to step onto Taylor's turf and declare that the torch of greatness had been passed over to him. But that was exactly what he did during a conference call with New York reporters. His words were met with numerous raised eyebrows.

"Over the last ten years, he [Taylor] has probably been the most dominant defensive player in the league," Smith said. "But I think I've taken it up a notch above him. Right now, it's time to give credit to somebody who deserves it. It would be a terrible injustice if I don't get NFL Defensive Player of the Year."

Those are the kind of words that find their way onto dressing-room bulletin boards and incite the opposition. Smith said he intended nothing of the sort, that he was merely dealing with facts. And one indisputable fact was, up to that point in the season, he was the more productive of the two, with 19 sacks to Taylor's 8½.

Still, a few Bills players expressed at least slight discomfort with Smith's remarks.

"Gee, Bruce, thanks a lot," Will Wolford said. He was, of course, being sarcastic. At left offensive tackle Wolford would be lined up across from Taylor for much of the game. He had expected to have his hands full with the NFL's all-time sack leader—even before Smith opened his mouth.

Hull wasn't going to be bothered, "unless Lawrence winds up with ten sacks in the first half or something. Then, I might say, 'Hey, Bruce, you want to take some center for awhile?' "

Actually, LT's public reaction didn't contain nearly as much fire as some anticipated. It wasn't even all that terse.

"What do you want me to do?" he said. "Hell, if that's the way people think, that's the way they think. I ain't got nothing to do with that. I mean, everybody's time passes. It happens. It doesn't concern me. It doesn't bother me one bit."

But some of Taylor's teammates felt the need to come to his defense. As far as cornerback Mark Collins was concerned, Smith had no right to make such a comparison.

"How many times has he [Smith] been to the Pro Bowl? Three?" Collins said. "When you go nine years in a row, like Lawrence has, then you can start comparing yourself to the greats."

The verbal skirmish was just one indication that the Bills-Giants game was far more important than it appeared. In terms of play-off implications, it meant very little. The Giants, who were also 11–2, had already captured the NFC Eastern Division championship. The AFC Eastern Division crown wouldn't be decided until the following week, when the Bills met the Dolphins at Rich Stadium. In terms of pride, however, the game had the feel of something much bigger. It was a match between a pair of truly top-notch teams in an NFL season punctuated by mediocrity.

Some were even calling it a preview of Super Bowl XXV.

To be certain, there wasn't, with the possible exception of the Dolphins, a more attractive opponent on the Buffalo schedule. Less than two weeks earlier the Giants had participated in the much-hyped "Game of the Year," which turned out to be a boring 7–3 loss to San Francisco on "Monday Night Football." Their active roster still included eighteen members of the 1986 Super Bowl championship squad.

Of course, there was always the NFC-is-stronger-than-the-AFC debate to stir things up. And anyone who dared suggest the Bills belonged to an inferior conference was going to get an earful in their dressing room that week.

"I think it's a stupid assessment," Reed said with disgust.

Added Mueller, "I don't think it matters what conference you play in. Any team can beat any team."

The Bills felt their record was strong enough that they didn't have to genuflect in front of another NFL club, even one from the "mighty" NFC. They didn't buy the premise the NFC was a cut above because of the six consecutive Super Bowls its representatives had won, including the 49ers' 55–10 romp over the Broncos in Super Bowl XXIV. At that point the NFC held a 23–17 edge in interconference games. However, in regular-season contests since 1984 (when the Raiders gave the AFC its last Super Bowl triumph), the AFC was in front, 173–172, with one tie. The Bills were also feeling pretty smug about their conquests of the two NFC opponents they had already faced—Phoenix and Philadelphia.

"When I came into the league four years ago, that's the first thing I heard: 'You were drafted by an AFC team, and they're not that tough,'" Leon Seals recalled. "But we'll take it to anybody—NFC or AFC. For anybody to feel inferior because they're going to play an NFC team, they don't belong in this league."

Nevertheless, after several weeks of head-spinning point production, Kelly and the NFL's top-scoring offense were expected to have a far more difficult time reaching either Meadowlands end zone. The Giants had the league's number-one–rated defense—a defense without a glaring weakness. They were only seventeenth on offense, but they did have a strong running game (116.6 yards per game), featuring veteran Ottis Anderson and rookie Rodney Hampton.

A grind it out, ball-control attack figured to be the best means of disarming the no-huddle. After all, Kelly couldn't throw what he didn't have.

"You have to be patient when you play the Giants," Levy said. "They're close to what the Colts' style of play was, but with stronger players. They keep good field position, because their kick-return game has been so good, and they're plus-seventeen in turnovers."

Giants coach Bill Parcells hardly trembled at the thought of facing the no-huddle. In his own Jersey-guy way, he sort of scoffed at it.

"Regardless of what you do, offense becomes a matter of executing against a defense," he said. "If your offense executes better than the defense, then you are going to move the ball whether there is a huddle or not."

The Giants opened the game's first series from their 29, and promptly began a ground assault. Lewis Tillman carried on the first four plays to the Giants' 42. After that it was Rodney Hampton's turn, and the rookie also rambled four times in a row to the Buffalo 6. On second-and-goal Simms threw a 4-yard pass to Hampton, then called a time-out to regroup. After Hampton fought his way to the 1 on the next play Anderson plowed through the middle on fourth down to give the Giants a 7–0 lead.

For their first possession the Bills came out in the shotgun formation. You could almost hear the motor rumbling from their no-huddle offense. After an incomplete Kelly connected with Thomas on a 48-yard screen pass to the New York 26. A pass-interference penalty on Everson Walls advanced the ball to the 17, and a pair of Thomas runs gave the Bills a first down at the 6. One play after throwing incomplete for Lofton, Kelly found Reed on a shallow crossing pattern, and the receiver turned upfield for the tying touchdown. It marked the fifth time in a row and seventh in the last eight games that the Bills reached the end zone on their first offensive series.

A few minutes later, having failed to move beyond their 40, the Giants punted. The Bills were in the shotgun again, working from their 22. Two passes and a Thomas run put them at their 40, from where Kelly hooked up with Reed for a 36-yard completion to the Giants' 24. Three plays later they had a fourth-and-one from the 15. The handoff went to Don Smith, who was stopped cold in a collision with Taylor, but struggled forward to make the first down by half the length of the football. Thomas took the next three carries, the last a 2-yard touchdown sweep to the left to make it 14–7 less than a minute into the second quarter.

After an exchange of punts the Giants took over at the Buffalo 49. Simms completed a 19-yard pass to Stephen Baker. On the next play Hampton ran for 9 yards and picked up an additional 10 when his face mask was yanked by Seals. The Giants got as far as the 6, then called on Matt Bahr for a 23-yard field goal that cut the margin to 14–10 with 5:56 remaining in the second quarter.

Twenty-six seconds later Buffalo's Super Bowl hopes and dreams appeared ready to go up in smoke. Once again. On second-and-ten from his 21, Kelly threw a pass to Reed, then stepped back to watch the rest of the 8-yard play unfold. At the same time Giants linebacker Carl Banks—who had been thrown aside by Jim Ritcher—hit the right knee of Will Wolford, setting off a horrifying chain reaction. The 295-pound offensive tackle lurched backwards into Kelly's left leg, hitting it with his back, and the two crumpled to the ground. Kelly immediately clutched his left knee and began moving in a circle while writhing in pain. Then he sat up, bobbing his head back and forth while letting out a scream that chilled several nearby teammates and Giants players. Next to Kelly was Wolford holding his right knee, which had temporarily gone numb.

"I just turned around, and it seemed like there were people laying everywhere," Kent Hull said. "It was pretty scary."

After several minutes Kelly got to his feet, gingerly applied weight to his left leg, and walked slowly—but without assistance—to the sidelines.

"I'll be back," he told Hull.

And the center knew that Kelly, who had completed 7 of 11 passes for 115 yards and a score, didn't mean he'd return in a couple of weeks or a month. He knew he meant later *that* day.

Out trotted Frank Reich. This wasn't a new situation for him, of course. In 1989, while Kelly was sidelined with a separated shoulder, Reich was 3–0 as a starter. He had come through before; his teammates and everyone else connected with the Bills expected him to come through again.

"Let's do it," Hull told him, just as he had in the first huddle of each of the three games in 1989.

On the next play Reich handed to Thomas, but he came up one-yard short on third-and-two, forcing a punt. Meanwhile, Kelly had put on a jacket and was walking slowly in front of the Bills' bench, constantly stopping to test his left knee. At one point, he did a deep knee-bend before walking again.

"The first minute, two minutes of the injury are the worst," Kelly would say later. "But after a while it started quieting down. It felt pretty good. I got up, I was able to walk on it.

"And after I got to the sidelines and I started trying to bend on it, I said, 'God, this is great. I mean, if I get hit the way I just did and I'm able to walk the way I am, this is pretty good.' "

But all that changed when, losing himself for a moment in the excitement of the game, he jumped while trying to get a better view of the outcome of Rick Tuten's punt. The knee suddenly buckled, and Kelly began hopping on his right foot. He quickly turned and hopped to the bench, where he sat for a few minutes while being examined by the team physician, Dr. Richard Weiss, and the trainers.

Kelly then was helped onto the back of a utility cart and driven to the Bills' dressing room, where he would spend the rest of the game with what Weiss diagnosed as a sprained medial collateral ligament. Before he left he leaned over in front of Reich and instructed him not to allow the coaches to stop using the no-huddle just because of the quarterback change. They wouldn't.

At the time the doctor didn't specify how long Kelly would be sidelined, saying it "could be two, four, or six weeks." A magnetic resonance imaging (MRI) scan of the knee, to be conducted two days later, would provide the most accurate prognosis. One thing was certain, though: the NFL's top-rated passer was going to miss the following week's showdown against the Dolphins. Wolford returned briefly against the Giants, then limped off for the balance of the day with a less severe knee sprain. Glenn Parker finished in his place.

"I feel bad the whole thing happened," Wolford said. "But there was absolutely nothing I could do. I had no idea what was going on. I had my own problems at the time."

The Giants punted, but the Bills, with Reich looking shaky in completing two of his first four passes, couldn't make anything happen. The half ended with the Bills clinging to a 14–10 lead—and worrying about Kelly's knee. After opening the third quarter by going three and out, with another Reich pass falling incomplete, the Bills appeared in trouble. And the Giants, as well as the crowd, could sense the game was turning in their favor.

Two Hampton runs and a holding penalty on J. D. Williams moved the Giants 10 yards to their 30. Phil Simms then converted a third-and-five at the 35 with a 9-yard pass to Dave Meggett. But, like Kelly, Simms went down in a heap after the play. Like Kelly, he was in obvious pain, with an injury to his right foot. Jeff Hostetler filled in from there and proceeded to move the Giants into Buffalo territory.

On second-and-ten from the Bills' 33, New York not only gained 4 yards on a Hampton run, but also picked up 17 on consecutive penalties—5 for face masking on Shane Conlan and 12 for unsportsmanlike conduct on Leon Seals. Now the Giants had a first down at the 12. Two Hampton runs gave them a third-and-one at the 3, but Williams made up for his holding penalty earlier in the drive by stopping Anderson for a 1-yard loss. That limited the damage to a 22-yard Bahr field goal, pulling the Giants to within a point, 14–13, with 4:07 left in the third quarter.

Things continued to look grim for the once-potent Buffalo offense when, on the first play of the next possession, Reich was sacked for a 9-yard loss. But on second down from the Bills' 25, Reich connected with Don Beebe on a 43-yard bomb to the New York 32. Suddenly the Bills were coming back to life. Reich found Beebe for 6- and 7-yard passes to move the ball to the 19. On third-and-eight, a completion to Keith McKeller came up 2 yards short of the first down, so Norwood came out for a 29-yard field goal to give the Bills a 17–13 advantage four seconds into the fourth quarter.

From that point on Buffalo's defense took command, turning the Giants back four times in the final 14:56.

The New York series after Norwood's field goal was snuffed when Darryl Talley and Bruce Smith combined to stop Maurice Carthon for no gain on third-and-one from the Giants' 38. A few days earlier, of course, Smith committed the sports equivalent of blasphemy by saying he had supplanted Taylor as the best defensive player in the game. Besides unnecessarily inciting the opposition, he had, in effect, dared himself to be great. A poor individual performance would have made him a laughingstock not only in the Big Apple, but throughout the NFL.

Smith didn't have a sack all day. But he was a tremendous force against the Giants' running game with 10 tackles, including 6 primary hits. He continually disrupted the flow of New York's offense, which ran away from him at least a dozen times in the first half. Down after down, he either made the play, forced it, or caused the Giants to change direction.

The Giants' second drive of the fourth quarter began at their 45. Hostetler moved them all the way to the Buffalo 13, but a holding penalty by right guard Bob Kratch pushed the ball back to the 23. And on the next play Bart Oates sent a bad shotgun snap to Hostetler, who scrambled to recover at the Bills' 42. That brought out Sean Landeta for another punt.

During New York's next series, an offensive pass-interference penalty against rookie receiver Troy Kyles wiped out a 15-yard Hostetler-to-Stephen Baker pass to the Buffalo 22. It also left the Giants with a third-and-eighteen from the Bills'

47. Chased out of the pocket while attempting to pass, Hostetler was brought down by Jeff Wright and Bruce Smith after a 3-yard gain, forcing Landeta's third punt of the quarter.

The Giants' final hope for victory came when they took over with 1:04 left on the clock. Already out of time-outs, they received a big break when Rick Tuten's punt sailed only 24 yards to the New York 43. Doing his best Jim Kelly imitation, Hostetler completed passes of 15 yards to Lionel Manuel, 9 to Baker, and 7 to Meggett to give the Giants a first down at the Buffalo 26. Hostetler then spiked the ball to stop the clock at twenty-four seconds. But after that he threw two incompletes to Manuel and a third to Kyles, leaving Reich to kneel for the final nine seconds of Buffalo's 17–13 victory.

The Bills had twelve wins for the year, equaling a franchise record, and only two losses. They were 3–0 versus NFC teams, guaranteeing them their first winning record against the conference since 1980. They maintained a one-game lead over the Dolphins (who would beat Seattle the next day, 24–17) and could clinch their third consecutive division title and home-field advantage in postseason play against Miami the following Sunday.

When people spoke of this being a classic matchup, of it being the Super Bowl before the Super Bowl, they likely weren't picturing a duel between Frank Reich and Jeff Hostetler. But those were the ones taking snaps at the end of the cold, wet, dreary afternoon. And Reich was the one being hugged, high-fived, and patted everywhere he went.

He wasn't stupendous. The no-huddle definitely lost a little something in his hands. However, considering he hadn't taken a single practice snap all week (the Saturday game shortened preparation time, so Kelly needed as much work as he could get), his performance was well above admirable, completing 8 of 15 passes for 97 yards.

"Maybe I didn't get to run our plays in practice, but Jim, Gale Gilbert, and I put in a whole lot of time every week studying film and talking about our offense and what we want to do against certain teams and certain defenses," Reich said.

"So even though I hadn't gotten the physical repetitions, I didn't feel, from a mental standpoint, that I didn't get enough work."

Still, Buffalo's defenders were taking nothing for granted.

"After Jim was hurt we were determined not to let the game slip away," Talley said. "I think that was the best half of defense we played this year. Guys making plays—coming up with big plays at the times we needed them."

"Frank Reich did it for us before, but we still couldn't let the Giants get the lead, because Jim Kelly wasn't in there for us," Shane Conlan pointed out. "No offense to Frank, but Jim's in a class by himself for bringing a team from behind."

Just how determined were Buffalo defenders to keep the Giants from scoring? Ray Bentley stayed in the game with a torn pectoral muscle, which severely limited the use of his right arm. Still, he managed to make an incredible 14 tackles, including 7 initial stops.

"It was very painful, purple, and swollen," Bentley said of his injury. "But you get that adrenaline going and you don't even think about it. That was my kind of game, because you knew they were just going to run the ball right at us [42 times to be exact, for 157 yards]."

"You could tell that the injury was really bothering him," Walt Corey said. "It's tough enough playing this game with two good arms, let alone one. So he would just put a shoulder on a guy, then get the other arm wrapped around and make the tackle. He's a barroom type of player who uses barroom tactics to get the job done."

Kent Hull explained the overall gut-level effort best: "Jim Kelly is our leader. A football team has to reach for something extra when it loses its leader. We had to show we could respond to adversity. And we did."

As a result, Bill Polian distributed game balls to all forty-seven members of the Bills' active roster. "If there's a more courageous performance in Bills history," the GM said, "I haven't seen it."

The Giants finished the game with a huge advantage in possession time, 37:59 to 22:01. They also outgained the Bills by a whopping 313 yards to 264.

So their frustration with coming up 4 points short on the scoreboard was understandable.

"We shouldn't have lost to Buffalo," a disgusted Taylor said. "They're a fine team and all. But when Kelly went out, it took the air out of their balloons. You could see that."

Giants linebacker Steve DeOssie was asked if he could see the Bills' playing a month later in Super Bowl XXV. He paused for a moment, then nodded.

"Yeah," DeOssie said, "I could see them in the Super Bowl—and I'd like to see them from across the field."

7

THE REICH STUFF

"This is absolutely the best news we could have had."

The words had a strange ring as Bill Polian uttered them while addressing a room overflowing with reporters and photographers on the morning of December 18. Hadn't he just announced, moments earlier, that the results from a magnetic resonance imaging scan showed Jim Kelly would be sidelined for four weeks with the knee injury he suffered against the Giants? By "best news," was the GM referring to Kelly's being available by the divisional round of the play-offs? Or was it simply an expression of relief that "the franchise" hadn't sustained more severe damage to his left knee and wouldn't be lost forever?

Because the bottom line was that Kelly wouldn't play against the Dolphins in five days. And given the game's significance and the fact Kelly had never been hotter as an NFL quarterback, any news Polian delivered—short of a miraculous recovery putting number twelve over center for the first snap of the Miami game—was going to be received as "okay news" or "decent news" by Bills fans.

But definitely not "best news."

If the Bills lost to Miami they would squander a perfect opportunity to capture their third consecutive AFC East title and home-field advantage throughout the play-offs (the last hope for a division crown after that would be a Buffalo victory at Washington and a Dolphin loss at home against Indianapolis in the final week of the season). If they wound up a wild card, they would have to win at least once in the postseason without Kelly in order to have a chance to get to the Super Bowl with him. And if they were on the road for any play-off game their chances of winning—as they had painfully discovered through the years in places like Cleveland, Cincinnati, and San Diego—would be greatly reduced.

With or without Kelly.

So Western New York wasn't exactly bubbling when Polian said that the MRI scan showed a partial tear in the medial collateral ligament of Kelly's left knee, as well as a tear in the cartilage behind the knee. And the Christmas season didn't seem any brighter when he pointed out that team physician Dr. Richard Weiss had been "right on target" with his diagnosis the day before Kelly underwent the high-tech X-ray.

All anyone had to do was check the expression on Kelly's face after he limped up to the podium during a separate session with reporters. Besides the other wonderful fruits a victory over the Dolphins would bear, there also was revenge for the 30–7 loss in week two.

No Bills player wanted to deliver an equally humiliating payback more than Kelly.

"It's a game that not only the forty-seven players on this team are looking forward to, but the whole community," he said. "This is what everybody dreams about. This is what everybody lives for. And I'm just going to be watching from the sidelines."

Always one to sneer in the face of adversity, Kelly somberly admitted he was beginning to feel a little snakebitten. What good was his ranking as the number-one passer in the NFL if he couldn't play in the most anxiously awaited sporting event ever staged in Buffalo (or at least since the 1966 AFL championship game against Kansas City)? A year earlier Kelly had also reached the top of the league's quarterback ratings—just before suffering a separated shoulder against the Colts.

"It's like, 'What have I done wrong?' " he said. "I go to church every Sunday. I pray. God, I don't know . . .

"But hopefully I'll be back for the first play-off game. You always want to think optimistic. You always want to be the guy who's in there taking the snaps."

Against the Dolphins that guy would be Frank Reich.

The fretting over Kelly's injury wasn't a slam on his understudy of five years so much as a show of frustration over yet another ugly twist of fate in Bills history. Kelly had been the sparkplug of the unstoppable no-huddle offense. He had completed 219 of 346 passes (63.3 percent) for 2,829 yards and 24 touchdowns, while throwing only 9 interceptions. He had had opposing linebackers, cornerbacks, and safeties talking to themselves for most of the season. Not to mention several head coaches and defensive coordinators.

And now, as suddenly as the Bills developed the offensive firepower they lacked while nearly going the distance in 1988, they had it taken away in such a freakish fashion.

True, Frank Reich owned a perfect record as an NFL starter, including a 31–17 pounding of Miami. True, during his starting debut in 1989, Frank Reich twice used the hurry-up in the final 2:23 to engineer touchdown drives of 86 and 64 yards in leading the Bills to a 23–20 Monday night victory over the Los Angeles Rams. And with no time-outs.

But he was still Frank Reich—a dependable, just enough to get the job done backup. He wasn't Jim Kelly—a phenomenal, anything it takes to win and beyond superstar. Regardless of what anyone said, if the Bills didn't beat the Dolphins, the loss would carry an asterisk to indicate that Kelly didn't play.

"Oh, well," sighing fans would say. "What are you going to do? Kelly was hurt. The Bills never really had much of a chance in the first place."

Of course, that wasn't the talk around the Buffalo dressing room. Not by a long shot.

And some of the more emphatic support for Reich came from Kelly: "Everybody has confidence in Frank that he can do it. I *know* he can do it."

Kent Hull: "We've got all the confidence in the world in Frank. I think we can win with him back there. That's no problem whatsoever, because we've done it in the past."

Thurman Thomas: "Look at what Frank did last year. No

one was giving us a chance then, and he came in and won three games. We're in a better situation this year, but all of a sudden one of our main players goes down and everybody thinks that we're going to fold. I don't think that we'll miss a beat with Frank in there."

James Lofton: "If you put Jim and Frank in a foot race, you might fall asleep waiting for a winner. But they're both good quarterbacks. Frank's arm is maybe two yards shorter than Jim's, but Frank can put the ball out there deep. He's also very intelligent. And he does not get ruffled out there. We wait for him to get excited and pumped up, but it never happens. He's Mr. Calm."

Once seen as a bust by fans and media whose judgments were based solely on his shaky preseason outings, Reich saw his popularity skyrocket after his three-game Cinderella story. He was liked as much for his pleasant, unassuming nature as he was for his on-field success. No one could forget how, after throwing the winning touchdown to Reed in the final seconds against the then-undefeated Rams, an excited Reich ran in circles on the field, then headed for the sidelines, dropped to his right knee, buried his head in his left hand and began crying tears of joy.

Now, for the second consecutive season, he was capturing the imagination of Western New Yorkers. Buffalo radio station 97 Rock was calling itself "97 Reich" the week before the Miami game. Popular songs were being rerecorded with new lyrics, such as "It's all *Reich* now." DJs renamed Rich Stadium *Reich* Stadium. Everywhere you turned there were references to the Bills' having "The *Reich* Stuff."

Two days before the game representatives of a Rochester radio station showed up at One Bills Drive with a four-foot-by-five-foot greeting card signed by hundreds of fans. On the front it said, "Go Get 'em, Frank." Reich also received loads of standard-sized mail, as well as countless telephone calls from well-wishers.

"The support that I've gotten, not only from my family and friends, but from the fans and even the media, means a lot to me," he said. "You try not to get caught up in everything outside the field. But it's nice to know that people are pulling for you. It just gives you that little added confidence, that added edge of feeling good going into the game."

Most Miami players seemed to have a healthy enough respect for the Bills' offense, with or without Kelly, to keep from automatically assuming they were in for an easier game with Reich at the controls. "It doesn't matter who's back there," linebacker E. J. Junior said. "I remember last year we played Buffalo with Frank Reich. And we had our butts handed to us."

Said strong safety Jarvis Williams: "You've got to remember, Buffalo is more than just Jim Kelly. They've got Thurman Thomas, who's a Pro Bowler. They've got Andre Reed, who's a Pro Bowler. How can you put the whole game in one man's hands?

"We know Frank Reich can win."

But there were a few dissenting Dolphins. One was outspoken cornerback Tim McKyer: "They were with one guy all year long and now there's another guy. I don't care what anybody says, there has to be an adjustment. Kelly is their emotional leader, their heart and soul. When Reich is in there, he's the backup. That's got to be on their minds. He might have guys on his team guessing, and that's a factor."

Another dissenter was nose tackle Shawn Lee: "The Bills without Jim Kelly is like a hand without four fingers."

And this swipe from defensive end Jeff Cross: "To beat us, they're going to have to throw the ball. They're not going to run the ball on us. They can't and they won't. They have a good offensive line, I'm not taking anything away from them. But I just don't see them running on us."

What would the Bills do in their December 23 rematch with Miami? Go conservative and trust Reich only to move the ball from center to Thurman Thomas's gut? Stick with the wide-open, pass-happy approach that carried them to the top of the AFC in the first place?

All along the Bills' decision makers insisted there would be no alterations in their strategy to account for Kelly's absence. They stressed that Reich was perfectly capable of running the no-huddle and everything else in their playbook up to the time Kelly was injured.

"Frank doesn't have any limitations," Ted Marchibroda said. "I think the game plan will be pretty much the same as it would be for Kelly."

"I hope we stick with the no-huddle, because I feel very confident with it," Reich said. "It's a lot of short passes, a lot of just reading the defense, and I think those are my stronger points. I love it. Any quarterback would, because you get to throw the ball a lot. And that's really what we're paid to do."

Before heading down the tunnel for the pregame introductions, Reich, who is deeply religious, dropped to his knees and began to pray. He asked God, with whom he had spoken a little more frequently than usual during the week, for a last-minute boost of confidence.

And as promised, Reich came out throwing from the no-huddle offense in the game's first series, which began on the Buffalo 27. After Keith McKeller dropped his first pass and Thurman Thomas ran for 5 yards Reich had completions of 16 yards to Thomas and 14 to Don Beebe to the Miami 38. Thomas followed with carries of 7 and 5 yards to give the Bills a first down at the Dolphins' 26. This was where Reich would put the first blemish on his performance. Trying to escape from the pocket he had the ball knocked out of his hands, and defensive end Brian Sochia recovered at the Miami 23.

"I got careless with the ball," Reich admitted later. "Ted Marchibroda tells us all the time that if we're going to run, put both hands on the ball. I didn't that time."

The Dolphins failed to capitalize, however, as Jeff Wright dumped Dan Marino for a 6-yard loss on third-and-nine from the Miami 35, forcing a Reggie Roby punt.

Buffalo's next possession came to a similar end. One play after Andre Reed dropped a 38-yard pass in the end zone on second-and-ten, Reich was sacked—for the only time in the game—by Sochia for minus-11 yards. That brought out Rick Tuten, whose punt started Miami on its 11.

This time it looked like the Dolphins would get something going. Marino completed 5 of 6 passes for 48 yards to put the ball at the Bills' 29. After an incomplete and 5-yard penalty he fired a third-and-fifteen throw to Tony Martin. The pass was incomplete, but John Hagy clotheslined Martin and drew a penalty that gave Miami a first down at the 19. Four plays later, however, Pete Stoyanovich took Hagy off the hook by sending a 28-yard chip shot field goal wide to the left less than two minutes into the second quarter—his first miss inside the 30 in 16 career attempts.

The Bills' third series got off to an ominous start when Will Wolford was penalized for jumping offsides. Thomas still got the first down, though, with an 11-yard run. But on the next play, Kent Hull was flagged for holding. Once again the Bills climbed from a hole, with Reich throwing 18 yards to Reed. After Don Smith converted a third-and-one with a 4-yard carry, Reich completed an 11-yard pass to McKeller, ran for 6, and connected with Thomas on a 13-yard screen pass that gave the Bills a first down at the Miami 23. But then Hull, who rarely draws yellow flags for anything, picked up his second holding penalty of the drive, pushing the Bills back to the 33. Reich perservered again, completing a 17-yard pass to Beebe. Thomas runs of 7 and 2 yards gave the Bills a second-and-goal from the 7. On the next play Reich fired to James Lofton in the end zone and Buffalo had a 7–0 lead with 6:56 left in the half.

"That's the play where Andre comes across the middle and the whole defense jumps on top of him, which it did that time," Reich explained. "Then I waited a second until I could find a hole in the coverage. I saw James was open, waited until he got to the next seam, and threw. Fortunately I had all day to throw."

After punts were exchanged the Dolphins threatened to get on the scoreboard just before halftime. An offsides penalty on Bruce Smith turned a second-and-three from the Buffalo 29 into a first-and-ten from the 24. But on the next play Clifford Hicks picked off a Marino pass at the Bills' 7 with 1:14 on the clock. The Bills killed off all but three of the remaining seconds, enough for Marino to throw a deep incomplete, and the Bills' 7-point lead stood at halftime.

Looking to rekindle the Bickering Bills angle, NBC reported during the first half of its coverage of the game that there had been a fight during practice between Bruce Smith and Keith McKeller, and that the defensive end had suffered a broken hand while landing a punch. The broadcasters later withdrew the injury aspect of the story, and several players afterward indicated that it was no worse a skirmish than those that sometimes occur during the workouts of all NFL clubs. Because of the Bills' reputation, however, McKeller felt compelled to say, "We're still a focused team. We're playing together and we're going to keep playing together until we have reached our destination, which is the Super Bowl. And our goal isn't just to get there; it's to win it."

Another Miami turnover came on the second-half kickoff when Marc Logan's muff of Scott Norwood's short, high kick was recovered by Carlton Bailey at the Dolphins' 32. And the results were far more damaging to the Dolphins. Five consecutive runs—the first four by Thomas and the last by Don Smith—moved the Bills to the Miami 11. One play later Reich found Reed, who beat cornerback J. B. Brown on a quick post pattern for a touchdown, to make it 14–0 with 3:09 gone in the third quarter.

"I saw J. B. Brown on Andre's back and tried to throw it into Andre's body, so he'd have a chance to make the play," Reich said. "When you throw it like that to Andre, you have all the confidence in the world he's going to come up with it."

Redeeming himself for his muff, Logan returned the ensuing kickoff 35 yards to the Buffalo 35. After a 5-yard pass to running back Sammie Smith and an incomplete Marino unloaded a 30-yard scoring throw to Mark Duper, cutting the Bills' lead to 14–7.

But Buffalo came right back on the next possession. Beginning on his 20, Reich threw 22 yards to McKeller, and three plays later he hooked up with Beebe on a 43-yard bomb to the Dolphins' 11. The Bills couldn't get any closer than the 3, with Lofton dropping a third-down pass in the end zone. Norwood then booted a 21-yard field goal to put the Bills in front, 17–7, with 6:25 remaining in the third quarter.

Miami would punt a little more than a minute later, and the Bills started out on their third and final scoring march of the day from their 24. But they would temporarily be without Thomas, who left the field with muscle spasms in his lower back. As trainers worked vigorously with the running back on the sidelines, Reich moved the Bills into Miami territory, running 8 yards on first-and-ten from the Buffalo 46 to the Dolphins' 46. Thomas returned and proceeded to take the next seven carries, bouncing outside to his left on the last for a 13-yard touchdown to increase Buffalo's lead to 24–7 at 1:48 of the fourth quarter. The score was the Bills' fifty-third in fifty-nine trips inside the 20, and the thirty-eighth touchdown within that territory.

"Frank did a helluva job of mixing it up," Wolford pointed out. "They were never too positive of whether we were going to throw or not. So we didn't hit many eight-man fronts when we ran the ball."

Said Reich: "As is the case in the no-huddle, it was up to me what we used, rather than having it scripted before hand. I felt they expected us to run right at them as we did last year [when he was at quarterback]. I thought we had to throw the ball in order to loosen up their linebackers. Then we ran."

With the game firmly in the Bills' grasp, Kelly, donning a white cap and parka, walked over to Reich and gave him a hug for a job well done.

"Jim," Reich said, "all I want now is to get this thing back in your hands."

After his touchdown Thomas took the balance of the day off. So did Don Beebe, but under much more painful circumstances. He had suffered a fractured right leg, which would sideline him until the 1991 season, while blocking for Thomas on the final play of the third quarter. In a touching scene, Lofton and Reed each came over to embrace their fellow receiver after he was helped onto the back of a utility cart. The fans cheered as the cart left the field, and Beebe—who, after struggling to stay healthy and hang onto the ball through the first fourteen games, had caught a season-high-equaling 3 passes for 74 yards—responded by thrusting his right arm into the air, causing the ovation to crescendo.

The Dolphins' other touchdown, an 11-yard Marino pass to Mark Clayton to make it 24–14, came with a minute left in the game and capped an 11-play, 88-yard drive. Stoyanovich tried an on-side kick, but Tasker recovered at the Miami 39, and Reich killed the final fifty-nine seconds to give the Bills a

Jim Kelly, the NFL's top-rated quarterback, and Thurman Thomas, who led the league in total yardage, teamed up to lead the Bills' high-powered offense in 1990. *(Bill Wippert/Buffalo News)*

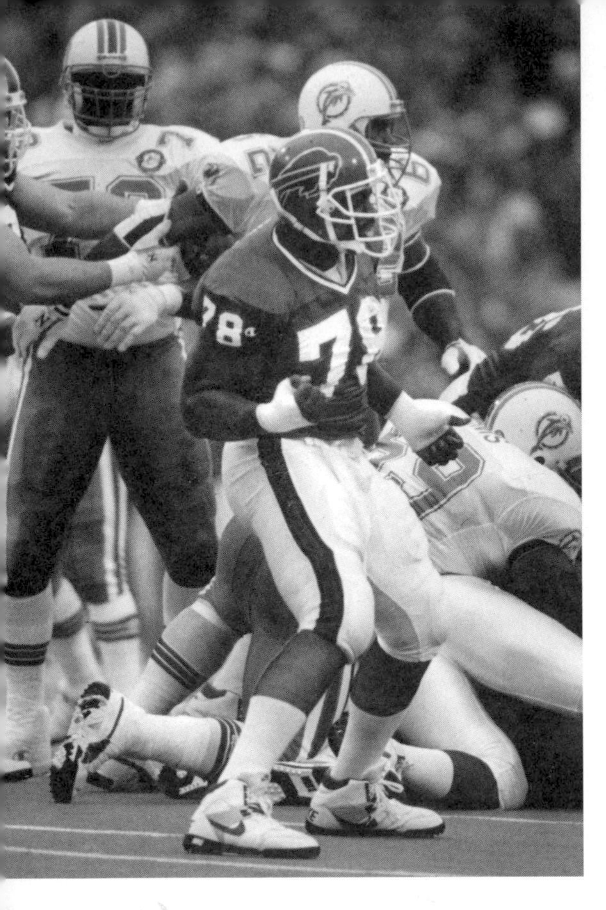

Bruce Smith, who finished the season with a team record 19 sacks and was named NFL Defensive Player of the Year in 1990, was a dominant force all season. *(Bill Wippert/Buffalo News)*

Cornelius Bennett and Darryl Talley, two of the Bills' All-Pro linebackers, close in on Mervyn Fernandez in the AFC Championship Game. *(Bill Wippert/Buffalo News)*

Head Coach Marv Levy and General Manager Bill Polian were the main architects for the Bills' super season. *(Bill Wippert/Buffalo News)*

Outstanding special-teams performances played a major role in the Bills' success. Nate Odomes's block of a David Treadwell field-goal attempt sparked a dramatic comeback victory against the Denver Broncos. *(Ron Moscati/Buffalo News)*

Andre Reed's ability to gain yardage after catching the ball made him one of the league's more dangerous wide receivers. *(Bill Wippert/Buffalo News)*

James Lofton, a 13-year veteran, recaptured his youth in 1990 and became a consistent long-yardage threat for the Bills. *(Ron Moscati/Buffalo News)*

After a shaky preseason, the Bills' offensive line came together and became one of the NFL's best. From left: Howard Ballard, Kent Hull, reserve Glenn Parker, and Jim Ritcher. *(Bill Wippert/Buffalo News)*

Frank Reich came off the bench and led the Bills to two victories and the AFC East title after Jim Kelly was injured. *(Bill Wippert/ Buffalo News)*

Fans stormed the field after the Bills beat the Dolphins to capture the AFC East title and secure home-field advantage throughout the playoffs. *(Bill Wippert/Buffalo News)*

Darryl Talley's 27-yard interception return for a touchdown was one of the many highlights as the Bills won their first AFC Championship. *(Bill Wippert/ Buffalo News)*

A jubilant Jim Kelly points toward Tampa and Super Bowl XXV after leading the Bills to a stunning 51–3 victory in the AFC Championship Game. *(Bill Wippert/Buffalo News)*

The Bills' Super Bowl hopes and dreams came down to a last-minute, 47-yard field-goal attempt by Scott Norwood. *(Rob McElroy)*

Scott Norwood was overcome by the warm reception he received from Bills fans at the rally. *(Robert Kirkham/Buffalo News)*

Ralph Wilson celebrated the Bills' season and shared his hopes for the future with his team's fans. *(Warren Wilkinson)*

Nearly 30,000 fans filled Niagara Square in downtown Buffalo to welcome the Bills home and celebrate their season. *(Ronald J. Colleran/Buffalo News)*

club-record thirteenth win, a third straight division championship, and most of all, the right to host a divisional-round play-off match and the AFC title game—the final step before Super Bowl XXV.

Reich had done it again.

Before the season his pay had been boosted from $210,000 to an average of $860,000 per year. Some critics thought that even with his 3–0 stretch in 1989 the Bills had been a bit too generous with someone they hoped would never do anything on the field except hold for extra points and field goals. After the victory over Miami, Polian was being congratulated for making one of the single smartest investments in the franchise's history.

"Pretty good insurance policy, wouldn't you say?" said Ralph Wilson, the man who pays the Bills and is also in the insurance business, wearing an ear-to-ear grin on his elflike face.

In a performance better than even his staunchest supporters could have ever expected, Reich had completed 15 of 21 passes for 234 yards and 2 touchdowns. Except for a fumble while scrambling on the Bills' first series, he was almost flawless. Staying true to his lovable form, Reich also was as modest as could be.

"I wasn't looking to come in and be the hero of this game," he said. "There were a lot of guys out there who played extremely well. I was just happy to be a part of it again."

Teammates and others in the Bills' dressing room were all too happy to remind anyone willing to listen that they had been and would still be comfortable with the offense in Reich's possession.

"I'm not surprised a bit by how he played," Hull said in his thick Southern drawl. "You can't rattle that guy. He's as strong as they come."

"Today," Thomas said, "Frank did everything right."

Thomas wasn't so bad himself. He ran for 154 yards on 30 carries (a whopping 5.1 yards-per-attempt average), including a 13-yard touchdown that put the game out of reach early in the fourth quarter. It was Thomas's fifth 100-yard day on the ground in 1990 and the twelfth of his three-year career. He also regained the NFL rushing lead with a career-high 1,297 yards.

"We could have run the ball anywhere we wanted to," Thomas said. "Outside. Inside. We just did an excellent job blocking."

Returning the compliment, Hull said, "Thurman Thomas ran as hard as I've ever seen him run. When that happens, I think the offensive line plays a little harder. There's a guy who weighs one hundred and ninety pounds taking on the big guys. When we see that we've got to go get after somebody."

As a team the Bills rushed 47 times for 206 yards, which obviously belied the prediction of a certain Dolphins defensive end. Levy had seen to it that a newspaper clipping containing Jeff Cross's remarks didn't escape the notice of Thomas or the Bills' offensive linemen during the week.

He had received the desired response.

"Anytime you have statements about how we can't run the ball and how we wouldn't even try to run the ball, that's always going to fire us up," Thomas said. "I can't believe a coach like Don Shula would let his players say something like that. He's a great coach, but I just can't see him letting his players mouth off like that. It does nothing but fire us up."

Buffalo's offense wasn't alone in the extra incentive department. The defense was as inspired as ever, having carried for thirteen weeks the stomach-twisting memory of the 30 points it gave up to the Dolphins on September 16. And the results on December 23 were these: Miami's erratic running game was held to a mere 35 yards on 12 carries. Dan Marino, the least-sacked quarterback in the NFL because of his quick release and penchant for getting rid of the ball no matter what, was brought down three times, hurried on numerous other occasions, intercepted once, and had one pass batted down at the line of scrimmage.

Chuck Dickerson, the Bills' effusive defensive-line coach, said he knew the team's defenders were ready for the game when he saw them head-butting each other on the sidelines—before the opening kickoff!

"Heck, they were even head-butting me," Dickerson said. "I

mean, these guys played sky-high hard today. They were very emotional. On the whole we've played pretty businesslike defense this year. But the last two weeks, we laid it on the line as far as emotion."

The weather wasn't anywhere near the factor some thought it would be in helping the Bills against their south Florida visitors. The Dolphins entered the game with a 1–6 record in temperatures below 30 degrees. But it was a relatively balmy 33 at kickoff, and there was only a mist of rain late in the fourth quarter. One female fan stood up in her end-zone seat to show off the bikini she was wearing. A man nearby displayed his outfit, which consisted of bathing trunks under Bills boxer shorts, a headband, and sneakers.

They and others in the record crowd of 80,235 had been gearing up for this party for a long time. They were frenzied, bordering on lunacy, even before the opening kickoff. And the buildup had reached mammoth proportions after the Dolphins were dealt a knockout punch with Thomas's final touchdown. The last time the Bills clinched a division championship at home, by beating the Jets in 1988, thousands stormed the field to tear down the goalposts in a scene that would forever be remembered as "Fan-Demonium."

Now everyone was on the launching pad of "Fan-Demonium II."

With 3:39 left to play the first in a series of feeble announcements was heard over the stadium's public address system: "Please stay off the field after the game . . . This is an unlawful act . . . Violators will be prosecuted." Along the sidelines Bills players looked at each other and laughed. "We knew better than to believe an announcement like that was going to stop any of them," Ray Bentley said.

Nor were the three hundred security guards, forty armed sheriff's deputies, and ten mounted police assigned to protect the goalposts, which run six thousand dollars apiece.

Cracked Ralph Wilson, "You could have Rommel's panzer divisions out there, and they wouldn't have kept those fans off the field."

With fifty-nine seconds left the crowd chanted wildly: "Tampa! Tampa! Tampa!" Kelly took that as his cue to start limping toward the tunnel, accompanied by a massive body guard (many assumed he was an offensive tackle out of uniform). Kelly knew, if he stuck around any longer, he risked reinjuring his knee in the expected crush of spectators.

The clock wound down toward zero, and at first only a trickle of fans came over the red wall surrounding the field. Within seconds, however, it became an all-out flood. And it was downright scary.

Worried about an injury to one of the horses, which struggled to keep their balance on the slick artificial surface, the mounted patrol quickly exited the field. That left the goalpost-hungry mob with clear paths to its steely prey, which it pulled to the ground and dismantled before hoisting large pieces to the top row of the stands and dropping them outside for sawing and distribution.

Other fans had different souvenirs in mind, such as pieces of turf. Forgetting—or, more likely, not caring—that the field was scheduled to be used again the weekend of January 12–13, they pulled out knives, got down on their knees, and began cutting.

Not that all of this wasn't met with some resistance. A couple of drunken men were pounded into submission by security guards and dragged into the tunnel. Another man, already in the tunnel, held a blood-soaked towel to his head while sitting in the back of an ambulance. Still another was receiving medical care after falling on the field and being stepped on repeatedly. Police and security guards also were being treated for everything from cuts and scrapes to a severe knee injury.

Meanwhile, the Dolphins' buses, which had never had problems quickly departing the stadium after many a victory there, were slowed to a crawl by fans who pelted them with rocks, bottles, and eggs. As if the Bills hadn't administered enough of a flogging.

"Nasty fans," J. B. Brown said. "Nasty, as in cursing, swearing, throwing anything they can get their hands on. If something isn't done, somebody could get seriously hurt."

Much of Bill Polian's joy over the victory was sapped by

what he witnessed after the game. He said it wasn't celebration, but thuggery.

"Thuggery sparked by a small minority of undisciplined individuals," the GM said. "First of all, there was no reason to celebrate. We'd won the AFC East for the third year in a row. Everyone associated with this team has clearly pointed out that the Bills have larger goals in mind."

Polian vowed to take stringent measures to prevent the scene from being repeated in the play-offs. The first would be banning beer sales, a standing rule for night games at Rich but unprecedented for a daytime contest. The second would be having a "stronger uniformed presence," with the snarling assistance of attack dogs.

"Believe me, anyone who tries running onto the field from here on in will do so at their own risk—both physical and legal. And I urge the ninety-nine percent of loyal Bills fans and Western New Yorkers who take pride in their team and their town to join with us in condemning this kind of behavior. Let's put our best foot forward now that the rest of the nation's going to be looking at us."

Nevertheless, to a man, Bills players praised the crowd for creating the tidal wave of sound that helped wash the Dolphins all the way back to Miami. Especially those on defense, because it was when Miami had the ball that the fans were at their loudest (as always, the Bills' offense was given the courtesy of being allowed to hear its plays).

For the Buffalo players it wasn't just noise; it was a source of strength.

"We walk out there, and it's like, 'Here comes that electricity,' " Talley said. "All you have to do is plug in."

"Sometimes I wish I could play defense just to get out there and feel what it's like to be in the middle of all that cheering," Kent Hull lamented. "It's too bad they can't holler like that when we're out there."

Said Reed: "The fans make a difference every home game, regardless of what's at stake."

Leonard Smith, the most exuberant member of the team and a crowd favorite, was the last Buffalo player to leave the field. Before he did, he climbed into the first row of the stands, exchanging high-fives with everyone in sight, and jabbing the sky with his index finger.

"I'm just happy we'll be here through the play-offs and the fans will get to see us play," he said. "They deserve it."

"I've never seen anything like this," said rookie defensive lineman Mike Lodish. "And I can't wait to see it again when we're AFC champions."

First, though, the Bills would have to win two more games. And Miami linebacker Cliff Odom didn't see the Dolphins's wild-card date two weeks later at Joe Robbie Stadium as the end of the line. He saw it as a springboard back to Rich for either a divisional-round match or the AFC Championship Game.

"The series is tied, one-to-one, and it will be continued," Odom promised. "The rubber game is yet to come."

Next up for the Bills was their December 30 regular-season finale at Washington. Thanks to the previous weekend's triumph, it amounted to little more than a glorified exhibition game. There was absolutely nothing to be gained by the Bills or, for that matter, by the 9–6 Redskins, who already knew they'd have to travel to Philadelphia for a wild-card game the following weekend.

For pride's sake the Bills did have a chance to finish with the NFL's best record, or at least share the honor with San Francisco, which also was 13–2. But that was hardly something Levy was going to use to try to motivate his troops. He had already established his priorities for the game earlier in the week when he said he planned to play "everybody who's medically able to play." In other words, the objectives were to keep the starters' exposure to injury to a minimum while giving the reserves a rare taste of extended regular-season action. Winning was permissible—just as long as it didn't take a whole lot of energy and no one got hurt.

So it wasn't a surprise that the Bills suffered a 29–14 loss at RFK Stadium. They substituted liberally—more liberally than the Redskins—with Reich and Thomas out of the game the entire second half. In addition, Reed and Lofton saw almost no action in the final two quarters.

With Gale Gilbert finishing at quarterback the Bills turned the ball over a season-high four times, making it easy for the Redskins, who didn't look nearly as impressive as the final score indicated. And the Bills didn't even use their no-huddle offense, deciding it was best to keep it under wraps while scouts from potential play-off opponents were watching, including the Redskins, whom the Bills could have met again in Super Bowl XXV.

McKeller was speaking for all of his teammates when he said, "Mentally, you try to do your best to get psyched up to win, because that's the name of the game. But deep down I think it was a little tough for all of us."

The first 15 Washington points came on 5 Chip Lohmiller field goals, tying a Redskins record. The last kicker to make that many field goals against the Bills was Jan Stenerud of Kansas City on December 19, 1971. The Redskins' only touchdowns came when they cashed in on 2 interceptions thrown by Gilbert, who before that day hadn't thrown a pass that counted since 1986, when he was a backup for Seattle.

The last time Gilbert had thrown a pass under game conditions was in August. Despite his rustiness, he did manage to complete 8 of 15 passes for 106 yards and a pair of touchdowns—13 yards to Kenneth Davis in the third quarter and 20 yards to Steve Tasker, giving him scores in both of his career receptions with the Bills, in the fourth. With 14 points, the Bills broke a single-season team record for scoring at 428, eight more than the previous mark set in 1975 and tops in the NFL for 1990.

Although Reich could have used as much playing time as any of the Bills' reserves, Levy's thinking in giving half the game to Gilbert was threefold: first, there was nothing at stake; second, he didn't want to risk an injury to Reich, who was the Bills' number-one quarterback until Kelly returned; third, he wanted Gilbert to get some low-pressure playing time in the event he had to be called upon in a high-pressure play-off situation.

The Bills received a scare late in the second quarter, when Leon Seals collapsed with a knee injury and spent several minutes on the ground, writhing in pain. With his left foot planted, Seals took a blow to the front of his left knee, causing it to hyperextend and resulting in pinched cartilage. He didn't return to action that day, but was expected to be fine for the Bills' first play-off game.

"We would like to have won the game, sure," Levy said. "But for the most part, particularly if Leon is okay, I feel very good that we came out healthy. I'm glad to see that we could get playing time for the players who needed it."

One such player was Mark Kelso, who returned to his free-safety spot for the first time since suffering a fractured and dislocated ankle October 7 against the Raiders. He relieved John Hagy in the second quarter and played the rest of the game, finishing with a tackle, an assist, and a great deal more confidence in his ankle.

"There wasn't any apprehension as far as my ankle was concerned, but the first few plays it felt like I was in slow motion and everyone else was in fast-forward," Kelso said. "It was kind of like the first game of the preseason. But then I settled down. I got some good hits. I had some good reads. And they didn't go deep."

Thomas entered the game leading the NFL with 1,297 rushing yards, but ended up with zero on five attempts in the first half, and sat out the final two quarters because he decided his health for the play-offs was more important than individual honors. As a result, Detroit's Barry Sanders, Thomas's former teammate at Oklahoma State, was able to win the league rushing title with 1,304.

"It meant more to my offensive linemen than it meant to me," Thomas said of losing the crown. "The most important thing for me right now is my health and how far we go in the play-offs. And as long as it went to a guy who I thought deserved it and is a good friend, I can live with that." Thomas still wound up leading the league in total yards from scrimmage (1,829) for the second consecutive year.

Despite playing most of the game Bruce Smith came up empty in a final crack at the NFL's all-time single-season sack record of 22. Smith, who didn't have a sack in his last three regular-season games, finished the year with 19, one behind the league-leading total of Kansas City linebacker Derrick Thomas.

"I'm just slightly disappointed, but I'm not going to dwell on it," he said. "We have better things to look forward to."

Such as one, and possibly two, play-off encounters at Rich Stadium, where the Bills were 8–0 in 1990 and 23–2 since 1988 (counting a play-off win over Houston).

"In the last two years, we've seen how much home-field advantage has hurt us," Reich said. "This year, we don't have any excuses. We have the home-field advantage. It's what we've been fighting for all year long.

"Now, it's up to us to do something with it."

8

JUST SAY NO-HUDDLE!

They knew where. The remaining questions for the Bills were: when, against whom, and would Jim Kelly be back in the lineup by that time?

After "Monday Night Football" the play-offs are a close second when it comes to tangible evidence of network television's ultratight control of the NFL. So even though the Bills knew on December 23 that they'd host a divisional-round game, they wouldn't find out exactly when until NBC put together a schedule that would be the most beneficial to its ratings, and then passed it along to the NFL.

Word finally came on New Year's Eve that the Bills were going to play Saturday, January 12, at 12:30 P.M. Throughout Western New York, weekend plans that had been on hold for eight days were hastily put in place. Sunday, January 13, was left open as a day to celebrate and anticipate the January 20 AFC Championship Game—or mourn and scorn the rest of a long, cold, empty winter.

The opponent would emerge from a wild-card field that, through won-loss records and tiebreakers, had been narrowed to Miami, Kansas City, and Houston. But it wasn't going to be determined until the afternoon of January 6.

On January 5, Miami and Kansas City were scheduled to

play at Joe Robbie Stadium, with the winner advancing to Rich only if, on January 6, Cincinnati defeated Houston at Riverfront Stadium. If the Oilers won, they'd pack for Buffalo, regardless of what happened the day before.

"They are three different types of teams," Ray Bentley said. "Houston has explosiveness with the run-and-shoot offense, and that's always tough to contend with [see the Bills' 27–24 loss on November 26]. Kansas City has a big running game and they play good defense, too. And Miami is Miami.

"Any one of these teams can present problems for us, but what do you expect? It's the play-offs."

Marv Levy insisted he didn't make a "wish list" of play-off opponents, that doing so would be a "huge mistake." To illustrate his point he told a story relayed to him by his receivers coach, Nick Nicolau: "When Nick was an assistant in Denver one year the Broncos were pulling for a certain team to be their opponent in a divisional game. Sure enough, that was the team they wound up playing. And that team kicked Denver's ass."

After the Washington game the Bills took it easy, with four days of light workouts before a weekend off to see which opponent they were going to face. Many players looked forward to the chance to become Saturday-Sunday couch potatoes for a change.

"I know I'll be irritating my wife," Bentley said with a grin. "Because *I'm* the one who will be holding that remote control."

The last time the Bills had two weeks off before a game was in early October, when the top four AFC East teams from 1989 had their in-season bye. In their first game back the Bills had struggled to beat the Jets, 30–27.

But turning stale wasn't a concern this time.

"This is totally different," Kent Hull said. "When we had the week off before, we knew who we were playing when we came back—the Jets—and we were already game-planning for the Jets. And I think we may have lost a little concentration as a result. Two weeks of preparation for a game is a lot; after a while, you begin to lose your edge somewhat.

"This time, we don't know who we're playing yet. Then,

come Monday, we'll start to prepare for whomever it is. And the concentration level will be high, I guarantee you."

Meanwhile, Bruce Smith's wish came true—or, one might argue, his relentless campaign for recognition succeeded—when the Associated Press named him its NFL Defensive Player of the Year for the first time. He easily won the balloting of sportswriters and broadcasters with seventy-two votes. Although he edged out Smith for the league lead in sacks, Kansas City linebacker Derrick Thomas was a distant second in the voting with five. The only other players to collect a vote were San Francisco linebacker Charles Haley and safety Ronnie Lott and New Orleans linebacker Vaughan Johnson. Lawrence Taylor, whose rule of defensive domination Smith had set out to overthrow, wasn't even an honorable mention.

Smith received one unexpected honor when the *National,* the sports daily, selected him its league Most Valuable Player—he was certain a quarterback, such as Joe Montana or Randall Cunningham, would beat out any defensive player for overall recognition.

"It's nice to receive all these awards, and after I'm told of them, I think for a second and say, 'Whew! I've finally made it,'" said Smith, who in 1990 reached career highs for sacks (19), tackles (101), and first hits (82). "With the knee surgery I had during the off-season and the type of preparation I put in to this year, I think it all paid off for me. I just decided I was going to prepare myself like I never have before. After that, I didn't see myself failing."

Between two days a week on a Stairmaster and three days a week following a Soviet weight-lifting program, he knocked ten pounds off his 6′4″ frame, to 265, and substantially built his upper-body strength. His body-fat count of 6.1 percent was good for a running back, much less a defensive lineman, and a far cry from his first two seasons, when it had hovered around 14 or 15 percent while he carried almost twenty more pounds.

But Smith's preparation didn't stop with his body. He began studying the opposition with greater intensity than ever—to the point where he watched "more film in a week than TV in a month." At the snap of a finger, he could rattle off opponents' running plays and pass protections from a certain formation over their last half-dozen games. Not to mention how they would protect in play action. After five seasons of being a sack artist who tended to be more aggressive on some downs than others, 1990 was the year Smith broadened his repertoire. He became a premier run-stuffer, a student of the game, and managed to go all out on virtually every play.

Jim Hanifan, Washington's veteran offensive line coach, had seen enough of Smith before and during the Bills-Redskins season finale to conclude he was the "most formidable" player since Hall of Fame defensive end Deacon Jones. "A constant source of irritation and confusion for an offense," was how Hanifan described Smith's play. "He's like a running back with that quickness, that explosion. He sees a hole and *psssffft,* he's there to make the play."

Jets offensive line coach Larry Beightol called Smith "an opposing coach's nightmare. You watch film of him, you don't sleep that week. I don't really think there's a way to stop him. He's at another level."

While being showered with accolades, though, Smith continued to show disgust over the fact his closest friend on the team, Darryl Talley, had been overlooked in Pro Bowl voting a couple of weeks earlier. Smith was one of eight Bills chosen in player and coach balloting to participate in the NFL's annual all-star game at Honolulu. Joining him on his fourth consecutive trip would be Jim Kelly, Kent Hull, Andre Reed, Thurman Thomas, Cornelius Bennett, Shane Conlan, and Steve Tasker (special teams).

"Darryl's been jerked around for the last three or four years, and it gets frustrating and sickening," Smith said. "He does it all—he plays the run, he rushes the quarterback, he covers guys. You can't ask for a better linebacker."

After earlier seasons when he seemed like a Pro Bowl shoo-in and didn't make it, Talley was disappointed. But this time—on the way to a team-leading 123 tackles, 4 sacks, 2 interceptions (including a 60-yard return for a touchdown)—he was devastated.

"What else can I do?" Talley said, fighting back tears. "The only other thing I can do is turn into God. And I can't do that, because I can't walk on water."

On January 5, Miami rallied from a 16–3 deficit to defeat the Chiefs, 17–16. Dan Marino led the way by guiding the Dolphins to 14 points, on a pair of touchdown passes, in the final, frenzied quarter. Pete Stoyanovich's extra point with 3:28 remaining was the difference. But the outcome wasn't safe until Kansas City's Nick Lowery came up inches short on a 52-yard field-goal attempt with under a minute to play.

On January 6 the Bengals buried the Oilers, 41–14.

Indeed, Dolphins linebacker Cliff Odom had been prophetic when he spoke of the Miami–Buffalo series being tied, 1–1, after their December 23 meeting, and had guaranteed a "rubber game."

The first thing most Bills players felt they had to do to prepare for the play-off rematch was forget all about what happened the last time the teams met. Forget all about how easy it was for them to score a 24–14 victory and clinch the AFC Eastern Division championship. Forget all about how pleased they were with themselves and their chances of reaching the Super Bowl.

"If we get complacent and think that we're going to beat the Dolphins because we beat them the last time, we won't win," Jim Ritcher said. "That was then, this is now."

Then the Bills had been a highly charged team. They had been on a three-game winning streak and fresh off a conquest of the big, bad Giants. Besides having a third consecutive division title and home-field advantage in the play-offs at stake, they also had sought revenge for a bitter loss to Miami in week two. And they had had an obvious rallying point named Frank Reich, who had been suddenly thrust into the spotlight because of Kelly's injured left knee.

Now it was the Dolphins who would have a score to settle. Now it was the Dolphins who would have momentum. "They've started their new season off already, and they're one and zero," Talley said. "Anytime a team comes in one and zero against a team that hasn't played yet, they naturally feel they're on a bit of a roll."

Observed Bentley: "The Dolphins played very well to beat Kansas City. Dan Marino looked great, and they're an explosive ball club. They showed basically what they've shown all year, and that's that they're going to hang their hat on trying to run the football. They also intend to stop the run. And they did a good enough job of that to beat Kansas City, which has a very good running game."

It figured that the Bills' familiarity with the Dolphins would make the preparation easier than if the opponent were the Chiefs, whom they hadn't played in the regular season since 1986, or the Oilers and their confounded run-and-shoot, which Buffalo's defense struggled badly against the only time it saw it in 1990.

Levy shook his head. "This is a play-off game," he said. "I divorce it completely from all previous games."

For the Dolphins it was just the opposite. The beating they had received on their last trip to Buffalo prompted them to do plenty of soul-searching. Was their real defense the Miami "Pound Machine," which held opponents to an average of 90 yards rushing per game in twelve regular-season victories? Or was it the "We-Get-Pounded Machine," which gave up an average of 184 yards rushing per game in four losses?

Defensive end Jeff Cross had the hardest time of all accepting the 206 yards the Dolphins allowed on the ground on December 23. In the poorest showing of an otherwise impressive season, he was credited with only one tackle, and held sackless by Will Wolford and Jim Ritcher. "I never, in my worst dreams, thought I'd play as bad as that," Cross said.

This time he wasn't talking about how the Bills couldn't and wouldn't run the ball, which had become added emotional fuel for Thomas, who finished with 154 yards, and Buffalo's offensive linemen. Instead he focused on what the Dolphins would have to do to stop the run and everything else the Bills' offense had to offer.

"It's going to take a season's best from everybody to pull this one off," Cross said. "This is a great opportunity for us—and for myself."

Although Miami's defenders were feeling better about themselves after doing a solid job of containing the Chiefs' potent ground attack, they continued to be nagged by the ease with which Buffalo's offensive line had pushed them all over the field. The Bills didn't do anything fancy. They just blocked straight ahead, and Thomas ran to any daylight he saw. Occasionally they stretched the Dolphins' defense, pulling their guards and tackles to draw linemen and linebackers out of their lanes, but for the most part it was a continual upfield push. And the chore of containing Thomas wouldn't be made any easier by the fact Miami's prime run-stuffer, linebacker John Offerdahl, wasn't expected to play because of a sprained arch.

Besides the inability to stop the run, another common thread through all four Miami losses was the inability to make the run go. Total rushing yards in those games were, to say the least, pathetic: 39, 14, 34, and 35.

"In the games that we've played well we've had balance on offense, and in the games we haven't played well we haven't had balance," Don Shula said. "That tells the whole story."

"We have to step it up a notch," said Dolphins running back Sammie Smith, who overcame extremely painful bruised ribs to rush for 82 yards against Kansas City. "We need to get some movement off the line in order to get room to run. If we don't it's going to be a real tough day."

Of course, not all Miami players were humbled by the earlier defeat. Tim McKyer sounded as boisterous as ever in challenging the Bills to throw in his direction—as if he hadn't been toasted enough by Reich the first time. "When they don't throw at me ten, eleven, or twelve times a game, I don't feel that I've been in the game," he said. "So I just hope Jim Kelly or Frank Reich come at me. Because I'm going to make them pay."

While appearing on a cable-TV program in Miami, rookie left offensive guard Keith Sims talked about how he or rookie left tackle Richmond Webb would be able to single-block

Bruce Smith (who regularly draws double- and triple-teaming) and that Cornelius Bennett was "soft" against the run.

Kelly didn't take part in any of the practices during the first week of the play-off bye. He spent the time going through a vigorous exercise program, which included leg lifts and running on a Stairmaster. He also rested his tongue, refusing to speak with the media until the following week, after he had completed his first full-scale workout with the team.

In the meantime, others spoke for Kelly.

"I ask Jim how his knee feels," said Marv Levy. "And he says things like, 'It's okay when I do this, it's a little stiff when I do that, I'm not confident when I do this.' He's not trying to turn it on and blast off yet. He's doing little by little, and each day he'll pick up the pace."

On Monday, January 7, five days before the game, Dr. Richard Weiss declared not only that the pace was ready to be picked up, but that Kelly had medical clearance to play against the Dolphins. This after several minutes of watching the quarterback jog and throw passes, still informally. "For the first time in three weeks, he felt very good," Weiss said. "He's going to play this weekend, I'm sure. He's right on schedule, and there's no reason to think anything else."

The next day Kelly, wearing a custom-fit brace designed to give him greater stability as he turned his leg on his follow-through, participated in his first formal workout since the injury.

Later, he spoke. One of the things he made clear was that the decision of whether he played would be his. Alone. Unmistakably miffed about Weiss's remarks from the day before, Kelly said, "If I feel that I'm ready to play, I'm going to play. It doesn't matter what the doctor tells me. If he says, 'Hey, you're able to play,' and I feel I can't, I'm not playing. Dr. Weiss is not in my body, he doesn't feel what my knee feels. And I'm not going to play if I feel it's going to hinder me for the rest of my career. I mean, this is a big game and if there's any way I can play, I'm going to play. But it's up to Jim Kelly."

Nevertheless, there was every indication Kelly would be

fine for the Dolphins' game. The most telling sign was his taking the vast majority of snaps in practice; Reich spent only a few plays over center, as he normally would when the main man was healthy. The second most telling sign was the encouragement expressed by those who watched Kelly drop back and throw, such as Levy, and Kelly himself.

"I thought he did pretty well," Levy said. "We told him to move a little carefully, and in some ways he did. But I thought he picked up the pace pretty well, too."

"I'm definitely not one hundred percent," said Kelly. "But overall, it feels pretty good. At first I wasn't sure how much to really press on it, how much to really show what I could do. You never really know until you've loosened up and you get into that rhythm. I didn't know whether it was going to give out or pop out or what, so I had to take it easy at the beginning. But by the end of practice, I was moving on it pretty well.

"All my timing and all my throws were right on. The dropbacks were fine. Everything was a little slower, but I thought it was right where I wanted. In seven-on-seven drills, I didn't throw a single incompletion. And, without a doubt, the three weeks of rest definitely helped my arm out a lot. I have a lot more zip than I had about three weeks ago, that's for sure."

Still, the final word on Kelly wasn't going to come until right before kickoff.

Leon Seals's status would also remain up in the air until game day, but the news on him was equally encouraging. "I'm about ninety to ninety-five percent confident I'll be playing," he said.

What was certain was the return of two other injured starters: cornerback Kirby Jackson, who had been on the injured reserve list since December 14 with a nagging hamstring problem, and free safety Mark Kelso, who hadn't started since suffering a broken and dislocated ankle against the Raiders October 7.

Kelso had spent nine weeks on the injured reserve list. He was active but didn't play in two games after that, and saw his first action in relief of John Hagy at Washington. "It has been a long time since I last started, but I feel good about it," he said. "I think my ankle's improved a lot. I'm confident in it. I finally feel like I have that burst back and I'm able to cover the ground I need to cover."

Hagy was the better athlete, but Kelso's two-year edge in experience was the major reason the Bills' decision makers felt he should return to the starting lineup. With the stakes so high against an opposing quarterback as dangerous as Dan Marino, they couldn't afford to take any chances of a critical mistake in pass coverage. The bottom line: Hagy was more error prone than his older teammate.

"When you're a secondary coach you're always trying to help your corners, and the free safety is the guy who can do that," Bills defensive backs coach Dick Roach said. "The free safety also has to direct a lot of traffic, particularly on third down when you get a lot of motion and movement. Those are crucial downs, and we know we'll see something different from Miami this time, which is where experience comes in. If it is something that has happened to Mark four years ago, he hasn't forgotten it."

The switch wasn't easy for Hagy to digest. He always had been long on confidence and felt he had proven, through the final eleven games of the regular season, that he should have remained the starter even after Kelso's injury healed. "Obviously, I'm not really happy about it," Hagy said. "But it's nothing I'm going to make an issue of right now, because there are too many other things that are much more important for that to happen. All I'm interested in is winning."

Similar feelings ran wild throughout the team. And in some cases they were generating some pretty crazy thoughts. For instance, the day before the game, Scott Norwood was telling Steve Tasker, "It's a shame I'm a kicker. I wish I were playing linebacker tomorrow. I'd really like to get out there and mix it up a little bit." This from a baby-faced thirty-year-old who stood barely six feet and weighed barely 200 pounds and wore a helmet that, even with a single bar, looked too big for his head. Besides, Norwood had enough to think about with his right foot making contact with the ball than to daydream about his whole body making contact with other whole bodies.

During the play-offs there can be no overestimating the importance of an accurate placekicker.

In three career play-off games Norwood had hit 3 of 6 field-goal attempts. And 2 of his misses came in the last postseason contest at Rich Stadium, the Bills' 17–10 victory over Houston. In six regular seasons with Buffalo, Norwood's numbers were impressive: a field-goal percentage of 76.7 (115 of 150) and an extra-point percentage of 97.7 (215 of 220). These statistics were even more eye-catching when one considered he did half of his kicking at Rich, where he was forced to overcome the deadness of a cold ball and some of the trickier winds a stadium could offer, and that most of his out-of-town kicking was done in cold, windy Northeastern cities.

But the knock on Norwood wasn't accuracy; it was distance—or lack thereof. Bruce DeHaven, the Bills' special-teams coach, maintained the knock was flawed. "You would always like a kicker who can kick real long field goals," DeHaven said. "But there aren't many guys in the league who can do that with any kind of accuracy. There are far fewer than what you would think."

As for the shallow kickoffs, the Bills capitalized on that by often having Norwood pop the ball up, enabling the coverage unit to get downfield fast enough to prevent any long returns. Not coincidentally, the Bills ended the 1990 season as the NFL's leader in kickoff coverage for the fourth year in a row, allowing an average of only 15.5 yards per return. "Kicks to the goal line with 3.8 seconds of hang time are the ones that get run back for touchdowns," DeHaven pointed out. "Kicks to the 15 yard line with 4.2 seconds of hang time usually don't. And that's the first goal, to limit the return."

Norwood suffered through a brief slump early in the season, which he corrected by widening the angle of his approach by five inches. He went on to make 10 of his final 13 field-goal attempts of the regular season, and all 34 of his point-after tries. "I'm hitting the ball as well as ever," he said. "I knew, if I got things straightened out earlier this year, it would be that way. I have all this experience to draw from, so it should be that way."

In 1988, when he led the NFL in scoring with 129 points and earned his only trip to the Pro Bowl, Norwood kicked 6 game-winning field goals, including 4 with less than four minutes left. He booted a 28 yarder (3:12) to beat Miami, a 41 yarder (:11) to beat New England, a 33 yarder (:13) to beat the Patriots again, and the biggest, a 30 yarder in overtime, to clinch the AFC Eastern Division championship against the Jets. Although Norwood had not been asked to decide a game since, DeHaven wasn't the least bit concerned about his ability to provide the winning points if called upon in the final seconds of a postseason match. "Scotty has already proven that he can kick field goals when you've got division championships and play-off games on the line," DeHaven said. "Let's put it another way: If we were to release Scott Norwood today there would be about a dozen teams that would claim him tomorrow. Including any of those in the play-offs."

"The way I look at it," said Norwood, "you don't know when a kick is going to figure into the outcome of a game, so they're all pressure situations. You have to realize that pressure's there, but I can't go out and approach those kicks differently than any others."

Such was Levy's approach to the game. He knew its significance was far greater than any of the previous sixteen his team had played. He knew his players were excited. He knew the fans were bursting with enthusiasm, even with all the stadium beer stands closed. He also knew those were the exact reasons why it was critical for him to stay "very levelheaded and cool and try not let the fact that the game has more impact mean that you do something differently."

The weather was a far bigger issue before this game than it was before the December 23 showdown, and with good reason. The forecast called for freezing temperatures and a drizzle that would turn into steady light snow as the game progressed. Which were precisely the conditions that prevailed. During the week Shula and his players had tried to downplay the drastic climate change they would face, with Marino saying at one point, "Maybe we should find a warehouse that's real cold and just practice in there." Nevertheless, the Dolphins did pack about three thousand extra pounds of equipment, consisting mainly of parkas, gloves, hats, and turtlenecks. Did someone say "psyched out"?

The field was covered with tarpaulins for most of the week.

But once uncovered the morning of the game, it immediately became a green skating rink—soon to disappear under a layer of white.

Jim Kelly started at quarterback and the Bills' no-huddle offense seemed whole again. He opened the game with a 20-yard pass to Thurman Thomas to the Buffalo 44. After a Thomas fumble that Keith McKeller recovered at the 46, Thomas ripped off 14 yards through right guard to the Miami 40. Then, bang! Kelly fired a 30-yard pass to Andre Reed, who ran the rest of the way for a touchdown to give the Bills a 7–0 lead.

The game's first controversy came on Miami's opening play when the officials missed what, on TV replays, looked like an obvious fumble by Sammie Smith. On the next play J. D. Williams was penalized for holding, turning an incomplete pass into a first down at the Dolphins' 37. Another infraction, this time an offside on Bruce Smith, turned a third-and-six into a third-and-one. On that play, however, a pass to Mark Clayton to the Buffalo 45 was, for some unknown reason, ruled incomplete, and it withstood a replay review even though press-box TV monitors seemed to indicate a reception. Sammie Smith then converted by running to the Miami 47. After two more runs there was further officiating controversy when Nate Odomes was penalized for pass interference on what appeared to be a clean near-interception of a pass for Mark Duper. That gave the Dolphins a first down at the Bills' 28, but they wound up settling for a 49-yard Stoyanovich field goal with 7:00 left in the first quarter.

Once again the Bills began making it look easy. Starting at his 37, Kelly completed a 4-yard pass to Thomas, then came back with a 44-yard bomb to Lofton to the Miami 12. Two plays later Kelly hit McKeller for 6 yards, setting up a 24-yard Norwood field goal that made it 10–3.

Three plays into the Dolphins' next series, Marino, on third-and-nine from his 33, threw a pass that a fast-closing Darryl Talley tipped into the hands of Nate Odomes, who returned it 9 yards to the Miami 38. The Bills were saved on third-and-six from the 34 when Kelly, while running for the first down, fumbled and Kent Hull recovered at the 18. A 3-yard run by

Thomas and an 8-yard pass to Lofton would give Buffalo a first down at the 7. The Dolphins' defense stiffened, however, and Norwood came out for a 22-yard field goal that gave the Bills a 13–3 lead with fifty-one seconds remaining in the first quarter.

Miami's next possession produced the game's first punt, a 37 yarder by Reggie Roby, that started the Bills at their 33. Kelly continued his no-huddle brilliance, throwing an 11-yard pass to Thomas on third-and-two from the Buffalo 41, and coming right back with a 43-yard completion to Reed to the Miami 5. Louis Oliver's task of trying to stay stride-for-stride with one of the NFL's best receivers was becoming more hopeless with each snap. But Kelly sympathized with the Dolphins' plight.

"With Andre Reed on one side, James on the other, and Thurman Thomas coming out of the backfield, who are you going to double-cover?" the quarterback asked.

One play after Reed's catch Thomas barreled through the middle for a touchdown, and the Bills were up 20–3, with 42:04 still to play. The drizzle of the first quarter had now turned to snow. It was a little colder, a little windier. Were the Dolphins about ready to pack up their three thousand pounds of winter gear and head back to the palm trees?

They would have to do so over Marino's dead right arm.

On third-and-five from the Miami 25 he fired an 11-yard pass to Mark Duper. And on the next play he connected with Duper again at the Buffalo 33, from where the receiver exploded away from tacklers for a 64-yard touchdown play that cut the margin to 20–10.

The "Shootout at the OK Igloo" continued, as Kelly opened the next drive with a 19-yard pass to Lofton that put the ball at the Miami 49. Thomas converted a third-and-one from the 40, and on fourth-and-three from the 32, Kelly hit Reed, with Paul Lankford covering, for a 13-yard completion. After a 9-yard run Thomas took a handoff for an aborted throwback play to Kelly and wound up losing 3 yards. But on third-and-four from the 13, Kelly hit Lofton for a touchdown with 5:11 left in the second quarter.

The Bills then forced a second Roby punt. But this time rookie return man Al Edwards had the ball knocked from his grasp, and Roby recovered at the Buffalo 47. "I guess I got stripped from the back side," Edwards said. "I didn't even see the guy."

Just when it seemed the Dolphins would squander the opportunity, Marino, on fourth-and-five from the 42, hooked up with Duper on a perfect 38-yard sideline pass to the Bills' 4. "That's a combination pattern, and it was a gamble," explained Gary Stevens, Miami's quarterbacks/pass offense coach. "If Dan has the guy open long, as he did that time, he goes to him; if not, he dumps off short, which might have really hurt us in that situation. But he makes those plays when he has to, which is why he's the best in the business."

After an incomplete and a 2-yard run by Sammie Smith, Marino thoroughly faked the Bills' defense when he rolled to his left on a 2-yard bootleg for a touchdown to cut Buffalo's advantage to 27–17 with twenty-one seconds to go in the half. He even did a little showboating on the play, holding the ball up with his right hand and turning to the Bills' defenders as if to say, "Is this what you're looking for, guys?" Then he drilled a hard spike in the end zone, making it clear the Dolphins weren't about to surrender a thing as they trailed by 10 points at halftime.

"That was a very big score for us," Marino said. "We felt we had to get a score before halftime to stay in the game."

Miami took another step out of the hole after the second-half kickoff, when they started at their 34. On the first play Marino zipped a 29-yard pass to Mark Clayton. And after a 17-yard run by Sammie Smith on third-and-two the Dolphins had a first down at the Buffalo 12. The Bills' defense rose to the occasion, however, and limited them to a 22-yard Stoyanovich field goal to make it 27–20 just under five minutes into the third quarter.

The Bills looked like they were going to have an immediate answer when, on the third play of the next possession, Kelly completed a 31-yard pass to Lofton to the Miami 27. Two plays later, however, Kelly was intercepted by strong safety Jarvis Williams at the 2.

Just when they thought they had dodged a bullet, the Dolphins were right back in trouble when Marino was picked off by Kelso at the Miami 48 with 4:52 left in the quarter. Faced with a third-and-seven at the 33, Kelly went to old reliable James Lofton for a sixth completion on the day and 13-yard gain to the Dolphins' 20. "James Lofton just always seems to come through in the clutch," Kelly said. "He's always there when I need him."

On this series Lofton was extra generous with his help. After stalling on the 11 the Bills decided to go for three points. And before heading to the sidelines, as the field-goal unit began trotting out for Norwood's 28-yard attempt, Lofton made a subtle but classic veteran move. He bent over and used his glove-covered hands to quickly brush away a spot in the snow for the placement.

"I saw old tapes of that New England–Miami game, and I didn't see the John Deere coming out this time," Lofton joked, referring to the controversial assist the Patriots received from a snowplow driver on the winning field goal of a 1982 contest. "So I figured I'd just help out a little bit."

Sure enough, Norwood's kick was successful, giving the Bills a 30–20 lead with 1:38 left in the third quarter.

But Marino wouldn't give up. On the first play after the kickoff—on which Norwood, living out his linebacker fantasy, tackled return man Marc Logan at the Buffalo 43—Marino completed a 23-yard pass to Clayton. After a pair of Sammie Smith runs the Dolphins had a first down at the Bills' 2. Three downs later, on a tackle-eligible play, Marino found 6′4″, 284-pound offensive lineman Roy Foster wide open for a 2-yard touchdown pass to pull Miami within 3 points at 30–27. After the score, which came fifty-six seconds into the fourth quarter, Foster broke into a bizarre dance that was a cross between "The Ickey Shuffle" and someone with a wasp caught in his shorts.

"I was just shaking," Foster explained.

"With enthusiasm?" someone asked.

"No," Foster replied. "It was cold as hell and I was just trying to stay warm."

After that the Dolphins seemed to have momentum on their side. And the Bills' faithful couldn't help but consider the prospect of facing the grayest and gloomiest of all winters.

Watching their team fall apart and lose a play-off game it had once led by 17 points—to the despised "Fish" no less—would have been galling beyond comprehension.

But there was no panic among members of the Bills' offense as they took the field at their 37 with nothing on the line except the whole season. "All we said when we got out there was, 'Let's execute. No turnovers. Let's just do what we've been doing all day,' " Thomas recalled. "Which was moving the ball on them."

On the first play Kelly threw 21 yards to Lofton to the Dolphins' 42. Then he ran for 8. But after an incomplete to Reed he faced a fourth-and-two from the 34. Not to worry again. The Bills' offensive line gave Kelly all kinds of time, which he used to find McKeller for a 5-yard pass to keep the drive alive.

"With the weather conditions the way they were, it was going to take a little more time for the receivers to get into their patterns, and even with the pass-rushers having a hard time, the offensive line did an unbelievable job protecting me," Kelly said later. "It was probably the best I've ever seen them play. They gave me the time to throw and that was the key to a lot of the big plays we made. All five of them deserve a big hand."

After a 12-yard pass to Al Edwards and a 2-yard run by Thomas, Kelly went to McKeller again on third-and-eight from the 15. This time McKeller drew a holding penalty on Tim McKyer, giving Buffalo a first down at the 11. Two plays later Thomas followed Ritcher into the end zone on a five-yard run to put the Bills ahead, 37–27, with 10:28 remaining in the fourth quarter.

And on ensuing kickoff the Bills' special teams did their usual big-play thing as Hal Garner collided face mask-to-face mask with Logan and forced a fumble that none other than Norwood recovered at the Dolphins' 29. "The guy who was trying to block me went inside too far and Logan tried to bounce back out, and we had our head-on collision," said Garner, who had returned to the Bills in 1990 after sitting out the 1989 season because of a third strike under the NFL's substance-abuse policy. "It means a lot to me to make a play like that in a game as important as this. It gives me just that much more confidence."

A couple of plays later Kelly threw a 26-yard scoring pass to Reed to make it 44–27. The extra point was Norwood's fifth, giving him 14 points for the day, a team play-off-game record, to go along with his tackle and fumble recovery.

With 9:42 on the clock the Dolphins began the next possession at their 22. A pair of Sammie Smith runs and a pair of Marino passes moved them to the Buffalo 35. The drive expired, however, after four consecutive incompletes, the last a drop by James Pruitt.

Rick Tuten's lone punt of the day, a 47 yarder, set up the game's longest scoring march—15 plays, 91 yards—which ended with an 8-yard Marino touchdown pass to Tony Martin with 1:15 left in the game. Stoyanovich tried an onside kick, but Reed recovered and Buffalo chewed up the remaining time with three running plays by Thomas to seal the 44–34 victory.

Besides giving the Bills their second triumph in three weeks against a team that once owned them for twenty games and eleven years, it also was the highest-scoring regulation-length game in NFL play-off history (79 points were scored in San Diego's double-overtime triumph against Miami in the 1981 play-offs).

The outcome was just as Jeff Wright expected all along: "I'm not saying we're cocky, but we were anticipating a win in this game. We have other goals in mind, and this game was just one of the bridges we had to cross to get there."

"When you write the script for a big day," Kelly said, "that's the kind of game you want to see."

Did someone mention something about Jim Kelly having a knee problem?

NBC analyst and former Bills punter Paul Maguire did, on the air, just before kickoff. He also said the Bills were making a *biiiig* mistake starting Kelly when a healthier Reich, who had beaten the Dolphins twice before, was at their disposal.

It was a big mistake, alright. In fact, it was such a colossal blunder that, not only did Kelly peform spectacularly with his arm (29 passes, 19 completions, 339 yards, 3 touchdowns), he also ran 5 times—yes, five—for 37 yards. On one play he even handed off to Thomas and went out for a pass, although Thomas saw the quarterback was covered and elected not to throw. The maneuver was a "Skillet Left," a takeoff on the nickname Kelly's teammates had given him for his receiving skills: Skillet Hands.

The Dolphins, some of whom weren't entirely convinced Kelly would even play, certainly had to have been surprised by all that running he did. "I think I surprised myself, too; I know I'm not the fastest guy in the world," said Kelly, who maintained he wasn't playing possum and that he hadn't determined his physical readiness until less than twenty-four hours before the game.

All Shula could do was shake his head when the subject of the Bills' leather-tough QB was raised. "We tried to put pressure on him, we really did," Shula said. "We blitzed him, he killed us blitzing. And when we laid back, he had all day to throw, and he made the throws. For not having played for a few weeks, the way he handled himself and handled that offense, I thought was remarkable."

It was such an amazing display that Reich marveled as if he were a distant observer rather than someone who could have easily been quarterbacking the Bills himself. Despite his previous conquests of the Dolphins he acknowledged there was a significant difference between his and Kelly's talents—as reflected by the many millions of dollars separating their contracts.

"I'm glad I didn't have to do what Jim did out there, because to be honest, I don't know if I could have done it," Reich said. "He was just everything. Every throw was on the money. He made the right reads and he made the perfect throws. That was why, in the fourth quarter of the last Miami game, I told him I wanted to get it back into his hands. He has been doing what he did today all year. And that's why he's the number-one-rated quarterback in the league."

Kelly needed to be at the very top of his game because Marino, a fellow member of college football's quarterback class of 1983, was performing just like the Hall of Famer he is destined to become. Marino completed 23 of 49 passes for 323 yards. He passed for 2 touchdowns, fooled the Bills on a 2-yard bootleg for a third, and came ever so close to pulling off one of the all-time great play-off comeback victories.

"We knew we were going to have to score some points because they have a lot of weapons on offense like we do," Kelly said. "You don't want to tell your defense that. But we knew this was going to be a battle."

As the teams' combined zero sacks and 662 passing yards suggested, the weather gave the quarterbacks and receivers the largest advantage of all. "It's a misconception that you have to run the football in bad weather, unless it's really windy," Hull said. "It's so much easier for us to pass protect and for the receivers to run their routes, which makes the passing game a lot more effective."

Just ask James Lofton and Andre Reed.

Lofton, while repeatedly beating McKyer (who got all of the attention from Kelly for which he had begged), caught a game-high 7 passes for 149 yards and a touchdown. Reed? The Dolphins insisted on single-covering him with free safety Louis Oliver, so he responded by catching 4 passes for 122 yards and 2 touchdowns. Actually, they insisted on the mismatch for two quarters; Oliver was yanked in the second half and replaced by Paul Lankford, who didn't fare much better.

"When I saw Oliver was going to cover me one-on-one, it was lick-your-chops time," Reed said with a mischievous grin. "Especially in this stuff. Their defensive backs are just backpedaling and don't know which way we're going to go. And we've played on this snowy field a lot more than they have."

Although the Dolphins' 430 total yards and 24 first downs didn't speak well of the Bills' defense, it wasn't a complete no-show while the no-huddle shined. Certain individuals, such as Shane Conlan, had reason to feel particularly proud. In what easily was his best performance of the season, Conlan registered a game-high 11 tackles, including 8 initial hits. The most he had recorded in any of his previous 16 outings was 9, and he did that only twice. His was a rare case of a defender's benefiting from the slippery field because, with it hampering the movement of the Bills' front three and forcing Miami's ball carriers to do more straight-ahead running, he often was the one who had to make the play.

"The second wave of defense was more important than normal," Conlan said. "On a couple of plays I was more or less just bird-dogging, just going to whichever back came out. And their linemen pretty much blocked high the whole game. It was just a head-butting type of game. Everybody just got in there and slammed heads. And that's the kind of game I like."

Another thing Conlan liked was that the Bills spent much of the day in a base or nickel defensive scheme (with only one extra defensive back replacing a run-stuffer). That meant he was on the field more. When the Bills switched to a dime package (with two extra DBs) Conlan was removed in favor of Darryl Talley, who was better in pass coverage. And the Bills' extensive use of dime during the regular season was considered a primary reason Conlan ranked only fifth on the team in tackles, with 93, prompting many observers to question his being picked for the Pro Bowl. In previous years he remained on the field in the dime.

A tape of the TV program carrying Keith Sims's inflamatory remarks somehow made its way to Buffalo and was viewed by Smith, Bennett, and several other Bills players the day before the game. They were, to say the least, inspired. Smith didn't have a sack, but he did knock down two passes and pressured Marino into an intentional grounding penalty. Bennett finished with 6 tackles and also deflected a pass.

"You don't throw gasoline on fire," said Smith, who was quite familiar with the subject. "I told Sims during the game, 'If you're gonna talk trash, you'd better be able to back it up.' This guy hasn't been in the league a full season, yet he's going to talk about us the way he did? I really don't understand the reasoning behind it. I mean, every time we play this team, they provoke us. It's like they feel we shouldn't win. We have a world of respect for the Miami Dolphins, but they don't give it to us in return."

Said Thomas, who finished with a career-high and team-play-off-record 32 rushing attempts for 117 yards (only the second 100-yard performance in Buffalo's postseason history after Cookie Gilchrist's 122-yard effort against San Diego in 1964), "I was kind of ticked off, too. Miami just doesn't want to give us the respect we deserve. They were shooting their mouths off and talking about how *they* didn't play well the last time. Well, I think they played pretty damn well this time—and they got their ass kicked."

Concern over another postgame stampede on the goalposts proved unfounded. Not one of the 77,087 fans even attempted to enter the field. But it was hardly by accident. Besides banning the sale of beer at the stadium, Bill Polian went on TV the week before the game and warned that any fans who tried to do what they did December 23 would be "risking life and limb." This time the security force was nearly doubled, with the Erie County Sheriff's Department deputizing 220 Western New York police officers to go along with 300 private security guards. It also included an intimidating four-legged contingent of twenty-four rottweilers and German shepherds.

In the game's waning moments the troops, along with twenty deputies on horseback, surrounded the field, daring somebody to cross the line.

"Nobody was going to storm the field today anyway, because this was just a stepping-stone game," season-ticket-holder Tom Wolff said. "But if we win next week and the Bills are going to their first Super Bowl ever—that could be different."

On January 13 the Bills relaxed in front of their TV sets and awaited an opponent for the January 20 AFC Championship Game. The conference's second divisional-round game was between the Raiders and Cincinnati at the Los Angeles Coliseum. Either way it figured to make for an intriguing title showdown. The Raiders had had a strong season (12–4), and except for what one might call a fluky loss to Buffalo, they could have wound up with the best record in the AFC instead of the 13–3 Bills. The Bengals had struggled to a 9–7 finish, but they would bring a strong revenge element to the game because of the Bills' crushing loss at Cincinnati for the 1988 AFC crown.

Unlike the previous week, when the Bengals quickly blew

away Houston and sent the Dolphins packing for Buffalo by halftime, this contest wouldn't be decided until the fourth quarter. That was when Ethan Horton made a fingertip catch of a 41-yard touchdown pass from Jay Schroeder to break a 10–10 tie, and the Raiders devoured more than five minutes on their way to a 25-yard Jeff Jaeger field goal with nineteen seconds left to secure a 20–10 victory.

"We said all year that the road to the Super Bowl goes through Buffalo," Raiders coach Art Shell said. "We're just happy to be taking that path."

But getting there wasn't easy. Despite having two starting offensive linemen (tackle Anthony Munoz and guard Bruce Reimers) sidelined with injuries, their star running back (James Brooks) slowed by a dislocated thumb, and their quarterback (Boomer Esiason) battling the flu, the Bengals gave the Raiders all they could handle. It also appeared to be a costly win, with running back Bo Jackson suffering a hip injury on the second play of the second half. By that time, he had 77 yards already on only 6 carries. But Marcus Allen picked up the slack impressively, gaining 140 yards and running his hardest through the final fifteen minutes. After the game Jackson vowed to play the following week, but the Raiders' medical staff wasn't quite as optimistic.

Still, in many ways, not the least of which was Buffalo's wild 38–24 victory when the teams last met, a Bills versus Raiders semifinal matchup looked like a classic. First, it was about weather—frigid Western New York versus toasty southern California. Second, it was about cities—blue-collar Buffalo versus let's-do-lunch-sometime Los Angeles. Third, it was about tradition—the Bills, dating back to the days when both teams competed in the AFL, were part of an endless list of Raider haters. They had long grown tired of the bullying, bragging, spying, pride-and-poise, just-win-baby mystique created by the top Raider, Al Davis.

"When we played football in the backyard and somebody was real mean, he was one of the Raiders," Jim Ritcher recalled. "Every kid growing up knew those were the tough guys, the mean guys. People still look at them that way."

People also looked at them as a team that had won three Super Bowls. The Bills had yet to play in one.

The game's other big plus was that it would bring together an impressive collection of NFL talent—Jim Kelly, Bruce Smith, Thurman Thomas, and Andre Reed going against Bo Jackson (if he overcame the injury), Marcus Allen, Howie Long, and Greg Townsend. Some were quick to describe it as the most attractive AFC Championship Game since 1980, when the then Oakland Raiders took on the San Diego Chargers. The Raiders won, 34–27, and advanced to Super Bowl XV, where they beat Philadelphia, 27–10.

"We were the two division winners with the best records," Levy said. "So maybe it's appropriate we do face each other."

The similarities didn't end there. Both teams had big, powerful offensive lines. Both had at least one highly talented running back (the Raiders would have two with Jackson). Both had a corps of fast, big-play receivers. Both had quarterbacks capable of utilizing those fast, big-play receivers. Both had active and effective pass-rushing defensive lines. And both were seen as the toughest kids on the AFC block, the ones who could put up the best fight against the mighty NFC (whose championship would be decided on the same day between the 49ers and Giants at Candlestick Park) in Super Bowl XXV.

"This is my kind of football game," Ray Bentley said. "I love when it gets dirty and nasty and you just get to line up and bang your head against somebody and see what happens. That's what the game's all about, isn't it?"

"It's a good matchup for us," Raiders nose tackle Bob Golic said. "We like to hit and they like to hit. It's going to be one of those good, old-fashioned games where, after it's over, no matter what the score is, everybody's going to be dragging themselves off the turf and laying around the locker room for a while."

On the night of October 7, when the Raiders left Rich Stadium, they were suffering from a lot more than exhaustion. They were stunned. They were mortified. One minute they had been holding a comfortable, 24–14 lead in the fourth quarter.

Six minutes and three seconds later they were on the wrong end of a fourteen-point loss.

Some in the visitor's dressing room that night couldn't contain their frustration. Al Davis had cursed loudly and refused to speak with reporters. Townsend had talked about how the Bills hadn't beaten the Raiders "heads-up" but rather with mere "fluke plays."

Looking back, even though Marv Levy said the Bills had earned "every inch" of their 4–1 record at the time, now several Buffalo players were admitting it wasn't the world's most convincing victory. Not with the Raiders' out-gaining them 347 yards to 280 and out-possessing them, 39:14 to 20:46.

"When we played them before, we got really lucky," James Lofton said. "They had us on the ropes and that was before they had Bo Jackson [still catching his breath from his baseball stint with Kansas City]. They were in control of that football game and we made some plays in the fourth quarter and scored twenty-four points."

One of the bigger charges in the 6:03 explosion was Steve Tasker's block of a Jeff Gossett punt that J. D. Williams recovered and returned for a 38-yard touchdown to put the Bills in front to stay, 28–24.

"You're thankful that those things happen," Tasker said. "But you can't go out there with a mentality that you're going to make a big play like that every time. It doesn't happen that way. You just have to play hard, worry about your assignment, and the big play tends to happen as a result.

"And I wouldn't expect it to happen this time, because the Raiders are too good of a team. It's also something that rarely happens to Gossett, because he is such a quick punter. In fact, that was only the second one he'd had blocked in eight years. They have excellent people on special teams, so you have to call what happened the last time a real fluke for the Raiders."

Still, it was part of a series of plays that had done so much to help set the course of the Bills' season. They knew they were much better than they showed in the week-two disaster at Miami. The question was, how much better? The blowout road-win over the Jets the following Monday night had taken them off the hook, but what it actually proved, in terms of the

Bills' ultimate destiny in 1990, was questionable. They had beaten up on the Jets several times before, home and away.

No, the games that spoke the loudest about the Bills' character were the 29–28 victory over Denver, in which they scored 20 points in seventy-seven seconds of the fourth quarter, and the near-carbon-copy triumph over the Raiders the following week—especially with the Raiders entering the game with a 4–0 record to the Bills' 3–1 mark.

As Tasker pointed out, "There's no question that it was a little bit of a springboard for us, to beat a good team like the Raiders. That victory meant perhaps as much as any other game we've had this year. It was a game that showed us that no matter how far down we were or how badly we were getting dominated, we could still pull it out if we kept playing hard."

Naturally, the Raiders weren't feeling the least bit inferior to the Bills.

Nor were they worried about the weather, which, presumably, would favor the home team as it had the previous week. "It's not like they're Eskimos," said center Don Mosebar. "Everybody gets cold in that weather. I mean, it's not like people in the East go outside in the winter and sit in their front yards and say, 'Gee, isn't all this snow nice?' They go inside, where it's warm."

"I grew up shoveling snow in Boston," said Howie Long. "That was my main source of income. I went right from five dollars a driveway to seven figures in the NFL."

Head coach Art Shell added, "You can't let it become an issue because we have no control over it. If it's cold, fine, you've got to play in it. We just have to make sure we don't make any big mistakes as far as not holding on to the ball. And who knows? Maybe we'll bring some of our weather and warm it up a little bit."

They also weren't worried about finding themselves in the kind of shoot-out the Bills had had against the Dolphins. "I think we can put points on the board, too," said Shell. "We proved that when we played Detroit. They were a high-explosive scoring team, and we had to score more points in order to win, thirty-eight to thirty-one. The object is to win, and if it means scoring three points, that's fine. And if it means scoring forty points, then you have to."

The Raiders also felt confident about facing the Bills' no-huddle offense. "I just don't foresee any problem with it," said Howie Long. "Our personnel is such that we don't need to run people on and off the field. We have the ability as a defense to set and make the calls on the line just as the Bills are making the calls on the line. What worries me more than the no-huddle is stopping Thurman Thomas. I think that's the key."

But Thomas suggested that the Raiders, despite having the fourth-ranked defense in the NFL, would be wise to reconsider their outlook. Not a single Buffalo opponent had found a way to stop the no-huddle yet. Even the Giants' highly touted defense struggled with it before Kelly left the game with a knee injury, and they also had a few problems when Frank Reich was in charge.

Why should that trend change just because the AFC championship was on the line?

"I think we'll come out and play the same kind of game that we played against Miami," Thomas said. "There's no reason to let up now. We're more focused now than we were in 1988 and 1989, we have the home-field advantage, we have eighty thousand fans who will come out and cheer for us. The city of Buffalo deserves a championship, and we're one step away from that."

As they watched maintenance crews paint the AFC and NFL logos on the field, a custom for the league's title games, Talley and Bennett couldn't help but feel goose bumps. They also couldn't help but think back to what had happened the last time they had played in the conference championship game, at Cincinnati in 1988.

"We looked at each other with big smiles and said, 'Last time we saw these, we got our butts kicked,' " Bennett said. "But we're at home now. They're on our turf. No way are we letting this one get away from us."

Kelly sounded equally confident.

"We learned a lot from the last time," he said, referring to the heartbreaking loss to the Bengals. "We learned that it was a big mistake to look too far ahead, to think we have the game won before we even set foot on the field, and start thinking about the next one. We also learned about keeping our poise."

There was one other lesson Jim Ritcher hoped had registered, and that was the importance of making every second count in postseason play. In his eleventh season with Buffalo, he had worn a Bills uniform longer than any of his teammates. He had also experienced enough of the tremendous highs followed by an equal number of devastating lows to realize nothing should be taken for granted.

"I think the longer you play this game, the more you understand how precious and few these opportunities are," Ritcher said. "There's no guarantee that I'll get another shot at this. And there's no guarantee that even the young guys will get another chance. The Lord doesn't promise you another day, so you have to take advantage of what you're given.

"My rookie year we won the division. My second year we made the play-offs as a wild-card team. I figured this play-off thing was going to be an every year occurrence and that we'd have won a Super Bowl or two by now. Then it all fell apart. We started going four and twelve and two and fourteen and suddenly it was like someone had put up a revolving door to the locker room. You needed a program just to know who your teammates and your coaches were."

Real or imagined, the Raiders were known for stealing secrets from their opposition. Real or imagined, Al Davis was reputed to have the biggest and best network of spies outside of the CIA and KGB.

Thus it was no surprise that, in the days leading up to the AFC Championship Game, the Bills took every precaution to foil any attempted espionage.

Real or imagined.

The effort began with the conversion of Rich Stadium into a fortress. Extra security guards were posted throughout the facility, with particular emphasis on the administration building because there, on the third floor, was where the coaches would prepare and store their Holy Grail—what the outside world knew as the game plan. Everyone entering and exiting the building was screened at the door. Even regular beat reporters, who walked in and out of the place year-round, were asked to give their names, affiliations, and state the nature of their business.

During the first general team meeting of the week Levy reminded his players to be especially careful not to leave their playbooks or any other printed matter pertaining to the game scattered around the locker room. Any new information of that sort would also be distributed later in the week than usual.

The custodial staff was under strict orders to quickly empty garbage cans in meeting rooms, where sheets containing Xs and Os were routinely disposed. And all the blackboards were promptly wiped clean after skull sessions. They did everything but use a paper shredder.

"Contrary to what the Bills think, we haven't been poking around in their garbage cans; we're so much more sophisticated than that," Howie Long cracked. "You might say the radar van that has been parked a few miles from their facility has some significance."

But it was no laughing matter to Levy, Polian, or even some of the Bills players.

"The Raiders have always been accused of clandestine activities," said Ray Bentley. "So you have to take some caution. You don't want to leave your game plan laying around, which happens more often than you would think. You just don't want the long arm of Al Davis to come in here and steal something right from under your nose.

"Also, you have to watch everything you say, because you might have reporters, who Al has in his pocket, who could be rather intrusive in their questioning and try to get any information they can to help the Raiders."

The fact was, far more reporters—about 150 from throughout the country and as far away as Tokyo (Could Al Davis have had a Japanese operative on his payroll?)—were covering the Bills at Rich that week than at any other time in their history, let alone the season. That resulted in a record number of unfamiliar faces in and around the team's headquarters. As Levy once pointed out about Al Davis, "He has friends with a reputation for maybe . . . inadvertently losing their way."

Raider-induced paranoia had a long history at One Bills Drive.

"Chuck Knox was the worst," remembered Dave Hojknowski, the Bills' veteran equipment manager. "Whenever we played the Raiders he would screen the cleaning people to make sure one of them wasn't Al Davis in disguise. And during practice he'd have someone in the stands, with binoculars, checking out the skies to see if any of Al's 'recon' planes were going by."

How genuine was the Raider spy threat? Consider the following: Pittsburgh coach Chuck Noll was certain no one was watching or listening as he quietly switched, for the first time, to a one-back attack the week before the Steelers were to face the Raiders in the 1976 AFC Championship Game. The move was partly to compensate for injuries to running backs Franco Harris and Rocky Bleier, and partly to catch the Raiders by surprise. And it appeared to be working to perfection, as the Raiders' defense spent the entire week preparing for a two-man backfield.

However, all of that suddenly—and suspiciously—changed at the eleventh hour.

"We had just finished our final day of practice and were taking off our uniforms and pads," former Oakland and Buffalo linebacker Phil Villapiano recalled. "All of a sudden, John Madden walked into the locker room and said, 'Everybody put your pads back on. We're going out there again.' We all groaned, but when Madden told you get back out there, you didn't ask questions.

"So we went back out, and this time we were practicing against the one-back offense. We worked on it until dark. Sure enough, the day of the game, the Steelers tried to open with the one-back, and we stuffed 'em."

Final score: Raiders 24, Steelers 7.

Despite Shell's claims to the contrary, the Bills weren't alone in taking extra precautionary measures before the 1990 championship match. *The Buffalo News* sent sports staffer Bob DiCesare to El Segundo, California, to cover the Raiders as they prepared for the game. But shortly after DiCesare arrived he was not-so-politely ordered to leave the grounds of the team's practice complex after identifying himself to Raiders executive assistant Al LoCosale. DiCesare's request to remain in the press room, which did not provide a clear view of the practice field, was denied. So was an appeal by sympathetic Raiders beat writers to "keep an eye on him" as he waited for the workout to end.

"Come back at the end of practice," he was told. "And not a minute sooner!"

But not everyone connected with the game was fretting over being watched by a Big Brother named Marv or Al. Darryl Talley thought the whole idea of one team's trying to steal another team's strategy was nonsense.

"What do you want to know?" he said sarcastically. "I'll tell you exactly what I'm going to do: I'm going to line up on the right side, I'm going to line up on the inside, I'm going to put my hand on the ground, I'm going to stand up. Okay? Got that, Al?

"It doesn't bother me at all, and I don't think it should bother anybody else. You've got to worry about playing, that's all. You can't worry about what anybody else is doing or trying to find out about you. Everybody's just got to play."

After Wednesday, January 16, there was discussion of a very different and very sobering kind of security pertaining to the game. That was the day war broke out in the Persian Gulf. And it touched off concern over possible terrorist activity at Rich Stadium, which would be the site of the first live, nationally televised event since the war began.

So while Levy met with his assistant coaches and players to talk about how to beat the Raiders, Polian huddled with officials from the FBI, local law-enfourcement agencies, and the NFL security office to form a plan for protecting eighty thousand fans, the teams, and dignitaries from terrorism. The security force, already doubled for the previous week's game, would grow even larger and include FBI counterterrorist agents—strictly as a precaution.

"We do not have any specific or general threats," stressed G. Robert Langford, special agent in charge of the FBI for Western New York. "We're just being cautious."

"Sure, there are concerns about terrorism," Polian said. "There is a volatile situation in the world, and the people who oppose us as a country use terrorism as a weapon. So it is only prudent to take the measures that are called for. There is, however, no reason to panic."

One option that was quickly eliminated was postponing—or canceling—either conference championship game or the Super Bowl. In a statement NFL commissioner Paul Tagliabue said: "We recognize that the American people will not be paralyzed by the events in the Middle East or allow the fabric of daily life to be destroyed. Local, state, and federal law-enforcement agencies have been enlisted in the league's efforts to provide the highest level of public safety to those attending our games. We will obviously continue to follow events in the Middle East and take those into account as we approach kickoff. If the networks believe that the events in the Gulf are so dramatic or so significant that they should go to an all-news format, then we would not play our games."

The day before the war started Buffalo linebacker Carlton Bailey had paid a visit to the Bills Locker Room. Not the one he shared with his teammates at Rich, but a store that sold team merchandise. Bailey purchased an assortment of shirts and caps that would be part of a package he was sending to Saudi Arabia. The addressee: his father, Conway Bailey, an officer with the 260th Army Reserve unit from Baltimore.

Dividing his thoughts between the biggest football game of his life and his father's well-being had been tough enough since hearing right after the Miami game that Congress and the Senate had given President Bush authority to declare war on Iraq. Now, having shipped off the box to the desert, Bailey was listening to his car radio when he heard a news bulletin about the Allied forces' bombing raid on Baghdad. Once home the first thing he didn't do was turn on the TV for more details. Instead, he picked up his Bible.

He also answered supportive telephone calls from several of his teammates.

"It's tough," the twenty-six-year-old Bailey said. "Sometimes I just sit back and try to block it totally out of my mind. But it's all over the news. Every time I turn around there's something coming up that reminds me I may not ever see him again.

"Back in Baltimore, my mother [Thelma] is real sad. My little sister [Conya] is probably taking it the hardest of all."

An assistant warden at the state correctional facility in Jessup, Maryland, Bailey's father had been an Army reservest for ten years. Before that he saw fifteen years of active duty, including two tours in Vietnam.

Since his father had left for the Middle East in November Bailey had only been able to communicate with him through letters. The last one he had received before the war urged him to concentrate on the business at hand, which, at the time, was preparing for the play-off game with the Dolphins.

"He told me just to keep my head up and try not to focus on anything that was going on over there," Bailey recalled. "He told me to try and focus in on playing football—to do the best we could in taking care of the play-offs and getting to the Super Bowl, while he and his company would do the best they could in taking care of things in the Gulf. He just wants me to play hard. He wouldn't want me to mope around and put my head down. He would want me to hold my head up and be proud of what's going on."

And Bailey was.

Speaking with calm admiration and respect, he said, "Whatever our government decides, that's what we have to go with. It definitely hits close to home. But my father once told me, 'You have to stand for something or you'll fall for anything.' And that's how I feel.

"In one of the letters I wrote to him, I said that, hopefully, when I'm on the field, I can make a big play not only for the team or myself, but for him. Whether we beat the Raiders or not, I'm going to put forth the extra, extra effort. And that way, when he's out there reading a newspaper article about our game, he can be that much more proud. In the meantime I'll just continue to pray for him."

Bailey wasn't the only Bills player with a loved one in the Persian Gulf. The father-in-law of Keith McKeller and the stepfather of Eddie Fuller, a rookie running back on injured reserve, were also serving in the armed forces there. And the brother of Raiders guard Steve Wisniewski was among the first wave of American pilots to invade Iraq.

Leon Seals faced a different sort of distraction. His mother, losing a lengthy battle with cancer, was fading in and out of a coma in a Baton Rouge, Louisiana, hospital where he had visited her during the team's day off earlier in the week.

For the first few days after the Raiders' play-off win over Cincinnati, there was at least one thing Bo didn't know: whether his sore left hip would allow him to play in the AFC Championship Game. He was officially listed as doubtful, which meant chances were 75 percent against his playing. Of course, the Raiders being the Raiders, few observers had even a lower percentage of belief in any information the club dispensed—especially concerning an injury to its top star.

But Jackson didn't take part in the first full-scale workout for the game, nor the second. As the week progressed it became clear that Raiders team physician Robert Rosenfeld wasn't kidding when he said that not only wouldn't Bo play against the Bills, but with only a week of recovery beforehand, he'd also probably miss the Super Bowl if the Raiders won.

Jackson's absence would take some sheen off the AFC title showdown. However, as he had proved with his 140-yard performance against the Bengals, Marcus Allen wasn't exactly chopped liver. Despite being two years older and having spent five more seasons in the NFL than his part-time backfield partner, he seemed to have gained speed and strength in the latter stages.

"I don't know what it is about the play-offs," said Allen, the MVP of Super Bowl XVIII whose career play-off average was six yards per carry. "I guess I just know how to get pumped up for a game of this magnitude."

His teammates respected him for that.

"Marcus is one of the most inspirational guys on the team," Wisniewski said. "He hasn't gotten the ball as much this year, but he doesn't complain about it. He has to block, and he doesn't complain about it. It's definitely exciting to see him do well."

"People don't understand what a team player Marcus Allen

is," said linebacker Jerry Robinson. "For seventeen weeks now, if there's one thing you knew, it was you could count on Marcus Allen. You know that if you were to walk into a dark alley, he'd be right behind you, ready to back you up . . . if not out in front of you, leading the way."

Buffalo defenders also had a high regard for Allen's running.

"Bo's definitely more explosive; he just gets the ball and goes," Conlan said. "But I still think Marcus might be a little better as a true runner. He cuts a little better and he's been doing it for so long."

"You can't take anything away from Bo, he's an outstanding athlete," Bruce Smith said. "But Marcus Allen gets the job done. He's a classy guy all the way around. And words can't describe the way we're going to have to play against this guy."

Except for the large contingent of reporters and the administrative hassles they and the ever-increasing security concerns were creating, the football routine wasn't all that different at One Bills Drive. The way the players went about their duties you'd have sworn they were preparing for any old game on the schedule as opposed to the biggest any had ever played. Had it not been for all those reporters asking all those questions, the dressing room and surrounding areas in the bowels of the stadium would pretty much have been dead.

"Yeah, it's really subdued around here," Dave Hojnowski, the equipment manager said. "I don't think these guys are really going to let loose until they win the Big One."

Win the Big One? None of the players had even been to the Big One in person, except for those who had tickets. How could they have been expected to keep their cool while standing on the Big One's doorstep, let alone if they earned the right to play in it?

Because that was how the Bills planned their January calendar way back in July.

"Our goal this season wasn't to win the AFC East," Kent Hull said. "Our goal wasn't to win the first round of the play-offs. And it's certainly not just to get to the Super Bowl. We set our goals high, and the number one goal we set was to win the

Super Bowl. Once that's achieved you'll see us let our hair down."

"We can't get caught up in the big media blitz," echoed Darryl Talley. "We're trying to win a football game. We're not running for president or governor or anything like that."

Like the sound of the double thud from a blocked kick, that sort of talk was beautiful music to Marv Levy's ears. He, too, had noticed the subdued atmosphere among his players. And with every practice he was seeing exactly what he had hoped to see from his team in the days leading up to a game of that significance.

Crisp workouts. Attentiveness in meetings. Lots of film study.

"Their concentration level is superb," the coach said. "They're executing in practice, asking good questions, and tuned in to getting ready. I think if you spend your whole week running around excited, you're exhausted by game day."

Was it simply a case of the players' being businesslike about the task ahead? Or had the war robbed them of some of their enthusiasm? By the end of the week the game had hardly generated the electricity around town that one would have expected for the first pro football championship in Buffalo since 1966. The TV airtime it received on the three normally rah-rah, Bills-crazy network affiliates was remarkably low. But with almost nonstop war coverage, that was understandable.

In all the security talk earlier in the week it was mentioned that there would be an even stronger goalpost-saving effort than the one that didn't allow a single fan to enter the field after the first play-off game. But between fears of terrorism and out of respect for the troops in the Gulf, a wild postgame celebration didn't seem as likely as the previous Sunday, when one fan said the Bills' clinching the AFC crown would prompt a rush even if there were "dogs, horses, pigs, or bears." Nevertheless, extra steps were taken, including the greasing of the goalposts to discourage any would-be climbers who managed to get past the sheriff's deputies, guards, rottweilers, German shepherds, and horses.

A Bills pep rally in downtown Buffalo, scheduled for the

Friday before the game, was canceled because of the war. Instead, team officials, players, and local government leaders who organized the event attended a prayer service.

"What's going on in the Persian Gulf is unfortunate and it's extremely important," Will Wolford said. "It's a heck of a lot more important than a football game."

"We're worrying about the weather, worrying about this, worrying about that," said Howie Long. "But there are guys over there dug into trenches worrying about taking some kind of a bomb that I've never heard of."

Yes, they played the game on January 20. They played it despite concerns over terrorism, which proved unfounded. They played it despite worries the Persian Gulf war would escalate and force NBC to pull the plug on its coverage and the NFL to pull the plug on the game, which also proved unfounded. They played it, and Rich Stadium was rocking from the opening kickoff.

But there was a sense of perspective. The stadium was a sea of American flags, in all sizes, sending a message that what was taking place in the Middle East had not been forgotten—that, in addition to forty-seven professional football players, support was going out to hundreds of thousands of professional soldiers. Banners and facial makeup depicted as many flags as Bills logos. One banner covered both themes: "Peace on Earth, Bedlam in Buffalo." And fans with radios listened for war updates every bit as closely as they followed Van Miller's play-by-play.

The West Point Marching Band performed the national anthem. As it did, Carlton Bailey felt chills going through his body. It had nothing to do with the weather, which was almost tropical at 36 degrees and with a light rain falling. Bailey was thinking about his father, a half world away. And when the music stopped the stadium-record crowd of 80,324 (there were only thirty-eight no-shows) exploded into a deafening chant of "USA! USA! USA!"

It brought tears to the eyes of Ralph Wilson, a veteran of World War II. "We are all thinking of the brave men and women over in the Gulf showing so much courage and resolve," he said. "Jack Kemp [former Bills quarterback, congressman, and at the time, the U.S. housing secretary] called me a couple of days ago and told me the troops over there wanted the championship and Super Bowl games to be played. And that's why the league has gone ahead with them, because that's what the troops want."

For a change, the Bills' first play of the game wasn't a no-huddle pass but a no-huddle run—a draw to Thomas from shotgun formation. It went straight at Howie Long, and picked up 12 yards. John Davis, who led the blocking, thought it made a statement for the rest of the day. "The Raiders are a penetrating team," he explained. "So if they can get upfield, you can kind of 'throw' their defensive linemen to where their momentum is taking them. And on that play, everybody just pushed their guys aside, and Thurman was in the open field."

Kelly then threw 14 yards to Thomas and 15 to Reed to move the ball to the Raiders' 34. After a 5-yard Thomas run and a Kelly-to-Thomas pass for 9 more, the Raiders, like previous Buffalo opponents, called a basketball-style time-out to regroup. Although theirs figured to be one of the more formidable defenses the Bills would face all season, they looked far more confused and disoriented than any Buffalo had faced to that point. It seemed as if the no-huddle, which everyone in the world expected from the Bills, had caught them by surprise.

"I really don't think they were prepared for it," said Thomas, who would finish with 138 yards rushing and 61 on 5 receptions. "We've been running it for a long time now, and you would think their coaches would know that that's what got us this far and have prepared for it. But it seemed they didn't start thinking about what to do against it until they called that time-out."

Which, of course, was way too late.

When play resumed Kelly completed a 9-yard pass to McKeller, followed by a 5-yarder to Thomas, followed by a Thomas run of 3. A holding call on Will Wolford pushed the ball back to the Los Angeles 13, but that wouldn't deter the Bills. Nor would a broken play. After dropping the next snap, from shotgun, Kelly calmly ran forward to pick it up, circled out of the pocket to his right and flipped a touchdown pass to James Lofton. Cornerback Lionel Washington, the Raiders' best cover man, never had a chance, because, as Lofton said, "All the defensive backs were coming up at the same time and they kind of bumped into each other." It marked the tenth score—and ninth touchdown—in the Bills' last twelve opening drives.

The Raiders surged back on the ensuing series, which began at their 19. Schroeder fired two consecutive 26-yard passes to Mervyn Fernandez and Willie Gault, and the Silver and Black suddenly had a first down at the Buffalo 29. But the best they could do after that was an incomplete, a 5-yard Allen run, and another incomplete, setting up a 41-yard Jeff Jaeger field goal that made it 7–3 only 5:49 into the game.

Buffalo's next drive was short and sweet, lasting only four plays and sixty-one seconds. On second down Kelly found Lofton for a 41-yard, over-the-shoulder reception to the Raiders' 23, with Washington again being burnt to a crisp. Kelly then ran for 11 yards, and on first-and-ten from the 12, Thomas slanted to his right and slipped the tackles of defensive backs Garry Lewis and Elvis Patterson for the touchdown.

The Raiders proceeded to go three and out. However, it looked as if they would get some life when a Kelly pass, on second-and-ten from the Los Angeles 24, bounced off Thomas's fingers and into the hands of Lewis at the 20. On third-and-six from the 24 the Bills sent Leonard Smith on a safety blitz. The Raiders picked it up, but in so doing, they allowed Bruce Smith to break free from one-on-one blocking and hurry Schroeder's throw. The pass sailed straight to Darryl Talley, who returned it 27 yards for a touchdown to give the Bills a 21–3 lead with 48:09 still to play.

"The first thing I thought was, 'The football's coming,' " Talley recalled later. "And as soon as I got the ball, the only thing I could think of was to get to the end zone as fast as I could. And the only thing I saw was a big lineman coming at me. Of course, all I could do was try to run away from him . . . like I said, he was big. Then I felt somebody come up behind me [Raiders ultrafast receiver Tim Brown] and take a swipe at the ball to try to knock it out. I held on. And after that, well, I just tried to get into that little corner of the end zone."

"When something like that happens, the other team begins to press," Levy said of Talley's score. "And our guys stayed very focused. They didn't get giddy on the sidelines."

Los Angeles' next possession ended with Jeff Gossett's second punt of the day, which started the Bills at their 43. By this time the Raiders were so desperate to stop Buffalo's passing attack they went almost exclusively to their dime defense, replacing run-stuffers with two extra defensive backs. Anticipating this, Kelly stayed mainly on the ground, handing off to Thomas and Kenneth Davis from shotgun formation and driving deep into Los Angeles territory.

"We were always one step ahead of them," Kelly said.

The Bills wound up with a fourth-and-goal from the 1 and called a time-out. It was expected Levy would play it safe and go for the short field goal, but he decided instead to try for the touchdown.

"Give me the rock," Davis told Kelly. "And I'll go."

Indeed, Davis went, slicing through the left side for the score. Scott Norwood's extra point was blocked, giving the Bills a 27–3 lead with 9:02 remaining in the first half.

On the kickoff Ron Holland muffed the ball and Jamie Mueller recovered for Buffalo at the Raiders' 27. Los Angeles caught a break this time, as Norwood's 45-yard field-goal attempt sailed wide right. Not that the Bills were all that concerned. For one thing, they were comfortably ahead and in full control of the game offensively and defensively. For another, the distance wasn't exactly comfortable for Norwood, who during the regular season had missed 4 of 10 tries between 40 and 49 yards.

The Raiders continued to be hopeless on offense, with Schroeder guiding them as far as the Bills' 46 before Gossett punted for a third time. "We had the kind of day where it seemed we couldn't do anything right," Schroeder said. "It was a heck of a time to have a game like that."

Starting at his 20, Kelly hit Thomas with a 16-yard screen pass. He followed that reception with runs of 7 and 4 yards to give the Bills a first down at the Buffalo 47. Two plays later

Kelly found an unlikely target—Steve Tasker, filling in at receiver for injured Al Edwards—for a 44-yard bomb to the Los Angeles 9. Kenneth Davis ran for 6 on the next play, and on second-and-goal launched himself into the end zone.

Now Schroeder was really pressing. And on the first play after the kickoff, he was intercepted by Nate Odomes at the Bills' 30, from where he returned it to the Buffalo 39. Four straight Thomas runs put the ball at the Raiders' 41, from where Kelly and Lofton went to work on Lionel Washington again, hooking up for a 33-yard gain to the 8.

"A lot of times," Washington said, "we were in a great defense for the plays they were running, but Kelly and Lofton made the great plays."

They made one more, at Washington's expense, when Lofton ran a turn-in pattern for an 8-yard touchdown catch. The scoreboard had everyone doing double takes when it showed: Bills 41, Raiders 3. But even with such an overwhelming lead at halftime (the 41 first-half points were an NFL play-off record), the Bills were determined not to let up. "Hell," said Bentley, "we had guys running up the tunnel yelling that we had to keep the pressure on because we were still thirty minutes away from achieving what we wanted to achieve."

Meanwhile, down at Tampa Stadium, Super Bowl groundskeeper George Toma had ruled out a comeback as emphatically as anyone could. He and his crew began painting an end zone with "Bills" in large letters, next to a giant picture of the team's helmet. With the longer schedule having eliminated the extra week between the conference championship games and the Super Bowl, there was no time to waste. Nor faith.

The Raiders did win a small—make that tiny—battle by shutting out the Bills in the third quarter. But just barely. On the opening drive of the second half, Jay Schroeder threw his third interception of the day, snagged by Mark Kelso at the Buffalo 5. Four plays later Rick Tuten punted for the first time in the game. But the Raiders gave it right back when Schroeder was picked off again, this time by Leonard Smith with 5:06 left in the third.

The Bills didn't figure to squander a second scoring opportunity in a game where everything was going their way. And sure enough, Kelly drove them from their 22 to the Los Angeles 1, converting a pair of third downs along the way with a 23-yard throw to McKeller and an 18-yarder to Lofton. On the first play of the fourth quarter Davis took the handoff and scored, tying a single-game play-off record with three touchdowns.

But Schroeder wasn't finished with his generosity. Two plays later Darryl Talley grabbed his second interception, providing further proof that his AFC peers erred by shutting him out of the Pro Bowl. After the pickoff Talley found himself momentarily frozen, forgetting what to do next. Then he took off for the end zone. And as he did he noticed Bruce Smith—who obviously wasn't an offensive lineman in a former life—running toward him.

"Hey, Bruce," Talley yelled. "Turn around and block somebody, would ya?"

Smith complied, helping Talley pick up 21 yards to the Raiders' 27. Showing mercy, Levy pulled Kelly and Thomas out of the game. Reich took over and handed off three times before Norwood kicked a 39-yard field goal to give the Bills a staggering 51–3 lead with 12:14 on the clock.

Vince Evans replaced Schroeder the rest of the way and was equally horrible, picking up an intentional grounding penalty on his first series and throwing the Raiders' sixth interception of the day to Ray Bentley on the next.

For all the AFC Championship Game was supposed to offer as a "classic" matchup, its drama—at least where football was concerned—came and left with the coin toss. And the Raiders lost that, too. In a blowout that stunned even their most loyal and confident supporters, the Bills tore through the silver and black as if they were vapor for a 48-point victory. One more time for any nonbelievers still out there: Bills 51, Raiders 3. Only two play-off games in NFL history were won by larger margins: 1940, when Chicago beat Washington, 73–0; 1969, when the then Oakland Raiders clobbered Houston, 56–7. It was also the worst postseason loss ever for the Raiders and their worst of any kind since 1961, when they lost to the Oilers by 55 points.

Who, in all sobriety, could have expected such a score?

"Nobody," said Kelly, who set an AFC Championship Game record with a 79.3 completion percentage for 300 yards and 2 touchdowns. "And that includes myself."

You knew the kind of day it had been for the Bills when a reporter asked the quarterback to describe a particular scoring play, and he paused, twisted his head to one side, stared out in space for a moment and said, "Gee, there were so many, I can't remember that one."

Said Hull, "We felt going into the game that the Raiders posed a bigger threat to us than anybody else we played this year." In the end, though, they looked helpless and pathetic. They were outgained, 502 yards to 320. They allowed an AFC title game record 30 first downs. And they turned the ball over seven times.

"Sad . . . depressing . . . embarrassing," Jerry Robinson said in a Raiders locker room that was quiet enough to hear one of Al Davis's pinkie rings drop.

Long, who before the game had said he didn't "foresee any problem" with the Raiders's defense handling the no-huddle, changed his tune afterward. "We prepared for it," he said. "I just don't think anyone can stop it. If Kelly throws that way down in Tampa, there's nobody who's going to beat them. Plain and simple."

Ralph Wilson called it "probably the best performance the Bills have ever had"—Which was appropriate, because it was the one for which he had waited twenty-five years, the one that would finally send his team to the big show, the twenty-fifth anniversary Super Bowl at Tampa Stadium (located, by the way, on Buffalo Avenue).

Extratight security, which included pat searches at the entrances and a ban of any aircraft over the stadium except the sheriff's helicopter patrol, kept the peace everywhere outside the playing surface. The wildest thing that happened on the field—besides the score—came late in the fourth quarter, when Bills players gave Levy a Gatorade shower that, judging from his dour expression, amused everyone but him. The goalposts survived, as only three fans dared attempt to break the circle of police and dogs around the artificial grass. They were promptly handcuffed and escorted away.

In fact, the only activity at midfield after the game was when several players from both teams got together to pray for the troops. Mark Kelso, who organized the show of faith, wrote the names of servicemen in the Gulf on the white tape around his wrists and ankles—names he had randomly picked from reading newspaper accounts of the war.

A seemingly endless roar from the crowd filled the stadium as sprinting Bills players hooted, hollered, hugged, and high-fived their way up the tunnel to the dressing room. With hundreds of reporters and photographers waiting outside, players, coaches, the owner, and almost everyone connected with the franchise did the kind of thunderous celebrating one would expect from a team that had just earned its first trip to the Super Bowl.

"It was bedlam," Bentley said. "Everybody was just out of their minds. It was chaos. Guys were running, screaming, banging heads, kissing . . . in fact, I was a little embarrassed by some of the kissing that was going on."

Unlike previous victories when game balls (at fifty dollars apiece) were handed out as freely as towels, only one was presented on this day. It went to the number-one Bill—Ralph C. Wilson, Jr. And after his players, coaches, and administrators gave him the ball, they honored him with a song.

Hooray for Ralph
Hooray at last
Hooray for Ralph
He's a horse's ass

Wilson grinned all the way through. It was the same grin he had been wearing since the final few minutes of the game, when a fan tossed a Bills cap to him through the open window of his private box. Wilson shook the cap in leading cheers in the section below. "I'm not using a cliché when I say this," he said. "But I am really happy about the Bills going to their first Super Bowl, for the fans of Buffalo." At seventy-two Wilson had become their figurative father and grandfather. And if it were possible he'd bring every single one of them with him to Tampa the next day. After all, this was a man who, for one of his daughters' coming-out parties in the 1960s, hired the Supremes for a command performance.

For the longest time, however, his image among the fans was something along the lines of "Daddy Dearest." He was seen as a cheapskate who, after an initial investment of twenty-five thousand dollars, grabbed more and more of their money each year while being perfectly satisfied to view football's game of games as a spectator rather than as a participant. Presumably, it wasn't until around 1986 that Wilson finally decided to get serious about building his team into a world champion and cracked open the vault. A few million dollars here for Kelly. A couple of million there for Bruce Smith. Millions upon millions everywhere to acquire and retain the marquee talent necessary to win the NFL's ultimate prize.

Such a notion made Wilson bristle. "I'd been wanting to go to the Super Bowl ever since the thing was inaugurated. I don't know where anyone got the idea that, all of a sudden, I woke up one day and wanted to spend a lot of money and get a championship team. I know people say that I didn't spend money and I was pinching pennies and so forth. But I have never been that way. In fact, I'm the one who started the renegotiation era in the middle seventies. O. J. Simpson said his wife didn't want to live in Buffalo anymore, and that if we didn't trade him to the Rams, he was going to quit. I said, 'Wait a minute! We're not trading you to the Rams and you're not going to quit.' So I gave him two million dollars over three years.

"I would have liked very much to have gone to the Super Bowl through those first ten to twenty years, but we didn't have the defense. We had Joe Ferguson, we had Ahmad Rashad, we had Bobby Chandler, we had Frank Lewis. We had some great players, but we just didn't have the defense. And the reason we didn't have the defense was that we had been drafting very poorly, especially in the late seventies and into the early eighties. Our drafts were just horrendous. The whole thing wasn't being operated right, and I blame myself. I was slow in making changes."

The turnaround began after the 1985 season, when for the

second consecutive year, the Bills finished with a 2–14 record. Wilson made Bill Polian ("A football guy, as opposed to an insurance man or some friend of mine") his general manager. It was a fast and dramatic climb to the top for Polian, a young scout who had occupied the smallest office at One Bills Drive and wasn't merely being modest when he introduced himself as "Bill Who?" at his first press conference as GM. But he promptly overhauled the football operation, with particular emphasis on scouting, and revamped other areas of the team's administration that were in dire need of repair. From 1986 on, the bulk of the players who comprised the 1990 AFC championship squad were found through Polian's smart drafting, shrewd trading, and keen free-agent signing.

All Wilson had to do was pay them—and keep paying them. "But money, alone, does not buy championships," he stressed. "You can spend a ton of money and the players don't pan out. You have to spend it on players who will produce for you. Everybody talks about all the money the 49ers spend, but they've also had good drafts, beginning with Joe Montana on the third round [in 1979]."

In the Bills' dressing room Wilson was still grinning as he stepped up to the podium, where Chiefs owner Lamar Hunt, president of the AFC and the man who invited Wilson to become one of the founding fathers of the AFL in 1960 (a.k.a. The Foolish Club), handed him the conference championship trophy. Now the Bills could officially be scratched from a list of ten teams that had never reached the Super Bowl (Atlanta, Cleveland, Detroit, Houston, New Orleans, Phoenix, San Diego, Seattle, and Tampa Bay were the others).

The idea in the dressing room, as it had been on the field, was to pummel and bury all the demons in the franchise's thirty-one-year history—the collapse after winning back-to-back AFL championships in the 1960s, the 2-14 seasons of 1984 and 1985, the near-misses in the 1988 and 1989 play-offs.

"Yeah, yeah. I heard all the jokes during the losing years," Talley said with a sigh. "The ones like: Knock! knock!

"Who's there?

"Owen.

"Owen who?

"Owen Ten.

"Yeah, I thought about the bad years. And if we could have dug up a few more of those ghosts, we'd have stomped all over them, too."

But some players weren't quite as exuberant as the rest. For them it was a time to reflect on thoughts that far outweighed football.

One was Carlton Bailey, who in seeing most of his action on special teams, led the Bills with seven tackles (including six first hits). It was, to say the least, an inspired performance. "I was going to do whatever it took—sacrificing my body, knocking myself out—to put that extra edge in there for my pops," he said. "They told me the game was being televised over in Saudi Arabia and, hopefully, he had an opportunity to watch the game. Hopefully, I made him proud."

On Saturday Leon Seals's mother, Annie Mae, finally lost her bout with cancer. He insisted her death hadn't detracted from his performance—and who would have blamed him if it had?—because she wouldn't have wanted it any other way. Seals had considered telling Levy he wouldn't be able to play against the Raiders, that "rather than be a menace to the team, I'd just as soon stay away." But he changed his mind as he reflected on his childhood, and on how his mother had told him one night when he was in ninth grade, "Don't you ever let me stop you from playing a sport you want to play."

Two years earlier, Annie Mae Seals, single mother of seven, had caught Leon in a lie. She discovered from seeing him in a newspaper photograph that her son was playing football, which she had ordered him not to do because she felt he was too small and football was too violent. So she made him stop. Leon was twelve at the time; as he turned fourteen, his body went through some significant changes and his mother gave him the okay to play. After an awards banquet that year, when she helped him carry home five trophies, Annie Mae Seals took Leon aside and told him to stick to his sporting guns and vowed she would never stop him again.

"And she never did," he said. "That's why I'm here. So now I'm dedicating the Super Bowl and every game I play the rest of my life to her.

"The last good conversation I had with her before she slipped into a coma, I said, 'If we get a chance to go to the Super Bowl, you're going to go with me, right?' She said, 'You'll know I'll be there.' And the way I look at it, she'll still be there."

James Lofton, who finished with 5 receptions for 113 yards and 2 touchdowns against his former teammates, couldn't help but think back to when his father took him to the first Super Bowl ever played. They sat in the cheap seats, well above the field at the Los Angeles Coliseum, and watched the Chiefs take on Green Bay. Lofton was only nine at the time, but the memory was still vivid a quarter of a century later.

Making it extra special was the fact his father, Emanuel, had died in early November.

"I wish he could be going to Tampa with me, but he can't," Lofton said. "Still, I'll always cherish the memory of that first Super Bowl that I attended with him." Now Lofton would be taking his son, eight-year-old David, to the game. Only Dad wouldn't be able to sit with him, of course.

Once the doors to the dressing room opened, and the eyes and ears of the outside world entered in the form of a small army of reporters and photographers, calm took over. No champagne corks popped. The running, screaming, head-banging, and kissing were replaced by a quiet sense of accomplishment.

Everyone seemed to go back to following the credo on the sign across the top of the dressing room's alcove. The one that said: "WE PEAK NEXT WEEK!"

"This is a great thrill, but as I keep saying, we have one more river to cross," Levy said. "It's not time to sit back."

Nor was it time to look too far ahead. People kept offering him brand-new, just-out-of-the-package Super Bowl XXV caps and shirts, and Levy kept politely refusing.

"I'll wear them," he said. "But only at the appropriate time."

Three thousand miles west of Buffalo the NFC Championship Game was down to its final four seconds. The Giants trailed the 49ers, 13–12. The Giants' placekicker, Matt Bahr, faced a 42-yard field-goal attempt.

Simply put, Buffalo's Super Bowl opponent would be determined by whether Bahr succeeded or failed in the biggest moment of his thirteen-year NFL career.

Success would give the Giants their second appearance in the NFL's premier event since the end of the 1986 season. Failure would put the 49ers in position to make NFL history with a third consecutive Super Bowl trip and a chance to "three-peat" as world champions.

For the fifth time in the game Bahr put the ball through the uprights, giving the Giants a 15–13 triumph that contained all the excitement lacking from the day's first conference-title showdown. But it wasn't a sure thing by any means. He had already hooked a kick wide in the same end of Candlestick Park, and the swirling winds weren't exactly cooperating on his seventh and final try of the day.

"It was drifting a little bit to the left at first," Bahr said. "So I hesitated before I reacted to anything." When the ball slid safely inside the left upright, setting an NFC Championship Game record for field goals, his first thought was: "We're going to The Show!"

And just as suddenly, the NFL found itself in a New York state of mind, for two teams that had already played a much-talked-about but virtually meaningless regular-season game would play the ultimate rematch.

The Giants' winning drive began with 2:36 left, after the only turnover of the game. On a first-down play from the New York 40, Giants nose tackle Erik Howard broke free from a double-team block and stripped the ball from San Francisco running back Roger Craig. Lawrence Taylor recovered it at the Giants' 43.

New York then moved thirty-three yards in six plays, including two critical completions by Jeff Hostetler—one for 19 yards to tight end Mark Bavaro, another for 13 to wide receiver Stephen Baker. Finally, Hostetler's quarterback sneak to the 49ers' 24 set the stage for Bahr's heroics.

Like his teammates and everyone else in Buffalo anxious to see who the Bills would face in Tampa, Scott Norwood watched attentively as the moment of truth unfolded on his TV screen. But he wasn't watching the way other players or fans were watching. He was watching as someone who understood the pressure that had been plopped on Bahr's not so giant shoulders.

"As a kicker you can empathize more than anybody else," Norwood said. "You're all alone out there. So I was happy for him when he made it."

"This victory is for the guys who have been here all year," said Bahr, who the Giants had picked up as a free agent after Raul Allegre suffered a groin injury in the third week of the regular season. "I'm just happy to be along for the ride."

"It was our obligation to prevent the 49ers from making history," said Erik Howard. "Let some other team set the record, not the 49ers."

Hostetler, who completed 15 of 27 passes for 176 yards and gained 11 more on three runs, shined as the Giants' signal caller after Phil Simms suffered a foot injury against the Bills. Since losing his relief performance to Buffalo, 17–13, Hostetler had built a 4–0 record as a starter. Yet he was still hearing a great deal of criticism about his playing ability.

"Everyone's got their opinions about me," he said. "They tell me I can't. But we're going to the Super Bowl."

And Giants linebacker Steve DeOssie, who did the snapping on Bahr's field goals, was granted the wish he had made after the December 15 game against Buffalo: seeing the Bills on January 27 in Tampa Stadium—from across the field.

ONE KICK FROM GLORY

"Until we win a Super Bowl, I'll just say we're a good team. When you win the Super Bowl, that's when you can call yourself a great team."

—Cornelius Bennett

The players knew this was a special trip the moment they arrived at the airport in Buffalo and saw the plane. They would no longer be stuffed like overgrown sardines in the 127-seat Pan Am Boeing 727 that had carried them to previous road games, a craft so small it couldn't cross the country once without making a fuel stop. For the two-and-a-half-hour ride to Tampa the Bills would travel in style on a 300-seat Pan Am airbus ironically called The Clipper Miami. They would even get an in-flight movie. Free.

It was for the most part a relaxed group that made its way south on the night of Monday, January 21. A lot of laughing. A lot of joking. Sounds of a season that had already produced more success than any other in franchise history. And, it seemed, a season that could only get better.

"No sense being in a tense mood right now," Jeff Wright said. "These first two days, when we don't normally practice anyway, will be good for relaxing. After that, when we start practicing on Wednesday, it's going to be all business the rest of the week."

There were the usual card games in the back of the plane, with the usual friendly accusations of cheating directed at Frank Reich (yes, Mr. Nice Guy, himself) and assistant trainer Bud Carpenter. Some players, such as Scott Norwood, sat quietly by themselves and read. Others listened to portable tape players or played with miniature video games. Others, especially the ones who had celebrated until the wee hours the night before, slept. Still others took in the movie, *Dick Tracy.*

The frivolity did get a little out of hand at one point when playful wrestling among players resulted in third-string quarterback Gale Gilbert's having the seat torn out of his pants. A flight attendant with a needle and thread tried to help him, but in her rush to beat the landing, she ended up stitching his underwear to his pants.

Finally, at around 7:45 P.M., Pan Am charter Flight 8207 touched down at Tampa International Airport. The Bills had arrived—in more ways then one.

They were at their first Super Bowl, the game's silver anniversary edition, yet were receiving the kind of respect normally reserved for a club that had already been to the big dance several times. Or at least once, like the Giants. Vegas odds-makers, obviously impressed with the 48-point mutilation of the Raiders, installed Buffalo as a 6-point favorite. That was no small honor, considering the AFC's horrendous track record in this annual celebration of pro football. For most of the last decade it had seemed that the only reason an AFC representative was even sent to the Super Bowl was because the NFL needed two teams to play the game. The conference was on a six-year losing streak, by an average score of 40–14, and had won only twice in ten years.

According to conventional wisdom, power-oriented teams featuring strong defense, such as the Giants, were always a better bet against finesse-oriented clubs featuring shoot-'em-up offense, such as the Bills. Dating back to the days when it was NFL versus AFL, the Super Bowl usually came down to a conservative, clock-controlling National team pushing around an undisciplined, let-it-all-hang-out American opponent.

But after watching them score 95 points in two play-off games, the nation's media were as excited as ever about the Bills and their no-huddle attack, declaring they were simply unstoppable. Wrote veteran columnist Gary Shelton of the *St. Petersburg Times:* "No team in football would have beaten the Bills [in the AFC Championship Game]. It's time for the jokes to cease, time for the bleeding to stop. A trend is about to pass. The Buffalo Bills are about to win the Super Bowl." Other writers went as far as to predict that the no-huddle's overwhelming success in the play-offs would revolutionize offenses throughout the NFL.

Not that Downstaters were the least impressed. The typical Giants fan didn't even know where Buffalo was, according to an unscientific survey conducted by *The New York Times* during Super Bowl week. The *Times* asked twenty-five men and women in Manhattan to locate Buffalo on a blank map of the state. Only three came close, still missing by fifty miles. The most common answer put Buffalo in the eastern half, somewhere above Albany. The next most common answer put it east of Rochester—on Lake Ontario instead of on Lake Erie. Like countless others living in the bottom right corner of the same map, those surveyed didn't care what any sportswriters or odds-makers thought. To them there could be only one favorite in a battle pitting the Big Apple against Podunk.

Still, there was no mistaking the confident strut as Bills players headed across the tarmac at Tampa International to the chartered buses that, led by police escort, would carry them to their week-long headquarters, the Tampa Hilton at Metro Center. Not so coincidentally, that had been the Raiders' hotel for the last Tampa Super Bowl, when they beat Washington, 38–9—the Bills were hoping a little silver and black luck, circa 1984, would rub off on them. On the way to the buses they passed in front of a line of wooden barricades behind which about two dozen photographers and TV camera crews stood, capturing their every move.

"Show time!" Bruce Smith and Cornelius Bennett said, while grinning and waving into the lenses. "Iiiit's show time!"

Indeed, the Bills and Buffalo were at center stage of the sporting world's most extravagant production. And they had none other than sixty-two-year-old Marvin Daniel Levy to thank for guiding them there.

It wasn't supposed to have worked out that way, of course. Not according to Levy's critics. They said he was too soft ever to accomplish a feat that men of steel like Shula, Noll, Landry, and Lombardi had accomplished. They said he was too conservative, too inflexible. They said he was too preoccupied with the negative things they were saying and writing to focus on the truly important aspects of his job.

But Levy had overcome a crisis in Miami that easily could have caused the season to come to an abrupt halt long before there ever would have been a need to call out the rottweilers at Rich Stadium. Other than, perhaps, to fend off a lynch mob outside Levy's office.

It wasn't an easy job, being an NFL head coach. Being one in Buffalo was probably harder than in most places, because for one thing, the roster was filled with some of the NFL's more highly paid players. Big paychecks helping to fuel even bigger egos. For another, the area's obsession with the Bills made the head coach's every decision subject to even closer scrutiny than in larger towns where there were other distractions and targets of criticism. Then, of course, there was the city's mentality—Levy liked to call it "the sky is always falling" syndrome. Especially where the Bills were concerned. If things got bad with them, they were automatically expected to get worse. The fans had seen it happen too many times before to think otherwise.

So when, as the Bills were suffering a 30–7 loss to the Dolphins, Bruce Smith tore into Levy on the sidelines of Joe Robbie Stadium (and later in the newspaper), and when Leonard Smith and Nate Odomes and Kirby Jackson ignored for three plays Levy's order to leave the field, it was feared the whole thing was coming apart right then and there. Some observers were reminded of a substitute teacher losing control of a rowdy class. How long before someone gave Levy a hot foot? Which player would tape a "kick me" sign on his butt?

Levy didn't allow any of it to happen. He issued fines. He drew resounding support from the owner. He stood tall, a whole lot taller than 5′10″.

And that, as much as anything, was why the Bills had arrived at Super Bowl XXV.

Darryl Talley remembered the team meeting the day after the Bills returned from Miami, the day Levy grabbed control of the team and never let go. Nodding as he re-created the scene, Talley said, "Marv got up there and told us, 'Here's what we're gonna do, fellas: We're gonna fine guys. And once you get fined, there's nothing else said about it. Period. You start complaining about the fine, then the fine goes up. Got it?' He laid down the law the right way, hitting guys right where it hurt the most. In the wallet. And everybody knew he had to do it. For him, it was a matter of saying, 'OK, guys, look. I understand how you feel. But when I give you a direct order—or any coaches give you a direct order—you best respond to it. If you don't, you suffer the consequences.' "

James Lofton praised Levy for knowing when to be firm and when to step back and allow internal problems, such as those that dominated the 1989 season, outgrow themselves. "Sometimes a coach can react to that sort of thing by stomping on everybody," Lofton said. "But when that happens, then everybody's got pain. Instead, Marv addressed the players and continued to treat everyone as mature adults, even if we weren't acting like it at the time. I really think that helped the guys on this team grow more than anything. And Marv's even more exceptional at deferring the credit as to who did the job. It would be easy for him to stand up and say, 'This is the way I handled this situation, and look what has become of it.' But he doesn't do that."

One of the more critical moves Levy made toward improving the team's harmony and focus was seeing to it that the thirty-four-year-old Lofton had a prominent place on the roster in 1990. That caused some eyebrow raising at first, considering Lofton had made only cameo appearances the year before and looked like a borderline number-three receiver at best. But he regained the form from his superstar days with the Packers, averaging a team-high 20.3 yards on 35 receptions during the regular season. And he proved to be a steadying force in the dressing room.

A classic example of Lofton's deft handling of the squad's psyche came after the play-off victory against the Dolphins. To Lofton the hooting and hollering in the dressing room sounded a bit too loud for a divisional-round triumph. To him, everyone seemed just a bit too pleased with the outcome, even if it had come against the despised "Fish" and the Miami players who had talked all that trash beforehand. So when the room got quiet for the usual postvictory presentation of game balls, Lofton seized the opportunity to bring down the party.

"Remember, guys, what you did today is great and let's all enjoy this," he said, sounding more like a coach than a teammate. "But we still have a long way to go. A *lonnng* way."

Kent Hull, himself viewed as a primary team leader, looked up at Lofton in amazement. Although he prided himself as someone who could maintain his poise during the highest and lowest of times, Hull realized at that moment he, too, had gotten a little too caught up in the euphoria. He couldn't believe Lofton's presence of mind to stop everything and pull everyone back on track.

"For him to be able to think through that high, that incredible element of emotion that was there, says a lot about James," Hull said. "And what he told everybody was right. That had been just one of the hurdles. From the start of the season our goal was not to beat Miami in the first round or win the AFC championship. It was to get to the Super Bowl. And win it. No one left that room feeling down, but subconsciously we knew we had to get right back to work. There was no time to be satisfied."

Never once had Levy allowed himself to be consumed by the Bills fever that swept through Western New York, either during the play-offs or the regular season or during earlier flirtations with greatness. No one would ever see him out hoisting a few with the boys at some crowded sports bar or shaking hands with the corporate honchos at some black-tie affair. For that reason media and fans saw Levy as aloof and dispassionate. They thought he was out of touch with how important the Bills were to Buffalonians. Or, worse, that he didn't care.

Levy offered no apologies for his approach. All through his coaching life he sought to be judged in the only way that he ever thought mattered—by his record.

"I live in a ten-by-thirteen film room," Levy explained. "I get in in the morning, I read the front page of the newspaper, I'll scan the sports section quickly, but other than that, all I want to see is our [practice] script for the day and our game-plan information. I don't mind talking with the fans when I'm out, but after spending sixteen hours a day on football, I don't like to talk about it when I get away from my job. And I hate the 'how we gonna do this week coach?' question. I hate the 'are we gonna kick ass this week?' thinking. It just isn't me. I enjoy the fans, I appreciate them, and I know there is no game without them.

"But I'm not a fan, I'm not a member of the media. I'm a coach. And as a coach there are perspectives you have that are different from those that the fans and the media have. And if you allow their perspectives to seep in I think you'll do a poorer job of coaching. That's because fans and media tend to become too optimistic at times and too pessimistic at times. I feel I'm very emotional about the game. But I also feel I know the things that help me prepare best, and there are certain beliefs I have that I think will help our team prepare best. And I believe they're based on experience and a certain expertise you have in the field. I know that every decision I make along the way will not be borne out and be successful. It just doesn't happen, because there's a guy on the other side of the field making decisions, too. I don't look at a play and say, 'Oh, my gosh! What a brilliant decision I made.' But nor do I say, 'What a dumb decision I made.'

"One of the reasons we've been more successful this year than in the past is that I have not changed. I think changing would have led to us being less successful. If you believe in doing what you think it takes to win, then you believe in it. You don't do something else. Coaching is a very hazardous occupation, in terms of job security, and right from the beginning I made up my mind that if I ever get fired, it's going to be because I'm doing what *I* believe in. I'm not going to get fired because I'm doing what somebody else believes in or thinks you ought to do and you're trying to placate that person."

Which explained why, the day after the Bills arrived in Tampa, Levy missed the first in a series of NFL-mandated appointments with the media. Every year at the Super Bowl, Tuesday morning is designated as Photo Day, with players (in their football uniforms minus pads and helmets) and coaches from each team showing up at the stadium for one hour to be photographed and interviewed by a thousand or more journalists. Every year, for twenty-four years, the head coaches from both participating clubs attended. But Levy broke the streak in 1991, because, on his schedule, every Tuesday during football season was the day he and his assistants put together a game plan. And his schedule had already been thrown off by the packing and traveling the team had done Monday.

The no-show incident, which made headlines in sports pages throughout the country, brought to mind a conversation Levy had had with Ralph Wilson the day he was hired as the Bills' head coach in 1986.

"Ralph asked me how I felt about addressing the local quarterback club on a regular basis," Levy recalled. "I told him I didn't want to, and that the reason was based on what I experienced as head coach at the University of California [1960–63]. That was the worst coaching job I've ever done, because on Monday, over at Joe DiMaggio's restaurant, which was an hour and a half ride up and back, they had the Bay Area media meeting. On Tuesday they had the Oakland Grid Club meeting at noon. On Wednesday they had the Sacramento Grid Club meeting at noon. And, as a coach, you were told you had to attend all these functions because the people running them were raising funds for the school. So I did. But then I'd always end up rushing back into the office and asking the assistant coaches what the game plan is, stay up until three in the morning to catch up on the game plan late in the week, go out on game day knowing the game plan, but feeling tired and not being sure of so many loose ends. And when I got fired at Cal,

I said to myself, 'If it costs me a job in the future, I'm never going to speak at any quarterback clubs or other things of that nature during the season.'

"Ralph said, 'Fine, Marv, I understand. You coach the team and don't worry about the other stuff.' "

However, the NFL wasn't nearly as understanding about Levy's skipping Photo Day. League officials were downright furious, issuing a statement that described the absence as a "clear breach of club obligations." Commissioner Paul Tagliabue was known to be particularly upset, because Giants coach Bill Parcells, despite having traveled all night Sunday from San Francisco to Tampa, showed up on time for the day's first session. Tagliabue had planned to hit Levy with a five-thousand-dollar fine after the season. The next day the coach apologized to reporters, saying he had gotten so immersed in his work that he lost track of the time and decided to continue working on the game plan.

Almost from the instant they set foot in Tampa, most Bills players, unlike their coach, couldn't wait to see firsthand what Super Bowl hype was all about. They thrived on the attention, gobbling it up like children turned loose in a candy store. And they were being turned loose, hailing from the NFL's second-smallest media market and playing on a team that put greater restrictions on media access than most others in the league.

Ray Bentley took one look at the mass of reporters and photographers at sun-splashed but chilly Tampa Stadium, then turned to Shane Conlan and said, "Toto, we're not in Kansas anymore."

The media conscious NFL spread the players throughout the stadium in an organized fashion—offense on one side, defense on the other. The bigger names, such as Jim Kelly and Bruce Smith, were up on the stands where there was more room to accommodate the larger crowds they were expected to draw. The second-tier stars, such as Andre Reed and Darryl Talley, stood on platforms around the field. And those in both locations wore TV-style clip-on microphones wired to amplifiers so no one would miss a word. Meanwhile, other players wandered around until they were stopped to answer a question or pose for a picture.

"I want all the media I can get while I'm here," said Cornelius Bennett. "I won't turn a single reporter down." He was especially happy the Bills were facing the Giants instead of the 49ers. Otherwise, Bennett pointed out, "we would just be the 'other' team here. Everybody would have been talking about a 'three-peat' instead of about us."

"Over the years," said Jim Ritcher, "I had talked to players on other teams who had been to the Super Bowl and they'd try to tell me what all the media attention would be like. Well, no one can prepare you for it. I never thought there would be so many reporters. And I never thought I'd be asked so many questions as an offensive lineman. I mean, who ever talks to us? I figured all I'd have to do each morning was sit back and watch everybody talk to Kelly."

Most of the questions pertained to obvious topics, such as the war in the Persian Gulf, the no-huddle offense, the turnaround of the Bickering Bills, Bruce Smith versus Lawrence Taylor, life in small-town Buffalo, Lofton's renaissance, Bentley's Alice Cooper–style eye black, and the series of children's books he had authored featuring "Darby the Dinosaur."

But the highlight of Photo Day was the presence of Downtown Julie Brown, the curvaceous VJ on MTV who was conducting interviews for the syndicated television show *Inside Edition.* Dressed head-to-toe in black—derby, halter top, skintight skirt ending at midthigh, net stockings, and cowboy boots—she was easily the biggest hit among the players. Not to mention the more conventionally dressed men from the fourth estate. She came armed with questions that were hardly standard fare for Super Bowl week (or any time for that matter), as evidenced by her conversation with Kent Hull.

Brown: "Hello."

Hull (smiling): "Hello there."

Brown: "Can I have your pants?"

Hull's eyes widened and he nearly spit out his chaw of tobacco. Given that the temperature had dipped to an un–Florida-like 43 degrees, his refusal to part with his pants was understandable. But Brown wasn't too upset, giving the 275-pound center an unsolicited but welcome rubdown of his biceps to ward off the chill.

She then sidled up to Leonard Burton, an offensive lineman who had been on injured reserve since the season began, and gently bit him on the chest. "I'm never washing this jersey again," Burton said, smiling broadly. "No way am I wearing this on game day."

The pint-sized Brown also was the only media type there that any player lifted and cradled in his arms while responding to questions—Butch Rolle did it first, followed by Dwight Drane. And she was the only one there who gave herself permission—without the slightest resistance—to fondle players' buttocks. In her thick British accent Brown offered a perspective that likely wasn't heard from anyone else covering the game: "All I know is there will be some fine buns on that pitch [field] on Sunday."

Before Photo Day ended a few Bills players couldn't resist the temptation to charge onto the playing field—which, having been freshly striped and painted with logos, was supposed to be off-limits until game day. A burly security guard watched nervously, not quite knowing how to tell some of the stars of the show that they had to exit their stage. After stammering for several seconds he finally turned up his palms and said, "Guys, would ya gimme a break. Please?" They did and trotted off without any fuss, to which the relieved guard responded, "Thanks."

The next two mornings would bring two more of these large media gatherings for both teams, at separate hotels, and Bills players would continue to have to be practically dragged from the microphones—even those not held by Downtown Julie Brown. Besides her request for Hull's pants, the week's other unlikely question was directed toward Bruce Smith by a Japanese reporter.

"The people in Japan only know Buffalo as the place [to which] they fly to get to Niagara Falls," he said. "Will you be able to show people in Japan that there is more to Buffalo than just the place they go to get to Niagara Falls?"

Putting his best cleat forward for the Buffalo Area Chamber

of Commerce, Smith didn't hesitate with his answer: "Yes. Definitely."

Once the players took to the practice field it felt like a fairly routine week. Except for what they found overflowing from their lockers before each workout: brand new Super Bowl XXV hats, T-shirts, sweatshirts, sweat suits, gym bags, shoes, and other commemorative merchandise, all compliments of the league and its sponsors. "It's like Christmas morning every time you open the door," a stunned Jim Ritcher said after the first practice. "I don't even know how I'm going to get all this stuff home. I guess I'll have to buy another suitcase."

A few players were so excited about slipping into their new duds, they walked around with the tags dangling from their sleeves and backs.

"Our practices have gone very well," Levy would say by the end of the week. "I was impressed by how the players have come to work and the atmosphere that took over the locker room when they came to work. And I'll say it again: I've never been with a football team that prepares itself better than this group. That's the biggest reason why we're here."

Marv Levy certainly had his hands full preparing a Super Bowl game plan, but Jim Kelly also carried his share of the pregame burden.

Everyone spoke, as Levy did, about the team having one more river to cross, and that was true. In Kelly's case, however, the victory over the Raiders meant he no longer had a cross to bear. All the excitement generated by his joining the Bills from the United States Football League on August 18, 1986, was based on one simple fact: with Kelly the Bills would eventually reach the Super Bowl. Period. It was something most of their fans were counting on, not hoping for. It was why thousands of them stood on overpasses and hung from windows to get a glimpse of Kelly as his black stretch-limousine headed from the airport to a press conference in the grand ballroom of the Buffalo Hilton. Kelly's mere utterance of "Super Bowl" brought a rousing ovation from the many fans who had joined the media at the coronation-style press conference. And it sent sparks flying throughout Western New

York, causing fans to return to the ticket windows they had all but deserted through the Bills' 2–14 seasons in 1984 and 1985.

The question, of course, was when would Kelly make good on his end of the $8-million deal he received that day? The 4–12 season the following year was disappointing but understandable; everyone knew the Bills still had plenty of other repairs to make besides quarterback. And it was still better than 2–14. The 7–8 finish in the strike-shortened 1987 season was acceptable because the Bills showed signs of improvement, particularly on defense, but Kelly hadn't wowed fans quite as much as he had in his "rookie" year. Then the Bills went 12–4 in 1988, and that, most of their followers figured, would be the year. Except it was defense that carried the brunt of the load; Kelly and the offense were inconsistent. And they did their worst flubbing at the least opportune time—against the Bengals in the AFC Championship Game.

From then on doubts began forming about Kelly's ability to win the big game and about his development as a quarterback. Although blessed with a great arm, he appeared to be slow at reading coverages and seemed to make as many poor decisions as good ones. The offense simply didn't have the spark that it was expected to have with Kelly and his howitzer arm. All the while, his off-the-field image took a beating. He was seen as a player who was much quicker at dispensing blame than accepting it. His happiness in Buffalo—which he had harshly criticized after the Bills made him a first-round draft pick from the University of Miami in 1983, then shunned for the USFL's Houston Gamblers—was questioned, as was Buffalo's happiness with him.

Then came 1989 and the Bickering Bills. Kelly was making strides as a quarterback, but they were lost, first because of a separated shoulder that sidelined him for three games, and then because of his involvement in the team's internal problems—of which he was viewed as a leading cause. Then there was his late-season, three-game slump that contributed heavily to the Bills' losing the home-field advantage in postseason play. And even in his most brilliant moment of that season, the play-off game against Cleveland, there was the lasting memory of his goal-line interception after Ronnie Harmon made The Drop.

But in 1990, after receiving a $20-million contract extension, Kelly did all the right things on the field and said all the right things off it. He took his game and his career to the top of the league. Of course, he had always come off sounding like God's gift to quarterbacking, which had caused some eyes to roll. But now there was no argument. Kelly kept asking, begging Levy for offensive freedom. He finally received it, in the form of the no-huddle. And once Kelly started calling his own plays, moving the offense at his own rapid pace, he proceeded to set the NFL on fire.

"I'm just enjoying playing the game of football," the $3-million-per-year man said. "They're paying me to have fun."

Before suffering a knee injury against the Giants on December 15, Kelly's "fun" included a team-record completion percentage of 63.3. His touchdown-pass-to-interception ratio was a career best 24 to 9. And his 101.2 quarterback rating was tops in the NFL. But Kelly's statistics for the two play-off games, when the great quarterbacks are supposed to shine, were really what spoke volumes of his progress: 36 completions in 52 passes (69.2 percent), 639 yards, 5 touchdowns, and 2 interceptions. Not to mention the Bills' 95 points.

After spending the better part of sixty minutes quickly tossing around a football he'd stand before the press and quickly toss around praise to his teammates, often including the defense (which he had never hesitated to criticize in the past) and special teams. And he'd speak of Ted Marchibroda as a father figure, as well as his offensive coordinator, something he had never done with any previous Bills coach. His views on Buffalo? They've changed dramatically from the time, in 1983, when he claimed he'd never have success passing late in the season in the wintry conditions at Rich Stadium.

"It's not anywhere near as bad as everybody in other cities says it is," Kelly said, sounding like another advertisement for the Chamber. "In the summer it's beautiful. In the winter it's cold, sure. But it's also cold in places like New York City, Pittsburgh, and Cincinnati. We just get a little more snow in

Buffalo. But I'll tell you, I'd rather take that snow for a game than some of the windy days we've had in other stadiums. And the other thing that's great about it is, when we play a Miami or the Raiders, we're always going to have the edge in that stuff. It's Buffalo Bills weather."

For a kid who grew up in East Brady, Pennsylvania, a town of eight hundred in the heart of Steelers country, there were plenty of Super Bowls to watch with a rooting interest. And there were the many fantasies they produced, especially when he was a high school quarterback.

"Seeing Terry Bradshaw, Franco Harris, Lynn Swann, and those guys playing in a Super Bowl, I'd say, 'Maybe one of these days, I'll get my chance,'" Kelly recalled. "Well, my chance has come. It's something that I relish and I thank God that it's happened."

His Buffalo teammates, particularly those who lived through the nightmares of 2–14, thank God Kelly eventually signed with the Bills.

"Ever since he came here, I think the Bills have gained a lot of confidence from him," Jim Ritcher said. "We've never felt we were out of any ball game with him. Even the first Miami game this year, I thought, with Jim on our side, we still had a chance to come back on them."

Kelly had also learned to bite his tongue more often around the media, but he hadn't lost the brash, bold playboy image he brought with him from the USFL. His romantic exploits still included women such as Sandi Korn, the *Penthouse* magazine "pet" who was scheduled to be at the Super Bowl as his guest. He still wore sunglasses every day, even when it was cloudy. And he found time, between media and practice demands, to have a little fun, Kelly style. His second night in Tampa he was a guest judge, along with Lawrence Taylor, for a nightclub's amateur topless contest. There were Kelly sightings at other hotspots around town the next two nights—make that early mornings—before Levy imposed an eleven P.M. curfew, as planned before the Bills left Buffalo.

"I'm single and I enjoy my nightlife," Kelly said, shrugging as always to questions about his conduct away from the game. "But like everyone else, I know there's work to be done, and

I'll stay focused, just like I always do. This isn't a pleasure trip, this is a business trip.

"The object is to win the Super Bowl, not just show up. A lot of teams get the chance to play in the Super Bowl. But twenty years down the road I don't want people to say, 'Oh, Buffalo was in it, BUT . . .' We have one more river to cross."

But Kelly no longer had a cross to bear.

The no-huddle offense was Kelly's baby, to be certain. But as much as he might have tried with the "Skillet Left" play against the Dolphins, he couldn't do the catching as well as the throwing. That was left to the phenomenal talent around him, whose hands and feet, as much as Kelly's right arm, made the no-huddle so deadly.

The number-one member of Kelly's supporting cast was Thurman Thomas, the NFL's most productive running back. He was the one who gave the no-huddle its ambushing effect, because in a rapid-fire succession of plays he could break a game wide open as a receiver as well as a runner. He could dart into openings in the secondary one minute, explode through cracks in the line the next.

Sure, Andre Reed had played a critical role, catching 71 passes in the regular season for 945 yards and 8 touchdowns, and getting 6 more receptions in the playoffs for 151 yards and 2 touchdowns. Sure, Reed's consistency in making the tough over-the-middle grab and tearing upfield for large gains was a key to the no-huddle's effectiveness. And, James Lofton, the home-run hitter, and Keith McKeller, the wide receiver in a tight end's body, were important, too. But their success, to a great extent, was dictated by Thomas's presence. The extra attention he drew on every down as a running/receiving threat helped open things up for everyone else.

The most telling proof of what Thomas meant to Buffalo's quick-strike attack had come in the AFC Championship Game. In the first thirty minutes, when the contest offered its only hope of competitiveness, the 5'10", 198-pound Thomas handled the ball on more than half of the Bills' plays and gained 170 yards. He ran 20 times for 109 yards and picked up 61 more on 5 receptions.

More proof: After being frustrated by Thomas in the first quarter of their 17–13 loss to the Bills on December 15, the Giants became the first and only team all season to assign a linebacker (Taylor) specifically to follow him, which he did through the balance of the game. "I don't think we need to change anything if that happens this time," said Thomas, who in the two play-off games had amassed 255 yards on 57 carries and 99 yards on 8 receptions. "If they're going to put one guy on me, somebody's going to be on man-to-man coverage. With the players we have, we should be able to exploit whatever they give us."

"I'll tell you," said Andre Reed, "when Thurman first came here, I thought he was just a runner. But he has turned into probably the most versatile back in the league. Not only does he take pressure off me, but off James and Keith, too."

The most pressure, however, was removed from Kelly, because with Thomas he always had an effective dump-off target. In an offense relying so heavily on snap decisions that was an invaluable option. "I've been an outlet for Jim all season," Thomas explained. "That's one of the things we always work on in practice—my telling him where I'm going to be all the time in case he wants to use me as an outlet."

The remarks were much more than Xs-and-Os talk. They underscored just how far the team had come since 1989, when Thomas became one of Kelly's more vocal critics and brought to a boil the Year of the Bickering Bills. He did what he believed was right in standing up for Howard Ballard after Kelly's public criticism of the lovable offensive tackle. And despite the additional problems it caused, Thomas didn't regret the decision.

"I knew Kelly was King Stud on the team, but I wasn't going to let that bother me, because that's the way I am," he said. During Thomas's freshman season at Oklahoma State, star defensive end Leslie O'Neal ripped a young teammate mercilessly during a practice before the Gator Bowl. Afterward Thomas walked up to the 6′4″, 260-pound O'Neal, tilted his head back, and told him what he had done was wrong. At first Thomas wasn't certain if he had just signed his own death warrant. However, he and O'Neal worked things out and have been friends ever since. The same was true between him and Kelly.

"Thurman became a team leader that day," former Bills running back and Hall of Famer O. J. Simpson pointed out. "He took on Goliath, and I think he gained a lot of respect from teammates who had grown tired of Jim's finger-pointing. Thurman is a self-assured individual. He's not a guy who will be intimidated.

"The guy also knows how to run. Most backs don't have the understanding of the game that Thurman does. He's what I call an educated runner. And like all the great runners he expects to go the distance every time he touches the ball. Some backs, like Herschel Walker, break into the open and it's like they are surprised. They can't believe they are there. Thurman expects to be there. He's surprised when he's not."

In the first two scoring drives against the Giants on December 15, Thomas accounted for 100 yards. Then Kelly left the game with a knee injury. Although he finished with 60 yards rushing and 65 more on four receptions, Thomas wondered what kind of day he'd have had with Kelly going the distance. "It will be very interesting to see what happens this time, now that Jim's healthy," Thomas said. "Because when Frank runs the no-huddle, it's more of a slowed down no-huddle. When Jim runs it, every time we run a play and turn around, he's right back at the line of scrimmage calling another play. And that kind of throws the defense off, because they can't get their signals in as quickly as they want to."

When the Giants first arrived in Tampa they displayed a sort of quiet confidence. They were emotionally drained from the NFC Championship Game and, perhaps, a little humbled by the manner in which they had beaten the 49ers. It had required a gift, Roger Craig's late fumble, and a field goal by Matt Bahr that had just barely cleared the inside of the left upright with four ticks on the clock. It was an unlikely victory against a team that was supposed to reach and win its third consecutive Super Bowl. The Giants knew they had stumbled into the path of history.

But after four days of listening to questions about Buffalo's being favored by a touchdown and the Bills' no-huddle offense being impossible to stop, enough was enough. The Giants' confidence grew significantly louder. They became outspoken, almost brash, about their chances of defeating the Bills in Super Bowl XXV.

It began with Taylor. Earlier in the week, in answering one of the umpteenth queries about the comparison between him and Bruce Smith, he sounded cordial enough, saying, "Right now, Bruce Smith is the best defensive player in the league. And I think he's getting better. I have nothing against Bruce. I think he's the greatest. But it's just like anything else. About five years from now, somebody else is going to be calling himself the best. So it's all relative."

Where the game's outcome and the Giants' proud defensive reputation were concerned, however, Taylor forgot all about diplomacy. Although he wasn't the first Bills opponent to dismiss the notion that the no-huddle couldn't be stopped, he made the ears of more than a few scribes perk up when he said, "We all have confidence Bill Parcells will find a way for us to win this game." In other words, Parcells, a noted defensive mastermind, and Bill Belichick, the Giants' highly regarded defensive coordinator, weren't going to be outsmarted twice in a row by some new-fangled offensive strategy. Taylor added, "If you look at the film, you say, 'Wow! You can't stop these guys.' But I know this defense and I know what this Super Bowl means to our guys. And we'll find a way to stop them. That's all there is to it."

Pepper Johnson was even more emphatic than his fellow linebacker in talking down the no-huddle's effectiveness. "We would have to have seven guys break legs and everybody else come out totally unprepared in order for a team to score forty-four or fifty-one points against us," he said. "Right now I don't see anybody just marching the ball up and down the field on us."

Another Giants linebacker, Gary Reasons, pointed out that the Bills got off to a fast start the last time the teams met. But he also thought the Giants' defense was quick to catch up. "We got better as the game went on," he said. "I think we caught up to them in the second half, in the second quarter even. So the important thing this time is to come out and play better early."

"We were like number one or number two all year long defensively," said cornerback Everson Walls. "And it's like it hasn't meant anything at all to the so-called experts. For some reason, no one recognized that coming up to the 49er game, either."

The Giants' coaches, whose team shared the NFL's second-best record with Buffalo at 13–3, sounded as fed up as their players with what they saw as a media-manufactured impression that the game was over, that their team might as well get an early start on packing. They were also tired of hearing about all the mystique surrounding the no-huddle.

"I don't think it's a revolutionary thing," Belichick said. "All the no-huddle does is put a lot of stress on your defensive communication and you don't have very much time to recognize some of the things they're doing. So what you have to do is be ready to play defense just like they're ready to play offense. Once the ball is snapped, now you're talking about football between the lines as we all know it. Up to that point, you have to have everything coordinated. They don't run any different patterns, they still have seven men on the line and five eligible receivers. It's just getting to that point."

Said Parcells: "What we're talking about is a two-minute offense; that's all the no-huddle is. It can be a little unsettling, sure. We just have to prepare for it and do the best we can. But let me tell you something: The no-huddle isn't going to win the game. The athletes running it are what wins games."

In the Bills' regular-season victory over the Giants, Buffalo's offensive athletes ran circles around the opposition. Many of the New York defenders were doubled over in exhaustion, their huffing and puffing visible in the cold air, as Kelly drove the Bills to a pair of lightning-quick touchdowns on their first two possessions.

"Fatigue does set in," defensive end Leonard Marshall admitted. "So the key to controlling the no-huddle is to recognize the formations, make good adjustments, and play the play. Then, once the play is over, forget about it. The big thing is to prepare and react to the situation, which is what defense is all about, rather than scrambling around." The Giants anticipated facing the no-huddle in the regular-season game, but they weren't counting on seeing it as much as they did and were, they felt, underprepared. This time they would be ready for a full, four-quarter dose.

Marshall had made one of the more decisive plays with 9:41 left in the NFC Championship Game when he blindsided Joe Montana, knocking him out of the game with a broken bone in his right hand, broken ribs, and a concussion. Marshall promised to be no gentler with Kelly, saying, "He's going to see pressure like he's never seen before."

The Giants also had reason to believe they could show the Bills a ball-control offensive attack they hadn't seen previously either. At least not since December 15, when the Giants churned out 157 yards on 42 carries (an average of 3.7 yards per carry) while holding a 37:59 to 22:01 advantage in possession time. Ottis Anderson, the ageless wonder, led New York in rushing with 784 yards on 225 carries during the regular season and seemed as spry as ever in the play-offs with a team-leading 147 yards on 41 attempts. He realized his role in defusing the no-huddle was every bit as vital as his teammates' on the other side of the line. Because as long as the Giants had the ball, Kelly didn't.

"If we shorten the game up, keep it close, who knows what the outcome will be?" Anderson said. "I do know this: I think we're going to do well. I think we're going to surprise a lot of people. Nobody gives us a chance."

The teams were in Tampa. Many of the out-of-town fans, who held the majority of the tickets, were already there or on the way. Super Bowl week was progressing at a steady pace, but still the question was asked: With the continuation of the Persian Gulf war, should the game be played?

NFL officials pondered it by the hour, if not the minute. But all along the green light shined. Said Joe Browne, the league's director of communications: "We expect to play the game, but we will take events in the Middle East into account right up to kickoff. We recognize that the American people will not be paralyzed by the events in the Middle East, but the words 'priorities' and 'perspective' are important during Super Bowl XXV activities."

Which was why, in the interest of good taste, one of the first war-related moves made by the league was canceling its glitziest event of the week—the annual commissioner's party, at which three thousand media and advertising friends of the NFL, along with celebrities and would-be celebrities in and out of football, are lavishly wined, dined, and otherwise entertained. A number of smaller Super Bowl celebrations were also called off, but that still left plenty to go around. Seeking the proper balance between sports and the real world would be no easy task at an event that had a long history of trying to outdo itself.

It was especially difficult for Tampa mayor Sandra W. Freedman. For one thing, her city was home to numerous members of the armed forces in the Middle East, who had been deployed from MacDill Air Force Base. For another, General Norman Schwarzkopf, commander of U.S. forces in the Persian Gulf, was a Tampa resident. "I think the community believes the game should go on," Mayor Freedman said. "Certainly we should make sure appropriate reverence takes place. But we also have to have some normalcy in our lives, and the Super Bowl is part of our lives."

The threat of terrorism, which created an air of tension around the conference championship games, was an even larger concern during Super Bowl week. As a result, unprecedented security measures were taken for the game. There was around-the-clock security at Tampa Stadium, which was sealed off January 16, the day the war began. Since then two temporary fences had been erected outside the permanent fence around the stadium. The first consisted of portable concrete barriers placed at the extreme edge of the grounds. The second was a six-foot chain-link fence placed about fifty feet from the permanent one.

No vehicle could enter without being thoroughly searched, and on game day no aircraft within a half-mile of the stadium could fly below ten thousand feet. Metal detectors were installed at all sixty-eight gates, and no fans would be permitted to carry portable radios, televisions, camcorders, or still cameras. The game-day security force of more than two thousand strong would be looking into coats, purses, and any packages fans might bring along. Even something as seemingly harmless as a soft drink or a bag of potato chips had to be left outside.

It would be a time-consuming process, so ticket holders and media were warned to show up several hours early—lest they wanted to risk missing the opening kickoff.

The war wasn't the only distraction in the Bills' camp. A few days before the game Bruce Smith learned his father, George, was admitted to a hospital in the player's hometown of Norfolk, Virginia, because of a breathing problem. "He had a breathing attack just putting on his shirt to sit around the house; that's all he was doing," a somber Smith said. His father's history of heart trouble added to the concern.

Smith's family had tried to avoid telling him about the incident, which landed his father in intensive care, so it wouldn't take his mind off preparing for the Giants. But he sensed something was wrong during a phone conversation with his mother and she could conceal it no longer. "It seems as though, when something goes good for a person, something else always seems to go bad," Smith said. "At one point in time I thought that when we were coming down here things would be so great and so wonderful and I was going to be on top of the world. But not when my father's in the condition he's in. I had wanted him to be here to experience this with me, but in that condition he can barely talk, let alone travel. So he's home and that's where my heart is."

Leon Seals, the Bills' other defensive end, wasn't part of the Photo Day festivities. He was in Baton Rouge, Louisiana, attending his mother's funeral. Seals arrived in Tampa the next day.

In addition to the heavy hearts being felt by two of the defensive front three, there was also the growing anxiety of other players, such as Carlton Bailey, with relatives serving in the Persian Gulf. Asked if he worried the team was being besieged by too many outside concerns before a game that would require the highest levels of concentration, Levy said, "When you're in a business with fifty or more people these type of personal problems happen all year. It's very unfortunate for the players involved. We commiserate with them, but it's part of life."

There was one positive distraction that week: Darryl Talley's last-minute selection to the first Pro Bowl of his eight-year career. He was the handpicked choice of Art Shell, who as the losing coach in the AFC Championship Game would guide the conference's all-star squad in Honolulu a week after Super Bowl XXV.

Season after season Talley had playfully referred to himself as the "Rodney Dangerfield of NFL linebackers," the one who never got any respect. But when he was overlooked in the 1990 voting he was reduced to tears. He figured that 1990 had been his best and last chance to ever be recognized beyond Buffalo as one of the premier players at his position.

A month later Talley was crying tears of joy. He had found even more satisfaction making the Pro Bowl this way, because "it's the ultimate compliment that a player can receive from a coach. I mean, he had the opportunity to take any other player in the conference, including someone from his own team. And he selected me."

Not that the choice could have been very difficult. After all, Talley intercepted 2 passes (returning one 27 yards for a touchdown) against Shell's Raiders in the AFC Championship Game. He was credited also with 5 tackles, including 4 initial hits, and a pass defense. His regular-season numbers—highlighted by a team-leading 123 tackles, including 79 first stops—were too impressive to ignore. "Darryl Talley is a great player," said Shell. "He should have been voted to play in the Pro Bowl in the first place."

Realizing what the honor would mean to Talley, Walt Corey, the Bills' defensive coordinator, decided to have a little fun while giving him the good news. Talley was in his hotel room, taking a shower, when the phone rang.

"Hello?" the drenched linebacker said, holding a towel around his waist.

"Darryl, it's Walt, and I've got some news that you're probably going to want to hear," Corey said, trying to sound as somber as possible.

"What is it, Walt? What's wrong?"

Corey began to snicker.

"Come on! I just ran out of the shower and I'm dripping wet. So what the hell's going on?"

"Well, Darryl . . ."

"What? Tell me, Walt!" Talley said, growing angrier by the second.

"I just wanted to let you know that Art Shell just picked you to play in the Pro Bowl next week."

At first Talley went numb. He didn't say a word.

"Well?" Corey said, expecting to hear yelling and screaming at the other end of the line.

"Man! That's the only word that comes into my head right now. Just, man!"

After drying off and dressing Talley walked into the hall. The first person he spotted was his fellow outside linebacker, Cornelius Bennett, who in December had been voted to the Pro Bowl for the second time in his three-and-a-half-year career. Bennett had heard the news about Talley already. Without saying a word he threw his arms around his teammate.

Of course, no one could have been happier than Bruce Smith, who was heading to his fourth consecutive Pro Bowl. Besides the campaigning he had done for himself to become NFL Defensive Player of the Year, Smith rarely missed a chance to plug Talley for Pro Bowl recognition. "He deserved it more than anybody in the league," Smith said. "I've been talking about it not just this season, but for the past three or four years as well. Finally somebody listened. God bless Art Shell."

Like Corey, James Lofton couldn't resist giving Talley some good-natured ribbing.

"Hey, Darryl," he said with mock seriousness during the Bills' final mass media session of the week. "I just want to know one thing."

"What's that?" Talley replied.

"I just want to know what your new act's going to be."

"What do you mean?"

"Well, you can't do anymore Rodney Dangerfield imitations."

Talley smiled. But he knew that the end of Super Bowl week was neither the time nor the place to be consumed by personal euphoria. "I have to put all of this aside, because Sunday is the most important game of our careers," he said. "And I'm hungry for the same thing I've been hungry for ever since I got into the league—a Super Bowl ring."

Bill Parcells was also hungry—hungry to adorn a second finger with the ultimate Super Bowl souvenir. He picked up the first ring in Super Bowl XXI with the Giants' 39–20 victory over Denver. Ever since he had been absorbed by the need to return to the game of games. This wasn't simple desire; this was addiction.

"After you've been there, I can just tell you this: Getting back is all you want to do," Parcells said. "As a coach, once you've been there, nothing else is going to satisfy you. It's hard to explain the feeling, but it's inside of you. More than ever you're determined to get back and win another one. I guess it's just one of those insatiable things that keeps you going."

The day after arriving in Tampa he had a phone conversation with his close friend Bob Knight, whose Indiana basketball team had captured three NCAA championships. Speaking from experience Knight guaranteed Parcells that each subsequent title would, in the Giant coach's mind, dwarf its predecessor. By a lot.

"Bobby Knight told me, 'You're going to want that second one even more than the first one,' and he was right," Parcells said. "Then he said, 'After you've won the second one, the third one's going to be the most satisfying of them all.' Our fans in New York? Oh, yeah, we've got them nice and spoiled now, too."

In Buffalo the fans might have been happy about the Bills' 13–3 regular-season record. They might have been excited about their third consecutive AFC Eastern Division title. They might have even been a little giddy about their 48-point rout of the Raiders for the conference championship.

But spoiled? Not by a long shot. This journey to the other side of the rainbow had taken twenty-five years. Old and young, Bills fans had been through a lot. They were taking absolutely nothing for granted.

Spoiled?

Officers of the Buffalo Bills Backers, Ron and Peggy Lavey had no intention of staying home and having Al Michaels, Frank Gifford, Dan Dierdorf, and ABC's cameras give them a long-distance perspective of their team's dream shot. They had to witness it for themselves, firsthand. And after shelling out three hundred dollars for a pair of tickets they were forced to economize on transportation. So, for $179 round trip, they rode a train from Buffalo to Orlando, sitting up the entire way. Said Peggy: "We hope not, but what if this was the only time the Bills ever get to the Super Bowl? No way could we not be there."

Spoiled?

David Champlin, who had recently graduated from college, wasn't going to miss the game for the world, either. Especially since he felt, in his own small way, a part of the Bills as a member of the crew that raised the nets for field goals and extra points at Rich Stadium. There was only one problem, though. Champlin didn't have the money to finance his trip to Tampa. The solution? He sold a collection of hockey cards he had been keeping since childhood for six hundred dollars. "It wasn't a hard decision at all," Champlin said. "The Super Bowl is the biggest day in Buffalo sports history."

Spoiled?

Super Bowl XXV happened to fall on the wedding anniversary of another Bills fan who refused to allow the game to pass without his being on the scene. But while he would be sitting in Tampa Stadium the Mrs. would be back home in Buffalo. His explanation? "Hey, I've known the Bills a hell of a lot longer than I've known my wife."

Many Bills fanatics came down in groups, such as the gang of nearly two hundred from a bar in South Buffalo called Mudd McGrath's. Among the contingent was Mudd himself, and friends named Moose, Animal, and Hugger. Just a bunch of burly, beer-drinking, chicken-wing-chomping guys who represented the salt-of-the-earth quality found among typical Buffalonians. The *Tampa Tribune* ran a large color photo of a dozen group members wearing bathing suits that showed off their girth to the fullest, as they plunged feet first into a hotel swimming pool. All the while holding up copies of a fake front page from *The Buffalo News* that said: "BUFFALO BILLS WIN SUPER BOWL!"

"We're not Adonises," Mudd said. "We're just down here to drink some beer, tell a few lies, get away from the cold and snow—and see a Bills win."

A blue-collar town rooting for a blue-collar team at its finest hour.

Even if their salaries were slightly higher than the average assembly-line worker, the Bills players were very much in tune with their following. They understood there couldn't be one without the other.

"Wearing a championship ring is more important to me than anything else in the world," said Jim Kelly. "Because it's not just for Jim Kelly and it's not just for the forty-four other players who suit up with me every week. It's for the fan support we have. Everybody says bad things about Buffalo, but you can look anywhere in the country and you'll never find greater fans than the people there. Eighty thousand of them show up every week, whether it's five degrees or seventy-five. So this game is not just for the forty-five players out there; it's for the whole city."

"Buffalo deserves a Super Bowl championship more than any other town in the world," said Bruce Smith. "The people there have gone through so many years of being down. We've worked hard and long to help put them back on their feet again. I truly believe the heart of Buffalo is the Buffalo Bills. And this is an opportunity for each and every one of us to show the whole nation what we can do. We're greedy. We want it all. We don't want seconds, we don't want leftovers. We want it all."

"Our fans are the best in the league," added Darryl Talley. "Now, we want our team to be, too."

• • •

On Sunday morning, January 27, there were no wake-up calls to the players' rooms at the Tampa Hilton at Metro Center. With an early evening kickoff they all had permission to sleep in. The majority did. The hardest part would be the wait, so most figured that the longer they stayed in bed, the shorter the time between getting up and playing the game.

There was the usual chapel service offered to the team and its traveling party at the hotel. There was the usual late pregame meal, also at the hotel, featuring spaghetti, baked potatoes, and other foods high in carbohydrates. And at about 2:30 P.M. there was the usual bus ride.

Except, of course, that this was no usual destination. It was Super Bowl XXV. It was the Big Show, the Big Dance, the realization of many years of hopes and dreams—theirs and those of a city fifteen hundred miles to the north. And because it was the Super Bowl and because it was being played under the tightest security in the game's history, the bus followed a police escort for the short trip to Tampa Stadium.

The players were generally quiet. That was the time each usually spent focusing on his own piece of the overall puzzle, whether it meant running down a mental checklist of what to do and when to do it or picturing the big throw, big catch, big run, big block, big tackle, big kick he knew he was going to make. And through it all they tried to maintain the professional poise that had helped get them where they were—the internal strength that had made the difference in their consecutive miracle comeback victories in the regular season and would be crucial that night. The Bills were appearing in their first Super Bowl; the Giants, their second. Only twice in the ten previous matchups that pitted a returning team against a first-timer had the first-timer won. Lack of poise was usually to blame.

Still, several players couldn't help but feel at least a little bit of a tingle when, as they approached the stadium, the bus became swallowed in a mob of fans. Those supporting the Bills yelled and screamed, pointing to the team logo on their caps and stretching it out from the front of their shirts. Those supporting the Giants yelled and screamed, too—but they were giving thumbs down and other not-so-polite gestures. It took almost as long for the bus to cover the remaining distance to the player entrance as it had, whizzing behind the police escort, to get from the hotel to the stadium. "Oh, it was unbelievable," Ray Bentley said. "Those people were just going crazy, getting pumped up for the game. And when I got off the bus, I was psyched and ready to go, myself, right then and there."

Until he looked at his watch and saw that kickoff was still more than three and a half hours away. The emotions would have to remain bottled a bit longer.

Meanwhile, thanks to intensive security checks, waiting was also the name of the game for the 73,813 fans. Waiting on lines that were blocks long. Waiting in the hottest, stickiest heat of the week. Waiting to be scanned, one by one, by a metal detector. Waiting to be told (in case they hadn't been listening the first ten thousand times) that amenities such as umbrellas, coolers, bottles, cans, transistor radios, and portable televisions were not allowed.

Waiting . . . and waiting . . . and waiting.

However, as Bills fan Wally Megger, from Lackawanna, New York, reasoned, "Hey, we've waited twenty-five years for this game. What's another couple of hours?"

Regardless of the outcome this would forever be remembered as the Super Bowl played against the backdrop of war. And, as its organizers had been saying from the very start, it was going to be played. "The only way it would be called off is if there is an indication of terrorist activity right in Tampa, confirmed by the FBI," Tampa Bay Buccaneers owner Hugh Culverhouse had told *USA Today* two days before the game.

Yet, one couldn't help but notice the armed SWAT teams standing on the stadium roof. Nor could one miss the U.S. Customs helicopter gunship circling overhead. And whenever that high-tech aircraft, capable of engaging with any other high-tech aircraft that might have been looking to stage a real live *Black Sunday* wasn't seen, it was heard. A constant, eerie hum that would go on throughout the night, reminding everyone that what they were watching on the field was only a game.

Just like the week before at Rich Stadium the stands were awash in red, white and blue, as fans waved the four-by-six-inch flags found inside each seat cushion. By contrast, with the biggest opening kickoff of their lives inching closer and closer, things were far more subdued in the Bills' dressing room. "It was definitely more quiet than normal," said team publicist Scott Berchtold. "You could tell, just looking around the room, that it was a different game at a different level. I wouldn't say it was quiet enough to hear a pin drop, but you definitely could have heard a nail."

At long last it was time for player introductions. The Bills were designated the visitor, and each member of their starting defense was called out from the tunnel at the southeast corner of the stadium, running between two columns of Buffalo Jills cheerleaders. "Let me tell you," Bentley said. "I flew out of that tunnel, I was so whacked out of my mind with excitement. I don't know if my feet ever touched the ground. That was, to say the least, the pinnacle of my career, being introduced before the Super Bowl."

The cheering was loud, but with downstate New Yorkers holding about a sixty–forty edge in attendance it would get noticeably louder when the Giants' offensive starters came out. Nevertheless, the mere sight of Bills players gathering at midfield was enough to bring Alice Winslow, a longtime fan from North Buffalo, to tears. "All I could think about was sitting in the rain at Rich Stadium when they were two and fourteen," she said. "I was just so proud to actually see them in the Super Bowl. They deserved it. We deserved it."

But the emotional high point came shortly thereafter, during Whitney Houston's moving rendition of the national anthem (even if, for those in the stadium, it had been Memorex and not Whitney herself). The combination of the song, the images of troops in the Middle East flashing on the giant TV screens, and the air force jets that thundered overhead when the music stopped didn't leave many dry eyes in the house, regardless of one's rooting interest.

The Bills had the ball first and opened with their no-huddle. However, unlike their two play-off games, they failed to score.

Not only that, they went three and out. They were, much to the surprise of anyone who had watched them in the last part of the season, unable to put a dent in the Giants' defense, which began the game in nickel coverage with five defensive backs and three linebackers.

Starting at their 31, the Giants pounded away in typically methodical fashion on the ensuing drive, which began with Darryl Talley picking up an offsides penalty. Jeff Hostetler, an unlikely Super Bowl quarterback, kept them moving with an even mix of runs and passes, converting a third-and-seven from the Buffalo 31 with a 16-yard throw to Mark Ingram. Two more plays moved them to the 11. Then, after a third-down incomplete, Matt Bahr, hero of the NFC Championship Game, kicked a 28-yard field goal. Despite coming away with only three points though, the Giants sent a message with the 11-play, 6:15 march: "Unless you stop us, we're going to sit on this ball all night long."

When the Bills took over from their 29, Jim Kelly was now facing a dime package, with six defensive backs and only two down linemen. After a 2-yard run by Thurman Thomas up the middle, the Bills' no-huddle drew its first major mismatch of the game when James Lofton wound up one-on-one with nickel back Perry Williams. Lofton easily broke into the clear down the left sideline. The pass was underthrown, and in one of the flukier plays in Super Bowl history, the ball bounced off Williams's right fingertips and into Lofton's hands, in stride, for a 61-yard gain to the Giants' 8. That figured to be all the spark needed to set off another first-quarter point eruption by the Bills. But it never happened. Kelly's next pass to Keith McKeller was incomplete, a run by Thomas gained only 3 yards, and a throw to Thomas failed to connect. The Bills would have to settle for a 29-yard Norwood field goal, making it 3–3 with 9:09 off the clock.

On their next possession the Giants were only able to move from their 20 to the Buffalo 46 before Sean Landeta punted into the end zone. This time the Bills' no-huddle offense more closely resembled its unstoppable self, as Thomas ran for 3 yards on the first play, and Kelly hit Andre Reed for gains of 11 and 4. After a false-start penalty on Jim Ritcher, Kelly found Reed again for a 20-yard completion that gave the Bills a first down at the New York 47. Thomas then ran around left end for 6 yards and caught a pass for 13 that put the ball at the 28. Another run and a 9-yard Kelly-to-Reed pass gave the Bills a first down at the 16. Thomas broke through the right side for 3 yards, McKeller caught a 5-yard pass that turned into a 9-yard gain and a first down at the 4, when free safety Myron Guyton picked up a personal foul. Jamie Mueller plowed to the 1. And on the next play Don Smith took it into the end zone to put the Bills in front, 10–3, with 2:30 gone in the second quarter.

The Giants' next series would end like the one before—with a Landeta punt. It also seemed as if the Bills might have taken Hostetler out of the game, if not physically at least mentally when, after he let go of a pass, Leon Seals came flying in on him straight up and slammed him hard on his back. The hit left the quarterback feeling woozy and blurred his vision for a while, but he continued to play.

After that it appeared the Bills were ready to take control. And they probably would have if Kelly hadn't gotten greedy. A 5-yard encroachment penalty on Erik Howard gave the Bills a third-and-one at the 50. With the Giants' still showing a two-down-linemen front, a situation begging for a handoff to Thomas for the easy first down and more, Kelly instead threw for Reed. And it was Reed's uncharacteristic drop of an over-the-middle pass that caused Kelly's rare poor decision in the no-huddle to backfire.

"If we scored on that drive, we had a chance to blow the game wide open," Kelly said. "But I admit it: I made a bad read of the defense on that third-down play."

"The pass came in a little faster than I thought it would," explained Reed. "I wasn't ready for it. I didn't have a chance to focus on the ball. But, yeah, I guess I should have caught it."

Rick Tuten's punt buried the Giants at their 7. Hostetler threw a 7-yard pass to Ottis Anderson to open a little breathing room. On the next play, however, Bart Oates was penalized for holding, pushing the ball right back to the 7. After that it looked like the Giants had begun to unravel and the Bills were ready to take command for good. While dropping back, Hostetler tripped over Anderson's right leg, and struggled to regain his balance in the end zone. With Bruce Smith in hot pursuit the quarterback tried desperately to escape while holding the ball out with his right hand. Smith grabbed Hostetler's right wrist and was on the verge, it seemed, of forcing a fumble that likely would have been recovered for a Bills touchdown. Hostetler somehow managed to hang on, however, and tuck it away as he was dumped—ending Smith's five-game sackless streak—for a safety. That made it 12–3 with 8:27 remaining in the first half, although Smith detracted from the score by drawing a 5-yard penalty for excessive celebration.

Landeta's free kick started the Bills at their 30, but they just couldn't move in for the kill. On the first play Reed dropped another pass, this one deep down the right hash mark. On the second Kelly overthrew McKeller over the middle. On the third Kelly, feeling pressure, started to run, changed his mind, and released a bad pass that the Giants nearly intercepted before the ball hit the dirt.

New York regained possession, and went three and out for the second time in the quarter. The Bills began their sixth series of the game at their 16. From there Thomas, despite having Lawrence Taylor assigned specifically to him as when the teams last met, went into one of his Superman routines. He popped through the right side for 18 yards, followed the same path for 4, took a screen pass for 10, and caught another throw in the flat for 8. That gave the Bills a second-and-two from the New York 44. But once again the Giants were let off the hook. A long pass for Lofton was broken up by Everson Walls at the Giants' 5, and after Will Wolford was flagged for a false start, the Bills found themselves with a third-and-seven at the 49. The best Kelly could do after that was connect on a short throw to Reed, who was dumped by Carl Banks two yards shy of the first-down marker. Tuten came out for his fourth punt.

In previous games third-and-long rarely presented a problem for the Bills' no-huddle offense. But it was clear the Giants were catching onto the scheme, using their nickel and dime coverages to eliminate Buffalo's favorite passing zones—the

5-, 6-, and 12-yard patterns that were stretched into big plays. Buffalo receivers would head for their designated spots and find a bloodthirsty New York defensive back waiting to try to decapitate them.

With 3:49 left in the half the Giants took over at their 13. It hardly appeared like a threatening situation for the Bills, especially with New York's plodding attack and Hostetler's inconsistency up to that point. A stop by the defense there, and heavily favored Buffalo figured to have a good chance of putting this thing away once and for all.

So much for appearances. Having taken his Johnny Unitas pills, Hostetler suddenly started to look very much like a Super Bowl quarterback. He opened the drive with a 6-yard pass to tight end Mark Bavaro. Then Anderson, who had been out of the game on the previous series with a sore back, tore loose behind left guard William Roberts for an 18-yard run. Hostetler fired 22 yards to Ingram, and Dave Meggett blasted around left end for 17 more to give the Giants a first down at the Buffalo 24. After an incomplete to Maurice Carthon, Hostetler threw again to the running back for a 3-yard pickup, and on third-and-seven he found tight end Howard Cross for just enough for the first down at the 14. With thirty-nine seconds remaining Cornelius Bennett batted down the next pass at the line, and Hostetler's second-down throw was delivered too late and too low for Stephen Baker to make the catch in the end zone.

All things considered, limiting the Giants to a field goal at that point would have been fairly uplifting for the Bills' defense. Instead Baker, beating Nate Odomes on a sideline pattern, caught a 14-yard touchdown pass to cut Buffalo's lead to 12–10. As they left the field for halftime the stunned Bills had to remind themselves that *they* were the ones with the two-point advantage.

The extralong intermission lasted twenty-seven minutes, with the NFL and Disney World bringing patriotism to center stage in a typically high-glitz Super Bowl halftime production. The president and first lady appeared on the giant TV screens, while two thousand of the most wholesome-looking children the show's directors could find—minus those who were pulled out by their parents for fear of terrorism—danced and sang through a "Small World Salute to Twenty-five Years of Super Bowls."

Meanwhile, there was plenty of strategic discussion and exhorting in the Buffalo dressing room, particularly among the defenders. But when the Bills came out for the third quarter, they still found themselves on the wrong side of momentum. After the kickoff the Giants, with an incomplete pass on first down and a false-start penalty on guard Bob Kratch, found themselves in a second-and-fifteen hole at their 20. But Hostetler wriggled his way out, first with a 7-yard completion to Meggett and then, on third-and-eight, with an 11-yard swing pass to the running back, who somehow danced out of Talley's awaiting arms, that put the ball on the New York 38. From there the Giants' went to their smash-mouth attack, with Meggett running left for 4 yards, Anderson running right for 5, and Anderson busting loose around left end for 24 to give New York a first down at the Bills' 29.

Carthon picked up five more yards on the next play, and Meggett raced for 15 to the Bills' 9. But a holding call on Bavaro pushed the ball back to the 34. After scrambling for 2 yards, Hostetler, facing third-and-thirteen, came up with one of the game's bigger plays when he hit Ingram over the middle for a 14-yard gain to the Buffalo 18. Ingram did the incredible, first breaking Kirby Jackson's tackle, then churning away from Talley's attempted takedown, then spinning away from two other defenders before J. D. Williams finally shoved him out of bounds.

Said Talley: "We waited until the worst time of the season to have our worst game of the year as far as missing tackles."

A 5-yard Anderson run and a 1-yard carry by Meggett set up third-and-four at the 12. This time Hostetler found Howard Cross for 9 yards, giving the Giants a first down at the 3. Two plays later Anderson fought his way around the left side for a 1-yard touchdown to put New York in front, 17–12. Equally important, the 14-play march devoured 9:29, which, counting all but twenty seconds of the final 3:49 in the first half, meant Kelly and the no-huddle had been off the field for a whopping 12:58.

"Very frustrating," he said. "When you run our type of offense you know sooner or later you're going to put the ball in the end zone. But it's very frustrating to know that and be standing on the sidelines—just watching."

When the Bills finally took over at their 40, after a 33-yard Al Edwards kickoff return, 5:21 was left in the quarter. Thomas ran for 8 yards, then Kelly scrambled for the first down at the Giants' 47. Thomas carried for 2 more yards, but an offensive pass-interference penalty on Reed moved the Bills back to their 45. Kelly then threw incomplete for Edwards and, on third-and-eighteen, Leonard Marshall delivered on his pregame promise and sacked Kelly for a 7-yard loss to snuff the drive.

Now the Giants were clearly, and perhaps prematurely, starting to taste that second world championship. Beginning at his 42, Hostetler zipped a 10-yard completion to Cross. On the next play Nate Odomes, struggling through one of the longer games of his four-year career, picked up a holding penalty that put the ball on the Buffalo 43. Two plays later Hostetler was sacked by Jeff Wright for a 1-yard loss, but he rebounded with a 9-yard completion to Ingram to the 35. Feeling cocky about their offensive muscle, the Giants went for it on fourth-and-two. But Bruce Smith caught Anderson two yards behind the line—and the Bills were revived.

Kelly came out with fire in his eyes, hitting Thomas with a 9-yard pass, then connecting with Kenneth Davis for 4- and 19-yard gains to the New York 31. On the next play Thomas took an inside handoff from shotgun formation around the right side, bounced off Myron Guyton, escaped the grasp of cornerback Reyna Thompson, and streaked down the right sideline for a touchdown that put the Bills back in front, 19–17, with eight seconds expired in the fourth quarter.

If only the Bills' defense could hold the Giants once, Buffalo would have a chance for another quick-strike score—the knockout punch it had delivered so many times with the no-huddle. Instead, Kelly and his offensive teammates got to do more standing and watching and sighing as New York played more keep away. On third-and-seven from his 26, Hostetler found Bavaro for a 17-yard pass. After a couple of runs and a 19-yard Hostetler-to-Bavaro completion, the Giants had a first down at the Bills' 27. A pass to Ingram advanced them to the 14 and, two plays later, they faced a third-and-five at the 9. No problem. Meggett ran for 6 to pick up the first down. The Bills did tighten after that, however, with Bennett batting down his second pass at the line on third-and-goal from the 3. Still, the Giants took a one-point lead, 20–19, on Matt Bahr's 21-yard field goal. They had also chewed away more of the clock, running 14 plays in 7:32, which left the Bills with 7:11 to stage a comeback.

Starting at the 20, Buffalo opened the next series with a 4-yard Thomas run, followed by a 15-yard Kelly-to-Thomas pass. But on the next two plays, Kelly and Davis each picked up only a yard running, leaving the Bills with a third-and-eight from their 41. Kelly threw to Edwards, but the rookie dropped the ball after taking a vicious hit from Perry Williams.

"The Giants had a great defensive scheme," Hull observed. "They gave up the pass-rush, went with those extra defensive backs and said, 'Hey, if you're going to catch the ball, you're going to get punished.' "

Tuten punted, and the Giants took over at their 30 with 5:25 remaining. From there on out, all New York needed to do was exactly what it had done the whole game—play Scrooge ball. So naturally the first play went to Anderson, who ran through the left side for 5 yards. And the second play went to Anderson, who broke through the middle for 9 more. But then Mike Lodish stopped Meggett for no gain, and the Bills did the same to the clock, using their first time-out with 3:33 left. After a seven-yard pass to Bavaro the Giants found themselves with a third-and-three at their 49. Hostetler tried running up the middle, but Seals stopped him 2 yards short of the first down. The Bills used their second time-out, stopping the clock with 2:22 showing.

Landeta punted to Edwards, who made the fair catch at the 10. And the Bills were 90 yards and 2:16 from glory.

As a youngster growing up in Alexandria, Virginia, Scott Norwood had always dreamed about deciding a big game with his foot. Not the Super Bowl, but a World Cup soccer match.

He played soccer for thirteen years before giving it up to pursue a placekicking career in football. In 1985, when he beat out nine others to win a spot on the Buffalo roster, he began dreaming about becoming a Super Bowl hero. Never a goat. Always a hero.

"As an athlete, you're constantly preparing yourself mentally for success," Norwood had said a few days earlier. "You don't dwell on failure. It's not something you even consider."

So the Wednesday night before Super Bowl XXV, as he lay in bed with his eyes open, all sorts of pictures flashed in Norwood's mind. They were pictures of success. Of the Bills' winning their first Super Bowl. Of teammates exchanging hugs and the highest of high-fives. Of long-suffering Buffalo fans riding the fifteen hundred miles back home on cloud nine. Of endless celebration throughout Western New York and anywhere else in the world that hard-core Bills loyalists could be found. He saw himself banging through every extra point and every field goal he tried. And, in the most vivid picture of all, he saw himself splitting the uprights for three points in the final seconds to win the game.

"You start to think about what would be the ultimate for a kicker, and that would be it," Norwood had said in his soft voice, but with the familiar icy look in his eyes that suggested he was in the right line of work. "It could happen. And should that situation arise, I won't have to hope or wish. I know that I'll be able to put it through. I've had a mental picture of winning the game."

The last time Kelly had faced as much comeback pressure as he did in the final 2:16 of Super Bowl XXV was in the final 2:41 of a divisional-round play-off contest at Cleveland a year earlier, on a drive that began at his 26. The Bills trailed then, 34–30, so Kelly, with one time-out and the two-minute warning to utilize, needed to march them all the way for a touchdown. And he nearly did.

This time, also with one time-out and the two-minute warning ahead, all that was necessary was to get close enough for a field goal.

"This is what champions are made of," Kelly reminded his teammates as they took the field. "Let's be one!"

On the first play Kelly, finding no one open as precious seconds disappeared, scrambled for 8 yards to the Bills' 18 before Pepper Johnson tagged him down. The clock then stopped at the two-minute warning.

Norwood was pleased with the way things had gone through the customary Wednesday-to-Friday kicking he did in practice that week. Working on the grass field at the Buccaneers' facility gave him a good feel for the natural surface at Tampa Stadium. He had spent the day before, as always, resting his leg.

After arriving at the stadium on game day and putting on his uniform, Norwood did his usual ten minutes on a stationary bike to get his heart-rate up and break a sweat before doing his usual fifteen minutes of stretching. Then, about an hour before kickoff, he went through pregame warmups.

He attempted about twenty-five kicks. The first was from 20 yards (extrapoint distance) and, while zigzagging the placements between the hash marks, he steadily worked his way as far out as 52 yards. Anything beyond that range was usually considered impossible.

"I was hitting the ball strong," Norwood remembered, pointing out, of course, that the ball tended to have greater explosion off the foot in warmer weather than in the cold he was used to at Rich. Which, for him, figured to be a plus on long-range kicks.

On second-and-two Kelly, again scrambling and losing valuable time, picked up a yard before running into Erik Howard. Then he handed to Thurman Thomas, who burst around the left side for 22 yards before Carl Banks tackled him at the Buffalo 41.

On the next play, Kelly threw 4 yards to Reed and, for the third time in the drive, the quarterback ran, picking up 9 yards and a first down at the Giants' 46. The Bills used their third and final time-out to stop the clock at forty-eight seconds.

• • •

When the clock had ticked below three minutes near the end of the Giants' last series, Norwood began thinking the game was likely to come down to him and his right foot. "It was a great feeling," he would say later.

But there was no time to revel in it. He knew he had to start warming up, start getting himself prepared—physically and mentally—for the moment of truth. Otherwise he ran the risk of being caught off-guard by it.

So while his teammates and the fans in the stadium and a billion television viewers in 101 countries watched the Bills' offense try to work its way downfield, Norwood entered his own little world behind the Buffalo bench. With Rick Tuten holding, he proceeded to make several kicks into a net before deciding, at about the one-minute mark, that his leg was loose and ready to go. After that Norwood walked over to the sidelines, where his teammates and coaches were standing, and watched. And waited.

Unlike those around him, he wasn't rooting for a touchdown. He wasn't rooting against one, either. It was just that he was gearing himself for the kick. Planning on it. Counting on it. Looking forward to it. "And if you're hoping for them to score a touchdown, that means you're not focused," Norwood explained. "My job is to go out there and kick a field goal. It's the only reason I'm going to be used in that situation, and it's the only thought on my mind. If something else happens, that's fine. But I'm focused on one kick. Nothing else. And it's really not a conscious effort. After doing it for years and years you become disciplined to think like that. You learn that that's the best way to go about it. You just block out everything else."

On the sidelines he spoke to no one. And no one spoke to him nor offered any encouraging pats on the helmet or the shoulders or the rump. As always it was understood by everyone else on the sidelines that, under such circumstances, he was best left alone with his thoughts.

"I'm thinking about my mechanics, about getting a good plant, going into it slow, hitting the ball solidly, probably taking the breeze [which would be coming toward him at about 5–10 mph] into consideration a little bit," Norwood said. "I was thinking about whether or not to get a draw on the ball or just

kick it straight. And I was thinking about how I was going to follow through. I also knew I wouldn't get a second chance, but I didn't think about that at all then. That would take me out of my focus."

On first-and-ten from the Giants' 46, Kelly threw a low pass that McKeller reached down and grabbed just before it hit the field, while backpedaling for a 6-yard gain. The Bills then caught a lucky break when the clock was stopped with twenty-nine seconds so replay official Mark Burns could take a second look at the reception. As expected, the play stood, and on second-and-four from the 40, Thomas shook free for 11 yards before cornerback Mark Collins brought him down at the 29. Kelly then hurried everyone to the line, took the snap, and spiked the ball to stop the clock at eight seconds.

The stage was set. Super Bowl XXV, which even with all the war-related distractions had been the greatest Super Bowl of them all, would come down to whether Norwood made or missed a 47-yard field-goal attempt. None of its predecessors had ever been decided this way.

The Giants, of course, used their final time-out to give Norwood a little extra time to think about the pressure of the moment, which had many an observer dreading the thought of wearing number eleven for the Bills.

Although he had missed 4 of 10 attempts between 40 and 49 yards during the 1990 regular season, and although his career numbers from that distance were 32 of 52, and although he missed the only try from that far during the play-offs, it never once occurred to Norwood the kick might be out of his range.

"Not at all," he insisted. "I had put some through from that far during pregame warm-ups. I knew I'd be able to get it there. And all I did during the time-out was flood my mind with positive thoughts. I don't back away from that type of kick. It's something I've never done all my career, and I certainly wasn't going to start then."

In front of the Bills' bench Marv Levy, his players, and other team employees joined hands. It was similar to the sideline scene at Cleveland the year before. Back then Kelly was trying to keep alive the Bills' chances of reaching their first Super Bowl. This time Kelly was part of the hand-holding as Norwood tried to win it.

"We knew that it was the last play, it was our last shot, and that our whole season was on the line," Steve Tasker said. "We all were just pulling for Scotty, just hoping that he did what Scotty does best. And that's to put it through."

The snap from Adam Lingner was perfect. The hold by Frank Reich was flawless.

Working from his soccer-style stance, Norwood took two steps, planted with his left foot while swinging his right one back and then forward and then into the ball. *Boom!*

It was a hard kick. Harder than Reich had ever remembered leaving the tip of his left index finger since the start of the season, his first as Norwood's holder. "He absolutely crushed the ball; just killed it," Reich said. "In fact, that kick probably would have been good from about fifty-five to fifty-eight yards."

But it only had to go 47. Not that that was gimme range by any means. It was far for most kickers, and especially far for Norwood. So he had concentrated on distance more than accuracy. He had set out to transfer as much power as he could from his 6′0″, 200-pound frame into his right leg. The last thing in the world he wanted to do was leave it short.

"Approaching fifty yards like that, you can't chop under the ball," Norwood said. "You have to attack it pretty good. And I did."

The ball exploded over the backs of his blockers—Lingner, Hull, Wolford, Ballard, Rolle, Parker, Pike. And over the outstretched hands of several Giants players leaping for all they were worth to try to knock it astray. And it sailed, end over end, into the night air at Tampa Stadium.

It sailed, higher and higher, carrying with it the Super Bowl hopes and dreams of a football team, as well as the expectations of a city that had suffered through so many years of pleasure and pain.

It sailed. And it sailed. And it sailed.

"THANK YOU, BILLS!"

On the morning after the sky was gray and light rain fell. It was, to say the least, an appropriate setting for the mood at the Tampa Hilton at Metro Center. A mostly somber group of Bills players, coaches, and team officials were checking out of their rooms and climbing aboard the chartered buses parked out front. They were headed back to Tampa International Airport, site of their jubilant arrival seven days earlier. Waiting for them were Pan Am Charter Flight 8207 and a long, dreary ride back to Buffalo.

Once they landed, more buses would carry them to a rally at Niagara Square in the heart of downtown. But on Monday morning, January 28, no one seemed in much of a rallying frame of mind. The emotional wounds of the 20–19 loss to the Giants in Super Bowl XXV were still every bit as fresh, every bit as painful as they had been in the visitors' dressing room at Tampa Stadium twelve hours earlier.

After watching Scott Norwood's 47-yarder sail barely two feet wide of the right upright, misty-eyed Buffalo players filed off the field slowly and quietly, most with their heads down. For several long minutes there was dead silence in the dressing room. And when players, coaches, and team officials began speaking, they did so in hushed tones. Almost everyone seemed numbed by it all.

Finally, Marv Levy, crushed more deeply than anyone would ever know, made a halfhearted attempt at delivering a postgame speech. What could he say? What could anyone have said? After so much expectation, after so much emotion, and the manner in which it had been decided, this was a loss that defied words. Levy knew that. And he kept his remarks brief, telling the players that he felt for each and every one of them and that he understood how much they were hurting inside and that he realized how badly they wanted to be toasting a world championship at that moment.

"There's not a loser in this room," the coach said, struggling to keep his composure. "So, guys . . . just hang in there."

They tried, but it wasn't easy. Everywhere one looked, eyes were glistening, heads were shaking back and forth, and faces were buried in hands. The greatest devastation was found at Norwood's cubicle, although he still managed to face the media and field every one of their difficult questions without flinching or being surly or trying to make a fast getaway.

"My whole body was kind of deadened by it," Norwood said of the moment he saw his kick go wide. "I just felt so empty out there."

"But that was hardly a chip shot," a reporter reminded him.

"Doesn't matter. You could have lined me up for a seventy yarder. If that was our last chance to win the game, I'd have gone in fully expecting to somehow get it through, just like I fully expected to get that one through."

Nevertheless, to a man, Norwood's teammates offered immediate and unconditional forgiveness. To a man, they said the game should never have come down to one player and one play, that the Bills' fate was decided by a combination of too many missed tackles, too many dropped passes, and not enough proper execution overall.

For the past three weeks the players had sounded like broken records, saying over and over that just reaching the Super Bowl wasn't good enough. That their goal had never been just to beat the Miami Dolphins by 10 points in the divisional round of the play-offs. Or just to pummel the Los Angeles

Raiders by 48 points in the AFC championship game. Those were merely rungs on a ladder, two of the three rivers that had to be crossed. The only thing that would ever satisfy them was making it to the top. Winning it all.

Now they were discovering exactly how painful it was to be number two in the NFL.

"When you come here," Bill Polian said, "you find out very soon that the joy is greatly tempered by the agony you feel when you lose."

Some tried to put it in proper perspective. "Look at it this way," tight end Pete Metzelaars said. "At least we're not getting bombs dropped on us like the guys over in the Middle East."

Others spoke optimistically about a return trip the following season, about accomplishing in Super Bowl XXVI in Minneapolis what they had failed to accomplish in Super Bowl XXV in Tampa. That sounded good. Certainly the Bills would be viewed again as a strong contender. But a second chance, even after success the first time, wasn't nearly as easy to come by as the 49ers made it seem with back-to-back appearances in XXIII and XXIV.

Even Ralph Wilson acknowledged that. "Who knows what's going to happen next year?" he said. "I don't know whether we're going to be back in the Super Bowl next year. We may never get back again. That's just the nature of this crazy game."

Although they might not have cared to admit it, players and coaches and everyone else who worked or rooted for the Bills realized Wilson was right. It wasn't pessimism, just pragmatism. And one of the harder facts being faced on that gloomy Monday morning at the Tampa Hilton at Metro Center was the great distance that been traveled to get to Super Bowl XXV—not the fifteen hundred miles, but the journey that dated back to July, the one that originated at Fredonia State College.

"Training camp," John Davis said, shaking his head just the way he had the night before. "That's the thing that keeps coming back into my mind. Training camp, and how we had worked so hard to get to this point. The practices, the meetings, the exhibition games, the regular season, the play-offs.

All that, and we *just* miss a great opportunity to become world champions. That hurts.

"We all know what we did wrong, why we didn't fulfill our goal. But there's absolutely nothing we can do about it right now—except just let it eat our stomachs out."

Levy was so distraught he couldn't bring himself to speak with the few reporters who showed up at the Bills' hotel the day after. At roughly the same hour Bill Parcells was at another Tampa hotel, addressing hundreds of journalists at the traditional day-after press conference featuring the winning Super Bowl coach. Among other things he reiterated a point he had stressed the night before: power wins football games. Power, as in the rushing attack that helped the Giants control the ball for 40:33, versus finesse, as in the Bills' no-huddle, which contributed to their mere 19:27 possession time.

Norwood was one of the last Buffalo players to check out of the Hilton. Yet he probably was one of the first awake that morning, besides the group of ten (Kelly, Thomas, Reed, Hull, Wolford, Smith, Bennett, Talley, Conlan, and Tasker) that had already left for Hawaii to play in the Pro Bowl. Of course most of them had just stayed up the entire night, having attended the team's private postgame "party" at the nearby Holiday Inn, where players' and coaches' families and friends spent the week. Norwood didn't attend. He and his wife, Kim, went out for a quiet dinner, just the two of them, then he left her at the Holiday Inn and spent the night at team headquarters.

The miss gnawed at Norwood through dinner and until he went to bed. Then it jabbed him awake in the early morning hours and he couldn't go back to sleep. He kept replaying it in his mind, kept thinking about the things he could have done mechanically to make it work. Maybe if he had placed a little more emphasis on pulling the ball left he wouldn't have been so aggressive with his plant foot. And if he wouldn't have been so aggressive with his plant foot, maybe that would have set his hips differently, to where they would turn in slightly. And if his hips would have turned in slightly, maybe that would have pulled the ball inside of the right upright.

Of course, thinking about it during the 1.3 seconds he had

to get the kick off and thinking about it several hours later were, to say the least, two different things.

Another memory that kept coming back to Norwood was the 52-yard field-goal attempt Kansas City's Nick Lowery had missed with fifty-six seconds left in the Chiefs' 17–16 wild-card play-off loss to Miami. The ball had fallen two feet short of the crossbar. "The situations we had were similar, except that he was on the other end of the spectrum," Norwood said. "He went up to the ball nice and smooth and struck it right on target, but came up short. On the other hand, I attacked mine and it was plenty long, but wide. Had Nick been given a chance to do it over again, he probably would have attacked it a bit more. Just like, if I had a second chance, I'd have probably gone for more accuracy. The right kick for each of us was probably somewhere in between."

The trip back to Buffalo would, of course, be the longest for Norwood. This time, the in-flight movie was *Ghost* and that seemed appropriate, considering the way he felt. Not that he wished he were dead or anything approaching that. He just wanted to be temporarily invisible. Because besides his teammates and coaches and Polian and Wilson, Norwood felt he had let down the Buffalo fans. The last thing he wanted to do was face a large throng of them (how large was anybody's guess after the outcome) at the rally. But the team had an obligation to show up, and Norwood was part of the team.

What the Bills found when they landed at Greater Buffalo International Airport was another police escort, this time with helicopters. And what they saw in Niagara Square when they filed onto the stage in front of City Hall was not to be believed: nearly thirty thousand pairs of open arms welcoming them home. The chant of "Thank you, Bills! Thank you, Bills!" echoed throughout the city.

Then something even more unexpected happened. As the master of ceremonies, Buffalo Area Chamber of Commerce president Kevin Keeley, began a program of speeches from team representatives and politicians, the crowd broke into a chant of "We want Scott! We want Scott!"

From the moment the buses had arrived at the rally, the

guilt was building inside of Norwood. He had tried to stay out of sight, standing in the far back corner of the stage. He didn't even attempt to anticipate the kind of reception he would receive. He knew all about what had happened to one of his Buffalo predecessors, Booth Lusteg, after he missed a 23-yard field-goal try that left a 1966 AFC game against San Diego locked in a 17–17 tie. Some irate teenaged fans followed Lusteg as he walked home from War Memorial Stadium and beat him up. When police later asked why he hadn't called for help, Lusteg replied, "Because I deserved it."

This certainly was no lynch mob after Norwood, but it was persistent. The chanting continued, louder and louder, until several of his teammates coaxed him forward. And when the kicker finally stepped to the microphone, he received the loudest and longest and warmest ovation of the day.

Sure, the fans had watched his miss in horror and no doubt cursed his name the night before. But now, waving American flags and Bills banners, they wanted him to know there were no hard feelings. That they realized he had tried his best. That they didn't expect him to carry the burden of the loss by himself. That they were thankful for the thrill he and his teammates had given them just by playing in the Super Bowl.

With tears in his eyes and his voice cracking, Norwood told them, "I know I've never felt more loved than right now. . . . I'm going to be back. You can count on it. And I'm dedicating next season to the fans of Buffalo."

The crowd let out a roar as Norwood dried his tears and triumphantly rejoined his teammates. It was exactly the kind of scene Tom Harter of Kenmore, New York, had wanted his sons, nine-year-old Michael and five-year-old David, to witness firsthand.

"I wasn't going to come if they had won," Harter said. "I came because they lost. I thought we should be a part of it for them, and especially for Scott Norwood. We just wanted to pat him on the back and tell him it was all right."

Levy told the fans he loved every one of them, just as he loved every one of his players. Wilson held his right arm high, with his hand outstretched, and said, "I give you all what in football vocabulary is a high-five!"

Mark Kelso and James Lofton spoke for the players.

"I'm proud to say I'm a member of the Buffalo Bills," Kelso said. "And I'm proud to say I'm from Buffalo, New York."

"We don't have the most talented players," added Lofton. "Every player on our team is not All-Pro. But what they are is family. We bond together. We're Buffalo's team. And we're going to be number one when we get back next year."

At least Governor Mario Cuomo thought so. He arrived wearing a sweatshirt that said: "Buffalo Bills Champion Super Bowl XXVI, Minnesota in 1992."

After the rally the outpouring of affection for Norwood and the Bills continued. A six-year-old girl, along with her mother, stopped Norwood as he was entering Rich Stadium the next day and handed him a piece of paper on which the youngster had scribbled, "We love you, Scott." Three roses from a teen-aged girl were sent to his Buffalo home with a note that read, "You did the best you could do. We'll always be behind you 100 percent." He even received a special message from Reverend Robert Schuller on national television.

In a post–Super Bowl newspaper interview Norwood used the phrase, "Tough times never last, but tough people do." It was the title of a book written by Schuller, which Norwood had first read six years earlier and picked up again after returning from Tampa. Schuller saw Norwood's quote, and on his show he praised the Buffalo fans for their reaction, then faced the camera and said, "We love you, Scott, and we're praying for you."

Soon after returning to his off-season home in Centreville, Virginia, Norwood received a giant mailbag from One Bills Drive. Inside were more than three hundred cards and letters, mostly from Western New Yorkers, expressing various forms of support and concern.

Some of the envelopes contained pictures and drawings of smiling faces, little pick-me-ups to brighten his spirit. Others brought messages that Norwood found deeply moving.

"We watched your interview [after the game], and you touched our hearts. Everything I have ever wanted to teach our children, especially our fifteen-year-old son, was taught by you

in just a few moments. You may not have scored three points needed to win the ultimate game, but you scored a million points in our hearts."

"I respect the way you've handled this temporary mishap. And the response of the people of Buffalo signifies a victory of the human spirit, far more important than a football game."

"The manner in which you conducted yourself during all of that attention after the game added dignity to the Buffalo defeat. You and your teammates showed yourselves to be a class act. In particular, your personal actions were those of a winner, not a loser."

The same was true about the fans' conduct. It wouldn't have been the least bit surprising if they had taken the defeat as a crushing disappointment and sought easy targets for blame. Fans typically react that way. Instead Buffalo's ultra-faithful recognized it as a special game, perhaps the best Super Bowl ever played, and as a worthy crowning jewel to a special season.

An almost-dream season.

DATE DUE
